MW00593752

LAW AND THE BIBLE

Justice, Mercy and Legal Institutions

Edited by ROBERT F. COCHRAN JR.
and DAVID VANDRUNEN

IVP Academic

An imprint of InterVarsity Press
Downers Grove, Illinois

Apollos
Nottingham, England

InterVarsity Press, USA
P.O. Box 1400
Downers Grove, IL 60515-1426, USA
World Wide Web: www.ivpress.com
Email: email@ivpress.com

APOLLOS (an imprint of Inter-Varsity Press, England)
Norton Street
Nottingham NG7 3HR, England
Website: www.ivpbooks.com
Email: ivp@ivpbooks.com

InterVarsity Press®, USA, is the book-publishing division of InterVarsity Christian Fellowship/USA® www.intervarsity.org and a member movement of the International Fellowship of Evangelical Students.

Inter-Varsity Press, England, is closely linked with the Universities and Colleges Christian Fellowship, a student movement connecting Christian Unions throughout Great Britain, and a member movement of the International Fellowship of Evangelical Students. Website: www.uccf.org.uk

Scripture quotations marked ESV are from The Holy Bible, English Standard Version®, ESV® copyright © 2001 by Crossway, a publishing ministry of Good News Publishers. Used by permission. All rights reserved.

Scripture quotations marked NAB are from the New American Bible, revised edition © 2010, 1991, 1986, 1970 Confraternity of Christian Doctrine, Washington, D.C., and are used by permission of the copyright owner. All rights reserved. No part of the New American Bible may be reproduced in any form without permission in writing from the copyright owner.

Scripture quotations marked NIV are from the THE HOLY BIBLE, NEW INTERNATIONAL VERSION®, NIV® Copyright © 1973, 1978, 1984, 2011 by Biblica, Inc.™ Used by permission. All rights reserved worldwide.

Scripture quotations marked NIV 1984 are from the Holy Bible, New International Version®. NIV®. Copyright © 1973, 1978, 1984 by International Bible Society. Used by permission of Zondervan Publishing House. All rights reserved.

Scripture quotations marked NRSV are from the New Revised Standard Version of the Bible, copyright 1989 by the Division of Christian Education of the National Council of the Churches of Christ in the USA. Used by permission. All rights reserved.

Scripture quotations marked RSV are from the Revised Standard Version of the Bible, copyright 1946, 1952, 1971 by the Division of Christian Education of the National Council of the Churches of Christ in the U.S.A. Used by permission. All rights reserved.

While all stories in this book are true, some names and identifying information in this book have been changed to protect the privacy of the individuals involved.

Cover design: David Fassett
Interior design: Beth Hagenberg

Images: Ornate fountain with statue: © WALTER ZERLA/cultura/Corbis
    Line of Torah: Matthew Ragen/iStocckphoto
    Supreme Court columns: © Joel Carillet/iStockphoto

USA ISBN 978-0-8308-2573-8 (print)
USA ISBN 978-0-8308-9559-5 (digital)
UK ISBN 978-1-84474-923-2

Printed in the United States of America ∞

 InterVarsity Press is committed to protecting the environment and to the responsible use of natural resources. As a member of Green Press Initiative we use recycled paper whenever possible. To learn more about the Green Press Initiative, visit www.greenpressinitiative.org.

Library of Congress Cataloging-in-Publication Data
A catalog record for this book is available from the Library of Congress.

British Library Cataloguing in Publication Data
A catalogue record for this book is available from the British Library.

P	21	20	19	18	17	16	15	14	13	12	11	10	9	8	7	6	5	4	3	2	1
Y	31	30	29	28	27	26	25	24	23	22	21	20	19	18	17	16	15	14	13		

Dedicated to

Herb Nootbaar

a champion of justice

&

Elinor Nootbaar

a lover of Scripture

CONTENTS

FOREWORD

CLS WAS AN ACRONYM with two very different meanings when I was a fledgling law student thirty years ago. For most, it meant "critical legal studies," a burgeoning new movement of sundry neo-Marxist jurists and philosophers collectively bent on exposing the fallacies and false equalities of modern law. Many of my first-year law professors were the high priests of this CLS movement. They were making serious waves at the time with their shrill denunciation of much that was considered sound and settled in the law. The best CLS professors taught established legal doctrine and then shredded it with rhetorical and analytical power. That instruction appealed to my native ethic of *semper reformanda*—always reforming and working to improve our traditions. Other professors simply taught their pet critical topics, sending us students scrambling to the bookstore in search of study guides that would acquaint us with the legal basics. After a year of such CLS instruction, I couldn't wait to take the upper-level electives that would no doubt unveil the new and better legal system CLS had in mind. Little was on offer. The "crits," I soon learned, were better at deconstruction than reconstruction of the law. Not surprisingly, this movement has now faded and fractured into sundry special-interest groups, held together, it seems, only by their critical approaches to the law.

CLS in the early 1980s also meant "Christian Legal Society," a handful of law students who gathered for periodic worship, prayer and reflection, and occasional good works in the community. We were very much a fringe group at my law school, the last remnant of the superstitious in the eyes of many. Ours happened to be a particularly weak local student chapter of a quite vibrant national Christian Legal Society of lawyers, law students and religious-liberty advocates. But, even at the national level, the Christian

Legal Society then was still a rather small group struggling to come to terms with what it means to be a Christian and a lawyer. The Christian Legal Society has become more substantial since then, and the United States Supreme Court lifted the name to permanent prominence with the recent case of *Christian Legal Society v. Martinez.*

CLS is rapidly acquiring an additional meaning today: a growing "Christian legal studies" movement in legal education—led, in no small part, by the authors of the pages that follow. These scholars are part of a group of some three hundred Catholic, Protestant and Orthodox Christian law professors in North America—and several hundred more around the world—who have dedicated themselves to studying the "weightier matters of the law: justice and mercy and faith." These Christian law professors are not just abstract legal theorists who have "neglected" the technical aspects of the law: the "mint, dill and cumin" as Matthew 23 (NIV) puts it. Many of them are leading scholars of the core doctrines of public, private, penal and procedural law. They have mastered the power of legal science and method—the special ability that lawyers have to build and break down arguments, to separate salient from superficial fact, to argue from analogy and precedent. Some of the weightier matters of the law that they address are familiar to scholars of law and politics, whatever their persuasion—questions concerning the nature and purpose of law and authority, the mandates and limits of rule and obedience, the rights and duties of officials and subjects, the care and nurture of the needy and innocent, the justice and limits of war and violence, the nature of fault and the means of punishing it, the sources of obligations and the procedures for vindicating them, the origins of property and the means of protecting it, among others. On many such questions of legal doctrine, science and philosophy, Christian law professors are not noticeably different from their peers with different convictions. A first-year class in contracts, criminal law or civil procedure looks mostly the same whether taught at Harvard or Columbia, Notre Dame or Pepperdine.

But Christian law professors also address questions that are more specifically Christian in accent but no less important to understanding law, liberty and politics: Are persons fundamentally good or evil? Is human nature essentially rational or relational? Is law inherently coercive or liberating? Is law a stairway to heaven or a fence against hell? Did law and government predate or postdate the fall into sin? Should authorities only proscribe vices or also prescribe virtues? Is the state a divine or a popular sovereign? Are social institutions fundamentally hierarchical or egalitarian in internal structure and external relations? Are they rooted in creation or custom, covenant or contract? What is the place of law and legal procedure in the church, and how must it be enforced? What is the place of democracy in the church, and how is it to be exercised? What is the role of the church in exemplifying and advocating justice for itself and for other institutions, for its own members and for other individuals? What is the relationship between crime and sin, contract and covenant, justice and righteousness, mercy and love? What do the Bible and Christian tradition teach about the fundamentals of law and liberty, faith and order?

It is this last question—about the legal teachings of the Bible—that is the central focus of this volume, and the ultimate source of the fundamental legal issues that occupy Christian jurists in particular. In the chapters that follow, pairs of theologians and lawyers march through the Bible—from Genesis to Revelation, from the laws of the Garden to the laws of the New Jerusalem—in search of basic biblical legal teachings. This is a sage method of exegesis, allowing theologians to keep the lawyers canonically honest and forcing the theologians to address close legal questions. The authors have left much of their heavy hermeneutical and jurisprudential machinery parked in their home disciplines and worked hard to present the Bible's teachings on law in learned but accessible interdisciplinary terms. This makes the book an ideal text for college, law school and seminary classrooms as well as for legal conferences, church study groups, and individual meditation. No one can come away from these provocative chapters and not be struck anew by the enduring relevance, prescience and wisdom of the Bible in dealing with many of the very legal, political and social questions that still challenge us today.

None of the authors herein pretends that the Bible is a complete legal textbook or a comprehensive legal code. None of them is pressing for the construction of a modern biblical commonwealth in place of our current governments. They understand that for every "*nomos* there is a narrative,"[1] for every Torah a Talmud, for every biblical legal principle a long set of precepts and procedures to make it real and concrete. The laws of the Bible

---

[1]Robert M. Cover, "*Nomos* and Narrative," *Harvard Law Review* 97 (1983): 4.

are part of a larger narrative about God and humanity, sin and salvation, faith and order. The Bible's commandments are the anchors of long traditions of legal reasoning, application and enforcement that go far beyond the original canon and commandments. The challenge that the authors leave for us today is to find responsible ways of making these biblical teachings on law effective vehicles both for critique and for reform of our postmodern legal systems.

For those who think this exercise is futile, it is worth noting that some of the Bible's basic laws are still at the heart of our legal system today. "Thou shalt not kill" remains at the foundation of our laws of homicide. "Thou shalt not steal" grounds our laws of property and theft. "Thou shalt not bear false witness" remains the anchor of our laws of evidence and defamation. The ancient laws of sanctuary still operate for fleeing felons, refugees and asylum seekers. The ancient principles of jubilee are at the heart of our modern laws of bankruptcy and debt relief. "Honor the authorities" remains the starting premise of modern constitutional law. Any good legal historian can show you the biblical genesis and Christian exodus of many of our modern rules of contract and promise, evidence and proof, marriage and family, crime and punishment, property and poverty, liberty and dignity, church and state, business and commerce. Some of these legal creations were wholly original to Christianity, born of keen new biblical insight and theological ingenuity. Others were converted and recast from Hebrew, Greek and Roman prototypes. Still others were reworked and reformed by Renaissance humanists and Enlightenment *philosophes* and their ample modern progeny. But whether original or reformed, canonical or casuistical, Western Christian teachings on law, politics and society have made enduring contributions to the development of law as we know it today.

These legal teachings of the Bible and the Christian tradition still hold essential insights for legal reform and renewal in this new millennium. What would a legal system look like if we were to take seriously the final commandment of the Decalogue, "thou shalt not covet," especially when our modern systems of capitalism, advertisement and wealth accumulation have the exact opposite premise? What would our modern law of torts and criminal law look like if we took seriously Jesus' command to "turn the other cheek"? What would our laws of civil procedure and dispute resolution look like if we took seriously the New Testament admonition for those with grievances to "go tell it to the church"? What would our systems of social welfare, charity or inheritance look like if we followed the Bible's repeated commands to tend to the poor, widows, orphans, strangers—the "least" of society—knowing that, as Jesus put it, "as much as you do it to them you do it to me"? What would our public and private laws look like if we worked hard to make real and legally concrete the biblical ideals of covenant community or sacramental living?

It's a fair question whether these and many other biblical passages now define the ethics of the communicant and the church rather than the laws of the citizen and the state. That, at minimum, requires that our modern churches get their legal and moral houses in order and provide the kind of witness and example that the modern polity needs. But I dare say that the Bible's call for Christians to serve as prophets, priests and kings provides lawyers with a unique vocation: to speak prophetic truth to power, to offer priestly service to all neighbors, and to foster rules and regimes that are marked with justice, mercy and faith.

John Witte Jr.
Center for the Study of Law and Religion
Emory University

INTRODUCTION

The law of the LORD is perfect,
refreshing the soul.
The statutes of the LORD are trustworthy,
making wise the simple.
The precepts of the LORD are right,
giving joy to the heart.
The commands of the LORD are radiant,
giving light to the eyes.
The fear of the LORD is pure,
enduring forever.
The decrees of the LORD are firm,
and all of them are righteous.
They are more precious than gold,
than much pure gold;
they are sweeter than honey,
than honey from the honeycomb.

PSALM 19:7-10[1]

---

[1]Scripture quotations in this introduction are taken from the NIV.®

THIS BIBLICAL SONG is likely to strike a contemporary Western reader as rather strange. We are hard pressed to think of a single song in American culture that praises law. Many in the West take the rule of law for granted, and some see law as an oppressive force; few sing law's praises. Law is also seldom praised in other parts of the world, where the law is often a tool of injustice wielded by corrupt leaders. In this context, it is startling to observe the high words reserved for law—albeit God's law—in Psalm 19.

What the Bible has to say about law is important for all the reasons that what the Bible has to say about anything is important. The Bible shows us God's will and character as it reveals him to us. The Bible reveals that God is our creator and that law springs from his will and reflects his holy character. The great hope of the Scriptures is that all God's works—including law—will praise his name. The Bible reveals that God is a God of love, justice and mercy—all qualities that are conveyed in his law and the stories of law in Scripture. God shows his *love* to us by teaching us the law as his intention for human life and action; his *justice* is manifested in his law as it protects and guides us; and his *mercy* saves us when we fail to abide by his law.

The Bible is full of law. It includes the laws of Israel given at Sinai (Ex 20), natural law (God's law made known in creation itself and perceived through the conscience), the laws of the Medes and Persians (Dan 6:8), and the law of Rome. It tells stories of faithful Israelite kings administering God's law and unfaithful Israelite kings ignoring it, of Israelites who are ministers of the law in pagan courts, and of Israelites and Christians suffering under tyrants' abuse of law. Biblical poets, as in Psalm 19, write about the law with fervent eloquence.

The focus of this book is on the *civil* law or *positive* law—that is, the law that orders human societies and is implemented and enforced through human government. The Bible, in one way or another, addresses almost all areas of civil law, including evidence, civil and criminal procedure, court administration, and welfare regulations. What inspired light does Scripture shed, we ask, on Christians' participation in contemporary legal systems?

MISUSE OF SCRIPTURE ON LAW

Many readers seeing a book on the Bible and the civil law may feel an instinctive skepticism. Christians along the full range of the political spectrum at times quote the Bible on behalf of (sometimes contradictory) legislative proposals. Often such use of Scripture pays little attention to the context of passages quoted or to the history of their interpretation. We fear that some Christians, on all points of the political spectrum, cherry-pick verses of Scripture to justify already-existing political opinions. This is a temptation of which all Christians ought to beware. Reading Scripture in both its immediate context and the context of all of Scripture will help to avoid such abuse. Ultimately, of course, by being attentive to all of Scripture we are attentive to God himself, who speaks in and through the Scriptures, judges our faulty assumptions and unbelieving propensities, and gives us greater insight into what all of life, including law, should be.

Another mistake made at times by Christians who enter the political arena is to assume that if Scripture gives a moral exhortation, it should be enacted into civil law. Moral exhortations in Scripture do not necessarily have immediate application for a human legal system since civil law is not designed for (or even capable of) enforcing all of morality. Nor is every piece of civil legislation in Scripture appropriate for civil law today; we should not assume, for example, that the civil laws of Moses promulgated to Israel as an Old Testament theocracy are fitting for the modern nation-state.[2] In this volume, the authors have tried to pay careful attention to questions of context and the purposes for which texts were written, and this should help to guard against the illegitimate use of texts for one's own agenda.[3]

Purpose and Audience

The essays in this book take a fresh look at what various parts of the Bible teach about civil law and reflect upon the insight they provide about it today. We have divided the Bible into nine sections. Each chapter of this book is coauthored by a legal scholar and a theologian[4] and explores what one of those sections teaches about civil law, in the context of Scripture as a whole. Since each essay is coauthored by a legal scholar and a theologian, this book seeks to integrate different areas of human learning and to keep before you concerns that legal scholars alone or theologians alone might miss. Though

---

[2]For discussion of this issue in this volume, see "Lessons for Contemporary Issues" in chapter three and "God's Moral Law, the Mosaic Law and Legislation" in chapter six.

[3]At times, the dating and authorship of a portion of Scripture help us to understand what that portion of Scripture says about law. In this collection, we will address these questions when that is the case.

[4]Authors representing the theological side have various scholarly specialties, including Old Testament, New Testament, systematic theology, ethics and philosophical theology.

the authors of this volume do not share all the same views, this book has been a collaborative effort. Each contributor read and critiqued early drafts of the other essays, which enabled each author to utilize the insights of the others and thus to better develop his or her chapter in the context of the whole Bible. The vast majority of the authors of this book are from the United States, and many of the legal examples we evaluate and much of the analysis we bring, no doubt, reflect that fact. Nevertheless, we have tried to address a broad range of legal situations that Christians face in other parts of the world as well.

The subject of civil law and the Bible is vast, and this project could have taken different forms. Our objective is not to provide a comprehensive biblical theology of law or to engage in technical biblical scholarship aimed only at Old or New Testament specialists. Nor do we seek to elaborate a biblical model for an ideal civil law code appropriate for every time and place. Instead, we survey the most relevant portions of Scripture and examine some of the fundamental questions Christians should consider as they explore their relationship to civil law, justice and government.

Each pair of authors has wrestled with the limitations of space available for their essay. Each chapter could have been its own book, and this book could have been a multivolume set. But we believe that a single volume like this one will serve an important purpose for the benefit of many readers. Our hope is that it will provide a stimulating introduction to the topic of the Bible and civil law and lead readers to further study and reflection.[5]

This book is designed for Christians who want to think deeply and seriously about the implications of the Christian faith for civil law, as well as for non-Christians who want to understand how Christians might thoughtfully engage this subject. These essays offer an all-too-unusual intellectual engagement among trained theologians and legal professionals. The contemporary academic and professional worlds are highly fragmented and specialized, with theology, law and other disciplines cordoned off in separate schools, departments, courses of study and sections of town. With this isolation, the transforming power of theological insight is unavailable

---

[5]Three significant new works in this area, for those who want to explore these topics further, are Jonathan Burnside's *God, Justice, and Society: Aspects of Law and Legality in the Bible* (Oxford: Oxford University Press, 2011); David VanDrunen, *Divine Covenants and Moral Order: A Biblical Theology of Natural Law*, Emory University Studies in Law and Religion (Grand Rapids: Eerdmans, forthcoming 2014); and *The Oxford Encyclopedia of the Bible and the Law*, ed. Brent A. Strawn (Oxford: Oxford University Press, forthcoming).

to law, as well as other fields. The teachings of the Christian faith have implications for all of life. By teaming a legal scholar with a theologian for each essay, this project has encouraged cross-disciplinary discussion and engagement. Thus, theologically trained readers will be challenged through the insights that the law professors bring to the table, and legally trained readers will be challenged through the insights of the theologians. By bringing lawyers and theologians into collaboration, we hope to enrich both disciplines and encourage future collaboration.

At the same time, we seek to address a broader audience than simply students and scholars in the fields of theology and law. Theology is not just for theologians, and responsibility for law is not just for legal professionals. All Christians should think about their responsibility before the law. Some, at times, will question whether they should obey the law; some, especially those in democratic societies, have opportunity to shape the law for just and benevolent ends. The Bible's call to justice is a call to all Christians, and it is crucial, both for Christians and non-Christians in a society, that Christians take seriously the justice-related claims of the faith. The Old Testament prophets, many of whom were ordinary citizens rather than legal or religious professionals, did just this in their own time. Many came from outside the circles of power. They stood against injustice, though they did not have a "professional" responsibility to do so. This book is for all who want to think in a Christian way about law and their relationship to it. Though used as an instrument of injustice in many parts of the world, law is a gift of God and should be used to promote justice.

CHRISTIAN SOURCES OF INSIGHT ON LAW:
SCRIPTURE, NATURE AND TRADITION

In this book, we argue that Christians can gain great insight about civil law from Scripture. Moreover, Scripture should always be the supreme standard for all aspects of life. Nevertheless, Christians must also look to other sources of wisdom if they are to be faithful participants in legal life. Most of the major branches of the Christian faith—including the Roman Catholic, Lutheran and Reformed traditions—have historically looked to natural law as foundational for civil law.[6] There have been many theories about natural

---

[6]Among representative figures, see Thomas Aquinas, *Summa Theologica* (New York: Benzinger, 1947), 1a2ae 91.3, 95.2; Martin Luther, "Temporal Authority: To What Extent It Should Be Obeyed," in *Luther's Works*, vol. 45, ed. Walther I. Brandt (Philadelphia: Muhlenberg, 1962),

law, many of which the authors of this book would not endorse. By "natural law" we refer generally to the idea that God has ordered this world—and human beings' place in it—in such a way that it communicates the basic requirements of his moral will, and that human beings perceive this law through their reason and conscience.

The idea of natural law is not in competition with the doctrine of biblical authority, for Scripture itself speaks about all people's knowledge of God and his law through nature. Proverbs, for example, describes an orderly world that yields wisdom as human beings observe and reflect upon law in the fear of the Lord. The most familiar text in Scripture on this subject is Romans 1:18–2:16, where Paul explains that God's attributes are known by all people "from what has been made," leaving them without excuse before him (Rom 1:20). When they fall into rebellion they "know God's righteous decree that those who do such things deserve death" (Rom 1:32). Those who do not have the law of God in Scripture nevertheless often "do by nature things required by the law" and thereby show "that the requirements of the law are written on their hearts" (Rom 2:14-15). Sin, of course, corrupts human knowledge of the natural law. As Aquinas notes, biblical law is also needed because of "the uncertainty of human judgment."[7]

The fact that Scripture does not give a definite answer to every legal question, should not disturb Christians (though it should give them a sense of modesty and humility that is often lacking). With the moral foundation revealed in nature, and confirmed and clarified in Scripture, Christians must use godly wisdom and prudence to seek to understand the world in which they live and the social circumstances in which particular problems arise. They must apply the norms of Scripture and natural law in ways that produce just and beneficial results for their fellow human beings.

In addition to Scripture and natural law, a third source of insight is tradition. Scripture is God's special revelation, and natural law is an aspect of God's general revelation. The contributors to this volume affirm the traditional Protestant belief that church tradition is not an authority on par with either of these. Nevertheless, we recognize the great value in learning from those who

pp. 127-28; and John Calvin, *Institutes of the Christian Religion*, vol. 2, ed. John T. McNeill, trans. Ford Lewis Battles (Philadelphia: Westminster, 1960), 4.20.16. For additional discussion of natural law in this volume, see "The Patriarch Narratives" in chapter one and "Romans 2:14-15: Natural Law and Empire" in chapter eight.
[7]*Summa Theologica* 1a2ae 91.4.

have gone before us. To ignore the contributions of godly and intelligent saints who for centuries have reflected on biblical teaching on issues of law and government would be foolish and arrogant.[8] Therefore, though the essays in this volume focus upon the biblical texts, they often reflect upon previous Christian interpretation of the issues under consideration. We wish this project not simply to plow new ground but also to further an ongoing, centuries-long exploration of the relationship of Christians to their civil societies.

PERVASIVE THEMES

Different sections of Scripture emphasize different things about God's work in history, yet together they present a beautiful, unified landscape. In a similar way, different sections of Scripture provide different insights about civil law while also cohering in a unified whole. To understand Scripture's teaching about civil law, it is therefore important to be attentive both to the distinctive insights of its parts and to the ways these fit together in the big picture. Most of this book focuses on particular sections of Scripture. But in order to help readers keep the big picture in mind as they read individual essays, we here identify a few themes that recur throughout this volume. By keeping these themes in mind, readers should be better able to trace the development of important ideas through the history of God's dealings with his people and to appreciate the overarching unity of biblical revelation.

Creation, fall, redemption and consummation. One theme evident throughout this book is the place of law in the larger story of the movement from creation to fall and then to redemption and consummation. The place and purpose of law is shaped by each of these great events.

Law is a conspicuous presence already at creation. Though the human race in its state of innocence did not need the coercive mechanism of the state as we know it, God ordered the world, placed the human race under legal obligation to him and called human beings to order the world under his authority in the exercise of benevolent dominion. Upon the fall into sin, coercive civil law became a necessity if human society was to continue. Both ordinary citizens and those who make and enforce the law—all of whom are sinners—need law's restraints. Shortly after the fall, we see God

---

[8]As G. K. Chesterton said: "[Tradition] is the democracy of the dead. Tradition refuses to submit to the small and arrogant oligarchy of those who merely happen to be walking about." See "Orthodoxy," in *The Everyman Chesterton*, ed. Ian Ker (New York: Alfred A. Knopf, 2011), p. 298.

taking interest in human justice, both in his dealings with Cain and in the universal covenant he made with the entire world after the flood.

Redemption comes through faith in Christ, not obedience to the law, but civil law remains very important for believers. When God called Abraham, he left him to live under the legal orders of the many societies in which he sojourned. When God set apart Israel as his special people, he organized it as a theocratic nation and gave it its own civil law and legal system. Under the new covenant, God calls believers to live in many places and under many legal regimes. The believer's ultimate citizenship lies in Christ's heavenly kingdom, rather than any earthly nation, but God appoints governing officials and calls Christians to work out the implications of love of neighbor in all realms, including law.

Our current situation is not the end of the story. Christians look forward to the consummation, Christ's victory over sin and the "principalities" and "powers" (Eph 6:12 RSV). "The kingdom of the world [will] become the kingdom of our Lord and of his Messiah, and he will reign for ever and ever" (Rev 11:15). Though the state and coercive civil law will have no place in that righteous society, law in some form will be present, for the blessed will still be under obligation to their God and undertake their responsibilities in fidelity to his will.

Faithfulness under very different legal regimes. A second theme coursing through the Bible (and this book) concerns the varied experiences of biblical saints with respect to civil law, both as subjects and as implementers of law. Living under civil law and the magistrates who enforce it is at times a blessing for God's people; on many other occasions, they suffer under the manipulation or flouting of the law by unjust rulers. Scripture, through both command and example, encourages believers to be involved in the administration of justice and to support its institutions; yet, other biblical texts warn against the dangers of worldly power and the necessity of disobeying ministers of the law when they contradict one's obligations before God.

In their sojourning, Abraham and his family enjoyed peaceful relations living in the territory of king Abimelech of Gerar, with whom they even entered into covenants (Gen 21:22-34; 26:26-31), but they were also the victims of great injustice when Shechem, another local magistrate, raped Dinah (Gen 34). The godly Joseph rose to a position of political prominence in pagan Egypt, but only after unjustly languishing there in servitude and prison for many years (Gen 39–50), and a pharaoh of later times oppressed Israel in a suffocating bondage (Ex 1–5). Under the Mosaic theocracy, some kings ruled Israel with relative justice and promoted peace and prosperity, but most were disobedient to their obligation to rule under God's law and provoked the denunciation of the prophets for their unjust ways. As a result of such disobedience, God subjected his people to the cruel tyranny of King Nebuchadnezzar of Babylon, who reduced Jerusalem to rubble and dragged the people into exile (2 Kings 25), yet in this foreign city the pious Daniel, Shadrach, Meshach and Abednego assumed high positions in Nebuchadnezzar's court (Dan 1–4).

In the New Testament, Jesus warned his disciples about the power-hungry attitude of earthly rulers (Mk 10:42-45) and exhorted them to turn the other cheek instead of enforcing "eye for eye, and tooth for tooth" (Mt 5:38-42), but he also commanded them to give to Caesar what is Caesar's (Mt 22:21). After Jesus' resurrection and ascension, the apostles Peter and John boldly declared that they must obey God rather than men (Acts 5:29), though Peter and Paul urged believers to be subject to civil magistrates (Rom 13:1-7; 1 Pet 2:13-17; Tit 3:1).

We do not suggest that the Bible is inconsistent, but we encourage readers to note the complexities and subtleties of Scripture's teaching on such matters. Wrestling with these issues is a challenge, yet of crucial importance for developing a balanced perspective on civil law. We see in Scripture models of faithfulness under a very broad range of legal experiences. The challenge for Christians is to discern their calling within the legal regime in which they find themselves.

Justice. A final theme that readers will find throughout this book is justice. Scripture often speaks about this ideal. The prophets call for justice and predict a coming Messiah in whose kingdom justice will flourish.

> In faithfulness he will bring forth justice;
>   he will not falter or be discouraged
> till he establishes justice on earth. (Is 42:3-4)

Scripture addresses various types of justice. The theme of retributive justice is prominent in the Old Testament, represented by the eye-for-an-eye formula of the *lex talionis* as found in the covenant with Noah (Gen 9:6) and the Mosaic law (Ex 21:23-25; Lev 24:18-21; Deut 19:21). Some commentators see the *lex talionis* as the model of just punishment; in the eyes of others it was a limit on punishment in the midst of the surrounding cultures where vicious revenge was the general rule. The New Testament affirms the state's continuing obligation to pursue retributive justice (e.g., Rom 13:4).

Again, in the Gospels, Jesus commands Christians to turn the other cheek rather than seek an eye for an eye. Some interpreters see this as a limitation on private revenge, with no relevance to the responsibilities of governing authorities; some see it as normative for the life and ministry of the church; others see it as a prohibition of Christian participation in the retributive justice work of the state; still others see it as a qualification to the state's focus on retributive justice, one that should yield justice tempered with mercy on the part of ruling authorities.

Scripture also addresses what today might be categorized as economic or social justice. The Mosaic law provided for periodic forgiveness of debts, the return of land to families (Lev 25:8-10) and other means of caring for the poor (e.g., Lev 25). It commanded that landowners not cut the grain on the edge of their fields, thus making this grain available to poor people (Lev 19:9-10). The Mosaic law, the Psalms, the Prophets, Jesus and James all identify widows, orphans, aliens and the poor as people deserving special protection (e.g., Ex 22:21-24; Amos 5:10-15; Lk 20:46-47; Jas 1:27). Jesus identifies loving one's neighbor as the second great command of the law and leaves his followers to wrestle with the implications of this command for civil law in their own time and place.

CONCLUSION

As the editors, we invite readers to join this exploration of the civil law in Scripture. This investigation will not yield a comprehensive biblical theology of law or an ideal biblical civil code, but it will immerse you in the story of Scripture, in key themes concerning Christian faith and civil law, and in foundational biblical texts for faithful thinking about life in a human legal order. This work will not answer every question about how Christians should be godly law students, lawyers or justice-loving citizens, but we hope it will stimulate your thinking in productive directions, provoke further study and make you a more faithful Christian and a more faithful participant in your own legal system.

1

THE BIBLICAL
FOUNDATIONS OF LAW

CREATION, FALL AND THE PATRIARCHS

Randy Beck and David VanDrunen

THE BOOK OF GENESIS describes God's creation of the universe, the primeval history of humanity and the establishment of the Israelite families descended from Abraham. From one perspective, these accounts of ancient history might seem distant from the concerns of civil law in the twenty-first century. They tell of cultures and practices separated by millennia from our own. The stories unfold in the context of nomadic and agrarian communities, unacquainted with the technological advances that shape modern life. The narrative sometimes touches on topics like economics or the environment, but without reference to the bodies of technical knowledge that inform contemporary discussions of public policy.[1]

When one begins to explore the teaching of Genesis, however, and when one reflects on the goals of the civil law, the book proves to hold foundational implications for modern legal systems. Though set in an unfamiliar historical context, Genesis highlights enduring truths about the nature of God, the nature of humans and the challenges of human community. It chronicles events that are determinative for our present condition. The

---

[1]The authors would like to thank Don Aldin, Nathan Chapman and George Fletcher for helpful comments on a draft of this chapter.

worldview reflected in Genesis speaks profoundly to the purpose, the promise and the perils of the civil legal enterprise.

From its very first pages, the book of Genesis reveals God as the one who governs the universe, ruling the created order by his words. He directs the components of the material world to accomplish his purposes. His words bring order and abundance to creation, earning a divine benediction: "And God saw everything that he had made, and behold, it was very good" (Gen 1:31).[2]

The human activities associated with the civil law seem analogous in some respects to these creative acts of God. Those who claim authority to govern the human community also use words creatively—to form statutes, cases, regulations and the like. The civil law employs these legal words for instrumental purposes, directing the participants in the social world. The words of the law seek to bring order and prosperity to the human community, pursuing ends deemed "good" by those who govern. One may view the civil law's attempt to exercise dominion in the social world through the use of language as a dim likeness of God's actions in creation. This weak imitation of divine government, we believe, reflects at least part of what Genesis means when it proclaims that humans are created "in the image of God." But if we can trace similarities between divine and human government, important differences also exist that carry implications for the wise exercise of civil authority.

A few moments' reflection highlights a number of issues fundamental to civil law that are addressed in the text of Genesis and discussed in this essay. Consider first the question of authority. Why may some humans govern others? Are some assertions of governing authority legitimate, or is all human government merely domination of the weak by those with superior force? Genesis presents God as the source of all legitimate authority and describes his delegation of some measure of that authority to his human creatures. Second, the civil law aspires to promote the good life or, at least, to create conditions in which citizens may pursue their own visions of the good life. Genesis takes up the questions of what is "good" and how the good may be known. Third, the civil law aims to influence the conduct of human beings, an enterprise that requires an understanding of anthro-

---

[2]Unless otherwise indicated, all Scripture quotations in this chapter are from the ESV.

pology. Who are these creatures the law seeks to regulate? Why do humans create problems for their neighbors, rather than live in peaceful cooperation? Genesis offers an understanding of human identity, one that highlights the need for civil government but that also suggests moral and prudential limits on the exercise of coercion by the civil authorities. Fourth, the civil law embraces the ideal of "justice," an aspiration that has been understood in different ways. We will seek to show that Genesis embraces a *talionic* understanding of divine justice. In his role as judge, God takes the misconduct of a wrongdoer, including the harm it inflicts, as the measure of appropriate punishment. Finally, the Christian church has always faced questions about its relationship to the civil authorities. Citizens of the "kingdom" of God have long wondered about the implications for their interaction with human "kingdoms." Genesis speaks to these questions as well, planting the seeds of Augustine's "two cities" framework and the later "two kingdoms" theology of the Reformation.[3]

In the pages that follow, we touch upon many of these questions concerning the implications of Genesis for civil law.

GOD, THE RULER OF CREATION

The first chapter of Genesis describes God solely in terms of what he does. It never records God's attributes but requires us to perceive the nature of God through an account of his actions, especially the words he speaks. His actions reveal that he is a great king who exercises sovereign legislative and judicial authority in the world he creates.

At the outset of the process of creation, Genesis identifies three problems afflicting the original earth—darkness, formlessness and emptiness (Gen 1:2). God systematically addresses all three problems by his decrees. He first creates the light to overcome the darkness. Since "darkness is as light" to God (Ps 139:12), the creation of light solves a problem not for God himself but for his creatures. The creation of light implies that God is acting for an

---

[3]On the relation of Augustine's "two cities" and the Reformation's "two kingdoms," see David Van-Drunen, *Natural Law and the Two Kingdoms: A Study in the Development of Reformed Social Thought* (Grand Rapids: Eerdmans, 2010), chaps. 2–3. In short, the "two cities" refer to two peoples, one who loves the Creator above all and one who loves created things above all; these cities mix in the present world but do not correspond neatly to church and state. The "two kingdoms" refer to God's twofold government of the world, a providential sustaining of the world (in significant measure through the justice of the state) and a redemptive reign (especially through the building of the church). Christians thus belong to only one "city" but participate in both "kingdoms."

audience, revealing himself to those he has made. Perhaps the fact that he only partially eliminates the darkness (day and night) implies that the creation involves only a partial self-revelation by God. We must await the new creation for night to be banished so we can see God as he is (Rev 22:4-5).

Having addressed the problem of darkness, God sets out systematically over the next five days to resolve the challenges of formlessness and emptiness. He does this in two corresponding sets of three days. On the first three days, God uses his words to create distinctions, separating what was previously muddled to bring form to the creation. On the first day he separates the day from the night, on the second day the sea from the sky and on the third day the sea from the dry land. The earth no longer remains formless. Boundaries now exist. Observers can distinguish one part of creation from another.

On the succeeding three days, God employs words to fill the emptiness of creation, following the same order by which he brought form. He separated day from night on the first day, so on the fourth day he fills the daytime sky with the greater light and the nighttime sky with the lesser lights. He separated the sea from the sky on the second day, so on the fifth day he fills the sea with fish and the sky with birds. He separated the sea from the dry land on the third day, so on the sixth day (since the sea has already been filled) he fills the land with animals and humans. Thus, just as God solved the problem of formlessness on the first three days, he follows the same sequence on the next three days in solving the problem of emptiness. (See table 1.1.)

Table 1.1. Creation

Overcoming Formlessness		Overcoming Emptiness	
Day 1:	Day Night	Day 4:	Greater light (sun) Lesser lights (moon/stars)
Day 2:	Sea Sky	Day 5:	Fish Birds
Day 3:	Sea Dry Land	Day 6:	(Fish already created) Animals and humans

God's work of creation has a legislative aspect in that it orders all things and establishes their proper functions. We see this legislative aspect on display first in the way he makes and locates each thing in its proper place. He distinguishes day and night, water above from water below, and water from dry land (Gen 1:4, 6, 9, 14). He makes plants, sea creatures, birds and land animals, each according to their kinds (Gen 1:11-12, 21, 24-25). He gives names to many created things (Gen 1:5, 8, 10). Most significantly, God decrees what created things are to do. The lights above, for example, he made to "rule over" day and night and to separate light from darkness (Gen 1:18). Climactically, God created human beings and commanded them to have "dominion" over other creatures, to be fruitful and multiply, and to subdue the earth (Gen 1:26, 28). The language of rule and dominion on days four and six suggests that the first three days established the realms of creation, while the second three days ordained the rulers of each realm. We see God acting legislatively as well when he prohibits Adam from eating the fruit of one of the trees of the Garden, using a Hebrew form of speech characteristic of legal commands later in the Old Testament (Gen 2:16-17).[4]

The opening of Genesis portrays God not just as a legislator but also as the great judge. God renders verdicts upon creation itself and thus, indirectly, upon his own work. Six times he pronounces "good" the things he has made (Gen 1:4, 10, 12, 18, 21, 25). Surveying the whole of his handiwork, he proclaims it "very good" (Gen 1:31). But he deems it "not good" for Adam to be alone, an assessment that leads to the creation of Eve (Gen 2:18). When giving the probationary command of Genesis 2:16-17, he states that Adam's disobedience will have consequences: if he eats of the forbidden tree, he will die. God's judicial role becomes fully evident after Adam and Eve disobey. God comes in judgment, pronouncing a verdict upon each wrongdoer—the serpent, the woman and the man (Gen 3:14-19). The early chapters of Genesis manifest what becomes explicit when Abraham later describes God as "the Judge of all the earth" (Gen 18:25). In sum, Genesis shows God as the sovereign King of the universe, who creates by his words, who pronounces laws governing the created order and who enforces those laws by his judgments.

THE IMAGE OF GOD

Though explicit references to human creatures being in the image and likeness of God appear only rarely in Scripture, the underlying idea leaves its mark on many pages and has shaped Christian anthropological reflection through the centuries. The first biblical reference to human beings

---

[4]See Bryan D. Estelle, "The Covenant of Works in Moses and Paul," in *Covenant, Justification, and Pastoral Ministry: Essays by the Faculty of Westminster Seminary California* (Phillipsburg, NJ: P & R, 2007), pp. 110-12; and J. V. Fesko, *Last Things First: Unlocking Genesis 1–3 with the Christ of Eschatology* (Fearn, UK: Mentor, 2007), p. 84.

as the image and likeness of God appears toward the end of the creation account in Genesis 1:26-27:

> Then God said, "Let us make man in our image, after our likeness. And let them have dominion over the fish of the sea and over the birds of the heavens and over the livestock and over all the earth and over every creeping thing that creeps on the earth."
>
>   So God created man in his own image,
>   in the image of God he created him;
>   male and female he created them.

We revisit the image-of-God theme when we consider the Noahic covenant, but it is important first to weigh what these words tell us about human nature and the human vocation in the original creation. We find that human beings, imaging their Creator, were called to abide by law, make law and judge.

Western theologians have often understood the image of God to exist in certain human attributes, such as rationality, spirituality or freedom. In recent years, however, a broad consensus has developed among biblical scholars that the image and likeness described in Genesis 1:26-27 should be understood in more functional terms.[5] In other words, the image of God does not refer to human rationality or volition (though it may presuppose such things) so much as to the office or task that God created human beings to perform. Specifically, God, the great king of creation, made human beings as his representatives, commissioned to exercise royal-judicial rule in this world on his behalf. Though we cannot defend this view in detail here, it rests upon a solid exegetical basis and carries significant theological implications.[6] One implication is that law making and judging were important parts of human identity even before the fall into sin.

---

[5]Gunnlaugur A. Jónsson noted this emerging consensus in his survey of the literature more than twenty years ago; see *The Image of God: Genesis 1:26-28 in a Century of Old Testament Research* (Lund: Almqvist & Wiksell, 1988), pp. 219-23. See the next footnote for examples of scholars who defend versions of this view.

[6]Among significant exegetical studies, see J. Richard Middleton, *The Liberating Image: The Imago Dei in Genesis 1* (Grand Rapids: Brazos, 2005), chap. 2; David J. A. Clines, "Humanity as the Image of God," in *On the Way to the Postmodern: Old Testament Essays, 1967–1998* (Sheffield: Sheffield Academic Press, 1998), 2:482-95; Phyllis A. Bird, "'Male and Female He Created Them': Gen 1:27b in the Context of the Priestly Account of Creation," *Harvard Theological Review* 74.2 (1981): 139-44; W. Randall Garr, *In His Own Image and Likeness: Humanity, Divinity, and Monotheism* (Leiden: Brill, 2003), chap. 7; and Meredith G. Kline, *Images of the Spirit* (Grand Rapids: Baker, 1980), chap. 1.

Since human beings were created in the image and likeness of God, understanding the image requires us to investigate what Scripture says about God himself. As children tend to resemble their parents, whose likeness they bear, so we expect human beings to resemble the God in whose likeness they were originally created (see Gen 5:1-3). As noted above, the opening pages of Scripture describe God as the great legislator who orders his creation and the great judge who holds it accountable. Little surprise, then, that these same texts portray human beings, created in the divine image and likeness, as God's representatives commissioned to rule the world justly under the supreme king.

We see this, first of all, in Genesis 1:26. English translations usually render this verse in a way that suggests God issued two indirect commands without any clear connection to each other: first, "let us make man in our image," and second, "let them have dominion." While one could interpret the Hebrew grammar this way, a more likely reading is that the second command constitutes a purpose clause following up on the first command.[7] Along these lines the verse might better read: "Then God said, 'Let us make man in our image, after our likeness, *and thus* let them have dominion.'" This implies that the very identity of the image of God is wrapped up in the commission to exercise royal rule in the world under God. The Hebrew words used in Genesis 1:26 and 28 usually translated "have dominion" and "subdue" are verbs indicating strong action.[8] Though we should guard against misuse of these verses to justify poor ecological stewardship, Christians should not overreact to this danger. God made human beings not to be weak middle managers, but strong rulers of creation. Yet their rule must always be benevolent and just, like God's, and therefore beneficial for creation itself.

In addition to the explicit direction to exercise dominion, the task of naming the animals also highlights the human commission to rule the world justly as God's representatives (Gen 2:19-20). As noted above, God named a number of things as he created them in Genesis 1. Yet he ceased doing so after the third day. Naming the creatures he made on the final three days was a job delegated to Adam. As God exercised his legislative authority in part through designating the names of his creatures, so Adam

---

[7]E.g., see Paul Joüon, *A Grammar of Biblical Hebrew*, trans. and rev. Takamitsu Muraoka (Rome: Editrice Pontificio Instituto Biblico, 1991), 2:381.

[8]See, e.g., Bird, "'Male and Female He Created Them,'" pp. 154-55; and Garr, *In His Own Image and Likeness*, pp. 156, 171.

was to image God's authority through giving each beast and bird its proper name. And as God's words in Genesis 1 were always efficacious, so Adam's naming in Genesis was efficacious: "whatever the man called every living creature, that was its name" (Gen 2:19).

We likely find a third sense in which God commissioned human beings to rule creation as his royal representatives in the mysterious title of that infamous tree, the tree of the knowledge of good and evil. Though theologians have toyed with various interpretations of this title, elsewhere in the Old Testament the idea of knowing good and evil usually concerns judicial judgment. It is often associated with the work of kings (e.g., see 2 Sam 14:17; 1 Kings 3:9). The test that God imposed on Adam with the tree was probably not *whether* he would "know good and evil," but *how*.[9] In knowing good and evil, Adam and Eve in fact became *like God* (Gen 3:22). The problem was not that Adam and Eve sought to know good and evil but that they exercised this weighty judicial authority in opposition to God's instructions. Instead of respecting the proper legal order established in creation (God as the overlord, human beings as his underlords, and the rest of creation submissive to them), they turned that order on its head, elevating themselves over God while submitting to another creature (the serpent). Instead of exercising their rightful judicial authority over the serpent, they let the serpent be their lawgiver.

The opening chapters of Scripture, then, portray human beings as the image and likeness of God in a way that showcases the significance of law in the original creation. God exercises his supreme royal authority by establishing order and prescribing the behavior of created things, particularly in laying down the law for his human creatures. He renders judgment first on his own creative work and then comes in judgment upon the work of Adam, Eve and the serpent. Human beings bear the image of such a God. God made them to exercise dominion, to name the animals and to "know good and evil" through rendering just judgment under his guidance. Yet their legislative and judicial authority was far from absolute. They could replicate God's infinite authority only on a finite level. Their lawmaking and judgment

---

[9]Among those advocating versions of this position are William N. Wilder, "Illumination and Investiture: The Royal Significance of the Tree of Wisdom in Genesis 3," *Westminster Theological Journal* 68 (Spring 2006): 51-69; and W. Malcolm Clark, "A Legal Background to the Yahwist's Use of Good and Evil in Genesis 2–3," *Journal of Biblical Literature* 88 (September 1969): 266-78.

rendering had to be exercised within the larger framework of God's justice. When they sought to overturn God's just order through their own autonomous judgment, catastrophe ensued.

THE FALL INTO SIN

The second chapter of Genesis describes an idyllic paradise, the Garden of Eden, where humans walk in harmony with God, where husband and wife work together in unity, where humanity exercises a benevolent and protective dominion over the natural world, and where the shame associated with transgression finds no place. Within two chapters, Adam and Eve have been deceived by the serpent, have disobeyed God's command that they not eat from the tree, and have been judged by God and expelled from the garden. Their son Cain, angry with God, has killed his brother Abel (see Gen 3–4). The story of the rapid descent from utopian concord to murderous rage shows that something highly significant has occurred in the interim. From one perspective, the account of the fall in Genesis 3 might seem trivial. Adam and Eve ate a piece of fruit that God told them not to eat. Who was hurt by this one seemingly *de minimis* offense? God could replace the fruit easily enough. No other creature was deprived of something needed for life or health. The radical consequences of the event, however, as described in the succeeding text of Genesis and the remainder of Scripture, show that this small act of disobedience reflected a far-reaching alteration in the relationship between God and humanity.

Humans pursue visions of the good life.[10] We come into conflict with each other because we understand the good in mutually incompatible and self-centered ways (Jas 4:1-3). Genesis attributes this state of affairs to a fundamental change of faith on the part of humanity—from God to self—that took place at the fall. Genesis began with God establishing a good creation in which Adam and Eve would exercise dominion. Their utopian existence continued so long as they trusted God to guide them in pursuit of the good. The serpent, however, called into question God's truthfulness and benevolence and persuaded Eve to break fellowship with God. Contradicting God's warning to Adam, the serpent told Eve that if she ate the fruit, "You will not surely die. For God knows that when you eat of it your eyes will be opened, and you will be like God, knowing good and evil" (Gen 3:4-5).

---

[10]James K. A. Smith, *Desiring the Kingdom: Worship, Worldview, and Cultural Formation* (Grand Rapids: Baker Academic, 2009), pp. 52-55.

Her faith in the Creator shaken, Eve fell back on her own perceptions of the good. She "saw that the tree was good for food, and that it was a delight to the eyes, and that the tree was to be desired to make one wise" (Gen 3:6). This fundamental transfer of confidence from God's assessment of the good life to our own—the change of faith from divine guidance to autonomous moral reasoning—underlies humanity's descent from paradise to violent conflict. Only the omniscient God possesses the wisdom to distinguish good from evil in a way that justly embraces the whole creation. Distancing ourselves from the only source of reliable moral guidance, we have created a state of continual discord as humans compete to pursue partial and self-interested visions of the good life.

The judgments imposed following Adam and Eve's sin show that the fall undermined in part the blessings of the original creation and frustrated humanity's commission to rule as God's regents. God had exercised dominion over the original creation, and then charged his image bearers to subdue the earth and rule over the other creatures (Gen 1:26, 28). Due to Adam's sin, however, the ground would now resist cultivation, and Adam would eat bread by the sweat of his brow (Gen 3:17). God brought fullness to the original creation by his words. He correspondingly had commissioned his image bearers to be fruitful and "multiply" and fill the earth (Gen 1:28). But the fall "multiplied" the woman's pain in childbirth, so that her fruitfulness would come at greater cost (Gen 3:16). Alienated from their Creator, humans would now find it harder to do what they had been made to do as bearers of the divine image.[11]

The fall into sin carries significant implications for our discussion of civil law. If nothing else, humanity's unwillingness to be ruled by a benevolent Creator indicates that we will not easily submit to our fellow humans, even

---

[11]Some readers of this chapter have wondered why the sin of Adam and Eve in Genesis 3 yielded a sentence of death. If Genesis embraces an ideal of *talionic* justice, as we contend, how does death represent a proportional retributive punishment for the sin of eating forbidden fruit? In explaining the punishment, God tells Adam "you are dust, and to dust you shall return" (Gen 3:19), language with *talionic* overtones. In proudly grasping after equality with God, these beings from the dust earned the retributive humiliation of a return to dust. Alternatively, one might say that Adam and Eve owed their entire beings to God—that they were obligated to love him with all their heart, soul, mind and strength (Deut 6:5; Mk 12:30)—so that the judgment justly demanded the lives they had wrongfully withheld. Or one could say that their sin lay in separating themselves from the source of life, making loss of life the natural and proportional consequence. More broadly, perhaps all sin involves secretly wishing for the death of God, a Deicide in the heart that makes the sinner's death a proportional retributive response.

when the good of the community is at stake. Those driven by their own perceptions of the good life can be expected to resist compulsion to serve the broader good. In seeking to govern this community of rebels, civil authorities must depend on the weak tools of human language and the threat of punishment. The words of humans have never been as powerful as the words of God, which can bring something out of nothing. In humanity's postfall alienation from God, human governments must rely on their own strength to enforce whatever decrees they issue, a strength that may prove unequal to the task. The civil authorities must also cope with the curse, which hinders humanity's attempts to exercise dominion in the earth. The self-centered rebelliousness of fallen human nature, the relative power-lessness of human language and creation's resistance to humanity's dominion after the fall all suggest that human law will necessarily prove a less-than-fully-effective means of ordering the social world.

One implication of this may be that we should limit our expectations for human government. In the words of the psalmist, we should not put our trust in princes (Pss 118:9; 146:3). The real hope is not that the right people will acquire political power and exercise that power in the right way. The true hope lies in God's creation of "new heavens and a new earth in which righteousness dwells" (2 Pet 3:13). Significantly, the New Testament often draws on Genesis to describe God's re-creation of the world through his Son. God "who said 'Let light shine out of darkness,' has shone in our hearts to give the light of the knowledge of the glory of God in the face of Jesus Christ" (2 Cor 4:6). Anyone in Christ is a "new creation" (2 Cor 5:17). Christ is the Last Adam who overcomes the curse of the fallen creation (Rom 5:12-21; 1 Cor 15:45-49). He will exercise dominion as king in the new heavens and earth and, with his bride, the church, will populate the new creation with spiritual children (Gal 4:26-29; Eph 5:25-32; Rev 21:9-14). God does indeed call us to pursue justice in the world and thereby uses us to accomplish genuine good for one another, but such efforts can never be our ultimate hope.

THE TWO COMMUNITIES AFTER THE FALL

One of the most influential works in the history of political theology has been Augustine's *City of God*.[12] Responding to pagan critics, who chal-

---

[12]Augustine, *The City of God*, trans. Marcus Dods (Peabody, MA: Hendrickson, 2000).

lenged the Christian faith based on Rome's fall to barbarian invaders, Augustine drew a scripturally based distinction between two cities: an eternal, heavenly city built by God and a temporal, earthly city built by men. Augustine saw the human race divided between these two cities, with believers as citizens of the city of God.[13] Of course, citizens of both "cities" live side by side in this world, so we might describe them as distinct communities that share a common earthly residence. The fall of Rome created no problem for Christian theology, under Augustine's framework, because Rome had never been God's city. It was merely an earthly city, under God's judgment like all the cities of this world.

Augustine's division of humanity into two communities finds roots in the text of Genesis.[14] As Augustine notes,[15] Genesis points to Cain, the first murderer, as the first person to build an earthly city (Gen 4:8, 17). When confronting Cain about killing his brother Abel, God condemns Cain to be a "wanderer" on the earth (Gen 4:10-12). Cain instead settles down, in apparent rebellion against the judgment of God. He establishes a city to the east of Eden, in the land of Nod, and names it after his firstborn son, Enoch (Gen 4:16-17).

Genesis offers no explanation for Cain's decision to build a city. The narrative suggests, however, that fear of violence played a role. Cain dreaded a retributive response to his crime against Abel, complaining that, "whoever finds me will kill me" (Gen 4:14). He intuitively feared that his violence against Abel would come back on his own head. Not content with God's promise to avenge him sevenfold (Gen 4:15), Cain sought the safety of walls built with his own hands. Naming the city after his son implies that Cain also viewed the city of Enoch as part of his legacy. By establishing a political community, Cain sought to make a mark on the world that would survive his death.

Cain's city flourished technologically and artistically (Gen 4:20-22). Ironically, though, the community established as a refuge against violence became itself a place of violence, as reflected in the boast of Cain's descendant, Lamech:

---

[13]See, e.g., Augustine, *City of God* 14.28.

[14]This section draws inspiration and interpretive insights from Warren Gage, *The Gospel of Genesis: Studies in Protology and Eschatology* (Eugene, OR: Wipf & Stock, 1984); and Jacques Ellul, *The Meaning of the City* (Grand Rapids: Eerdmans, 1970).

[15]Augustine, *City of God*, bk. 15.

Lamech said to his wives:

"Adah and Zillah, hear my voice;
    you wives of Lamech, listen to what I say:
I have killed a man for wounding me,
    a young man for striking me.
If Cain's revenge is sevenfold,
    then Lamech's is seventy-sevenfold." (Gen 4:23-24)

Lamech's boasting underscores his thorough sense of superiority. By taking two wives, he departs from the Edenic pattern of marriage (Gen 2:24), demanding the exclusive attention of two women. His violent reprisal against the young man assumes that a wound to Lamech warrants the death of his adversary. He lays claim to eleven times the vengeance described to Cain and even steps into the role of God, personally exacting revenge rather than leaving his vindication in God's hands. Cain's city, now dominated by the pride of Lamech, carries forward Cain's legacy of bloodshed.

Though Scripture as a whole makes clear that building cities is not inherently sinful, and does not evaluate the relative virtues of living in urban or rural areas, the early chapters of Genesis associate city building with the line of Cain. But these chapters also tell of another line descended from Adam through Seth, who replaced murdered Abel (Gen 4:25). When Seth later begot Enosh, "people began to call upon the name of the LORD" (Gen 4:26), a phrase that reverberates through the pages of Scripture. In the Prophets, to "call on the name of the LORD" becomes scriptural shorthand for the life of faith. The prophet Joel promises that "everyone who calls on the name of the LORD shall be saved" (Joel 2:32), an assurance echoed by Paul in the New Testament (Rom 10:13). The prophet Zechariah describes a people who will be refined like silver and tested like gold:

They will call upon my name,
    and I will answer them.
I will say, "They are my people";
    and they will say, "The LORD is my God." (Zech 13:9)

We thus find two groups among the descendants of Adam in the world of Genesis 4–7. Cain and his descendants become city builders. Alienated from God and relying on themselves, they seek to create a refuge in this world. But the violence of Cain's city gradually fills the earth, ultimately

provoking the judgment of the flood (Gen 6:5-7, 11-13). The other group of
Adam's descendants follows the pattern of Abel and Seth. These are the believers, who call on the LORD in faith. Seth's line eventually produces Noah,
who "walked with God" and was saved from the flood along with his family
(Gen 6:9; 7:1-24).

These two communities among humans reemerge in the text of Genesis
after the flood. Cain prefigures the men who unite to build Babel, a short
form of the name "Babylon." Just as Cain traveled east from Eden, Genesis
tells us that men once again moved toward the east (Gen 11:2). Reaching the
plain of Shinar, they said, "Come, let us build ourselves a city and a tower
with its top in the heavens, and let us make a name for ourselves, lest we be
dispersed over the face of the whole earth" (Gen 11:4). Cain's refusal to
wander foreshadows the early Babylonians' desire not to be scattered. His
aspiration to preserve a legacy, naming the city after his son, corresponds to
the Babylonians' hope to make a name for themselves. The building plans
for Babel are frustrated only when God confuses their tongues, concerned
over the projects men might pursue as "one people . . . hav[ing] all one language" (Gen 11:1-9).

Just as the discussion of Cain's city is followed by the account of Seth, the
story of Babel is followed by the account of Abraham. Like the family of
Seth, Abraham "call[s] upon the name of the LORD" (Gen 13:4). Leaving
behind the city of Ur, Abraham travels to Canaan, the land God promised
to give him (Gen 11:31–12:7). He and his household never settle down to
build a city of their own. Instead, they pursue a nomadic life, living in tents
as they travel about the Promised Land.

The New Testament author of Hebrews explains Abraham's failure to
build a city as an act of faith in God's provision. "By faith," Abraham "went
to live in the land of promise, as in a foreign land, living in tents with Isaac
and Jacob, heirs with him of the same promise" (Heb 11:9). He was "looking
forward to the city that has foundations, whose designer and builder is God"
(Heb 11:10). In this regard, Abraham characterized the entire Old Testament
"cloud of witnesses" (Heb 12:1) listed in Hebrews 11:

> These all died in faith, not having received the things promised, but having
> seen them and greeted them from afar, and having acknowledged that they
> were strangers and exiles on the earth. For people who speak thus make it
> clear that they are seeking a homeland. If they had been thinking of that land

from which they had gone out, they would have had opportunity to return. But as it is, they desire a better country, that is, a heavenly one. Therefore God is not ashamed to be called their God, for he has prepared for them a city. (Heb 11:13-16)

The author of Hebrews highlights the believer's sense of dissatisfaction with this world. Faith expresses itself as a longing for a better country. Unlike other utopian aspirations, however, the Christian longs specifically for a city built by God, not by human beings.

Abraham's patient anticipation of God's city underscores the profound contrast between Abraham and Cain. Each embodies a disjunction between appearance and reality. God sentences Cain to be a wanderer, but instead he builds a city. Yet he constructs the city in the land of "Nod," which means "wandering." Though Cain tries to rebel against the judgment of God, he cannot. To all appearances, he looks like he has settled down; he looks like he has a home. But in reality, he is still a wanderer.

In contrast to Cain, Abraham appears to be a wanderer. He dwells as an alien and stranger in the land of promise. He travels about and lives in tents. But though he seems to be a wanderer, Abraham really has a home. He rests secure in the promise of an eternal city built by God. In this respect, Abraham serves as the template for all who call on the name of the Lord. As the New Testament says of Christians, "here we have no lasting city, but we seek the city that is to come" (Heb 13:14). Human law and earthly cities are necessary and valuable, and God calls his people to seek the welfare of the cities in which they live (e.g., Jer 29:7). But these must never become the most important things for us.

THE COVENANT WITH NOAH

Genesis 6–9 records the famous story of Noah and his family. God, in response to human wickedness, decrees a great flood to destroy the earth. But God also recognizes Noah as a righteous man, and he enters into a covenant to save Noah, his family and the earth's animals from the coming devastation through the building of an ark. Much as God had given Adam the task of naming and ruling over animals in the Garden, the task of preserving the animals now falls to Noah.[16] Genesis 8 describes a sort of re-creation scene

---

[16]See Gage, *Gospel of Genesis*, p. 11: "Surely it also has anthropological significance that man in his relationship to other animate life is a point central to both the Adam and Noah records."

after the rain stops, as the wind passes over the earth (compare Gen 1:2 with 8:1), the waters divide and the dry land emerges. When Noah's family and the animals disembark, God enters into another covenant with all living creatures, promising preservation of the natural order and human society and giving the new humanity several commands (Gen 8:20–9:17). This covenant carries considerable significance for understanding human law.

We begin by describing several features of the postdiluvian Noahic covenant before reflecting on its implications for human law. First, God sets this covenant in place for the duration of human history on earth. God will uphold the natural order and spare it from another destruction by water "while the earth remains" (Gen 8:22). Someday this covenant will no longer be in force, but not until the end of history. Second, this Noahic covenant has a universal scope. God enters the covenant not only with all of subsequent humanity but also with all living beings in coming generations (Gen 9:9-13, 15-17). In contrast to the covenant God made with Noah before the flood (Gen 6:18) and the major biblical covenants yet to come, such as the Abrahamic, Mosaic and new,[17] the Noahic covenant does not distinguish a part of the human race from the rest but is all-encompassing. Third, this covenant aims to preserve the natural order and human society with it. This highlights another important feature that distinguishes the postdiluvian (postflood) Noahic covenant from the later biblical covenants. While these other covenants have redemptive elements—promising in various ways to save God's people from evil and the coming divine judgment—this Noahic covenant has no redemptive provisions. It never promises forgiveness of sins, eternal life or any of the other benefits associated with salvation through the rest of Scripture. Even the sign of the covenant, the rainbow (Gen 9:13-16), is not bloody, distinguishing it from later covenantal signs that symbolize or involve the shedding of blood, such as circumcision, the Passover, baptism and the Lord's Supper.

What the Noahic covenant does promise is preservation. God commits himself not to eliminate evil from the world but to mitigate its effects so that the created order might be maintained for a time. The covenant prevents

---

[17]The Abrahamic covenant refers to the covenant God made with Abraham and his descendants (see Gen 15 and 17). The Mosaic covenant refers to the covenant God made with Israel at Mount Sinai (see Ex 19–24). The new covenant refers to the covenant God made in Christ with the New Testament church (see Lk 22:20; Heb 7–9).

the destruction of the natural order (Gen 8:21; 9:11, 15), sustains the cycles of nature (Gen 8:22), regulates animal-human relations (Gen 9:2-4), and commands human reproduction and the administration of a legal system to maintain the human social order (Gen 9:1, 5-7).

With these basic features of the Noahic covenant on the table, we can now appreciate a number of its important implications for a biblical view of law. Of special significance are God's words in Genesis 9:5-6:

> "And for your lifeblood I will require a reckoning: from every beast I will require it and from man. From his fellow man I will require a reckoning for the life of man.
>
> > "Whoever sheds the blood of man,
> >   by man shall his blood be shed,
> > for God made man in his own image."

With most biblical commentators, we take these last words to be prescriptive, and not merely descriptive.[18] In other words, God authorizes capital punishment as an appropriate response to murder. No doubt other parts of Scripture are also relevant to issues surrounding the death penalty, and there are important questions about the procedural protections necessary to prevent erroneous convictions, the need to avoid racially slanted sentencing and the appropriate role of mercy in the legal system.[19] Within the context of Genesis, for instance, one sees God protecting Cain from human retribution for the murder of his brother (Gen 4:15). But the Noahic covenant would seem to indicate that capital punishment can, under appropriate procedures, represent a just legal response to the killing of another human being. Reflection upon the Noahic covenant yields much insight about the nature and purpose of human law. We mention six things in particular.

First, human legal systems lie ultimately under the authority of God. The development of legal systems is a human task, yet it should never be an autonomous endeavor. By means of a covenant, God has ordained that human beings pursue justice in the world, and he has given them, however

---

[18]For two examples of commentators who take this position, see Nahum M. Sarna, *Genesis* (Philadelphia: Jewish Publication Society, 1989), p. 61; and Gordon J. Wenham, *Genesis 1–15*, Word Biblical Commentary 1 (Waco, TX: Word, 1987), pp. 193-94.

[19]For additional commentary in this volume on capital punishment and the *lex talionis*, see "Lessons for Contemporary Issues" in chapter three (Old Testament law) and "God's Moral Law, the Mosaic Law and Legislation" in chapter six (Jesus).

sparse, a basic standard for justice: "blood for blood." While there is surely a place for creativity and ingenuity on the part of people entrusted with developing legislation, courts and judicial procedures, they must execute such tasks conscious of their accountability to God and his righteousness.

Second, the development of law and legal systems seems to be a central, not peripheral, task of the human race in its fallen, yet preserved, condition under the Noahic covenant. As recorded in Genesis 8:20–9:17, the Noahic covenant consists primarily in God's commitment to the world rather than in human obligation toward God. The covenant is unilateral in the sense that it posits no conditions that must be met if the divine blessings are to be enjoyed. But it does give three commands to human beings in Genesis 9:1-7. While the obligations of human beings living under God's preserving grace are undoubtedly much broader than these three commands, this covenant singles out being fruitful and multiplying, not eating the blood of animals and enforcing justice as exemplary duties. Creating, enforcing and living under law is apparently a central aspect of being human in the present world. This is further highlighted by the fact that Genesis 9:6 appeals to the image of God when setting forth this obligation. Though this appeal to the image of God is often taken as the explanation for the wrongfulness of murder (i.e., an image bearer of God has been slain),[20] a strong case can be made that the appeal actually serves to explain why God has delegated the execution of punishment to human beings (i.e., because, as his image bearers, God has granted them royal-judicial authority).[21] Pursuing justice is an essential part of what it means to be human.

Third, the development and enforcement of law and legal systems is a *universal* human responsibility. Christians should not see this responsibility as one that is rightfully theirs alone or feel morally compromised by working alongside nonbelievers when undertaking it. God entered this covenant with the whole human race, without respect to any individual's religious allegiance. In seeking justice through a legal system, Christians not only *may* collaborate with non-Christians but are *obligated* to do so. Human law should be designed not as if it applies to Christians alone (or to people of

[20]E.g., see Wenham, *Genesis 1–15*, p. 194.
[21]Writers defending this position include Steven D. Mason, "Another Flood? Genesis 9 and Isaiah's Broken Eternal Covenant," *Journal for the Study of the Old Testament* 32 (2007): 192-93; Garr, *In His Own Image and Likeness*, p. 163; and Meredith G. Kline, *Kingdom Prologue: Genesis Foundations for a Covenantal Worldview* (Eugene, OR: Wipf and Stock, 2006), pp. 252-53.

any other single religion) but as a social bond for human beings qua human beings preserved by God under the Noahic covenant.

Fourth, pursuing justice is a central task for preserving life in the present world but not a means for bringing in the life of the world to come. The fact that God ordains the development of human law in the context of the Noahic covenant should suppress the utopian dreams that often accompany the pursuit of justice. The Noahic covenant reveals God's plans for preserving the world, not for transforming it into the new creation. The development of law and legal systems is a central task for fallen-but-preserved humanity, yet our expectations for what these systems can accomplish must be modest. Human law cannot banish evil from the world. What it can do is mitigate the effects of evil and provide some degree of remedy for those who suffer wrongly at others' hands. This is a great blessing, but a penultimate rather than ultimate blessing. Salvation and eschatological consummation must come through another means.

Fifth, Genesis 9:6 indicates that a proportionate retributive justice should be the basic standard for human law. This verse mentions specifically only one kind of crime, murder, but in doing so states a more general legal principle: the *lex talionis*. What is stated later in Scripture as "eye for eye, tooth for tooth" (Ex 21:24) is here presented as "blood for blood." The idea, whether or not enforced literally, is that every wrong should receive a proportionate penalty. What is a more accurate price for a lost eye than another's eye? Though the *lex talionis* may strike us as barbaric when stated literally, it has in fact served as a governing principle in many legal cultures and has served to quiet blood feuds that would otherwise fester were too little or too much penalty imposed upon wrongdoers.[22] It is beyond the scope of this chapter to explore other forms of justice and to reflect upon their proper place in the human legal order. But the Noahic covenant suggests at least that retributive justice should have a foundational role in human law.

At the same time, we must also recognize that perfect proportionate justice is unattainable in the present world (and we would surely not want it to be, given the sinfulness of every person). For one thing, a human system of justice can never be omniscient, and hence know the circumstances surrounding an offense with enough certainty to do what is perfectly just. Fur-

---

[22]For a recent study of the *lex talionis* as a principle of justice, see William Ian Miller, *Eye for an Eye* (Cambridge: Cambridge University Press, 2006).

thermore, God's own example in dealing with this world through the Noahic covenant displays a forbearance and patience that holds back the full manifestation of his justice (such as he revealed in the flood). Insofar as Genesis 9:6 calls human legislators and judges to image God, they do well to let a degree of forbearance and patience temper the quest for perfect justice.

Sixth, and finally, the fact that God reestablishes the social order after the flood by means of a covenant, and then commissions human beings to administer legal order among themselves as his image bearers, suggests that covenant making is an appropriate way to accomplish the task. This idea gains plausibility at later places in Genesis, when Abraham and Isaac resolve legal disputes precisely by entering covenants with their pagan neighbors. We consider this further in the next section. For now we note that the idea of interested parties covenanting together to establish agreements for living and working alongside one another, a popular idea in various forms in recent centuries of Western legal and political thought, may well find divine sanction in the Noahic covenant.

THE PATRIARCH NARRATIVES

While this chapter has focused on the early chapters of Genesis and explored a variety of legal implications arising from the accounts of creation, the fall, primeval history and Noah, some brief reflection on legal issues emerging from the rest of Genesis is also in order. From the end of Genesis 11 to the conclusion of the book, the narratives focus upon God's covenant with Abraham and the lives of Abraham and his descendants. These covenant people—believers in the true God who made gracious promises to them—are constantly interacting with pagan neighbors in the lands where they wander. Given that the New Testament calls present-day Christians citizens of heaven who are "sojourners" and "exiles" here on earth (Phil 3:20; Heb 11:13; 1 Pet 2:11), hearkening back to the experience of the patriarchs who lived by faith in lands not their own, we can profit from considering how the patriarchs conducted themselves in their social interactions with their nonbelieving neighbors. Like the patriarchs, Christians today are called not to theocratic domination of the world but to just and charitable lives alongside nonbelieving neighbors who live with us under the covenant with Noah. We identify six significant implications for human law in these narratives.

First, human law exists against the backdrop of the justice of God, the ultimate judge of all. Abraham asked a question of God in Genesis 18:25— "Shall not the Judge of all the earth do what is just?"—and the surrounding narratives give an affirmative answer. One aspect of divine justice revealed in these narratives is a concern for due process. For example, though he is omniscient, God "goes down" to Sodom "to see whether they have done altogether according to the outcry that has come to me" (Gen 18:21). By going to Sodom and ascertaining their conduct firsthand, as it were, God makes absolutely clear to human beings that he judges only according to the facts of the case.

The patriarchal narratives address substantive as well as procedural aspects of divine justice. We see God providentially enforcing the *lex talionis*, for instance, in connection with Jacob's deception of his father Isaac.[23] When Isaac announces his desire to bless his firstborn son Esau, Rebekah prompts Jacob to dress like his brother and bring savory food to Isaac. By this ruse, Jacob takes advantage of Isaac's blindness to substitute the younger son for the older, procuring the blessing intended for Esau and depriving Isaac of his choice of heir (Gen 27:1-41). Soon thereafter, however, Jacob suffers a similar deception at the hands of Rebekah's brother, Laban. When Jacob announces his desire to marry Rachel, Laban prepares a wedding feast, with Leah presumably dressed in her sister's bridal veil. Laban takes advantage of the darkness of night to substitute the older daughter for the younger, depriving Jacob of his choice of wife (Gen 29:15-30). What Jacob had done to Isaac has now been done to Jacob. See a comparison of the two deceptions in table 1.2.

Table 1.2. Deceptions of Isaac and Jacob

Deception of Isaac	Deception of Jacob
Orchestrated by Rebekah	Orchestrated by Rebekah's brother
Jacob brings Isaac savory food	Laban prepares a feast for Jacob
Jacob dressed like Esau	Leah dressed like Rachel
Isaac cannot see (blindness)	Jacob cannot see (nighttime)
Younger son substituted for older	Older daughter substituted for younger
Isaac deprived of choice of heir	Jacob deprived of choice of wife

---

[23]See Alan Dershowitz, *The Genesis of Justice: 10 Stories of Biblical Injustice That Led to the 10 Commandments and Modern Morality and Law* (New York: Warner Books, 2000), pp. 132-46; Calum M. Carmichael, *The Spirit of Biblical Law* (Athens: University of Georgia Press, 1996), pp. 142-43.

As discussed in the previous section, the Noahic covenant prescribed *talionic* justice as the basic standard for human law. In the final analysis, however, Genesis shows God as the ultimate enforcer of the *lex talionis*, taking the principle of proportionate justice beyond the capacity of any human legal system. Indeed, we see in these patriarchal narratives a foreshadowing of a greater and final judgment yet to come, particularly in the destruction of Sodom and Gomorrah (Gen 19). This extraordinary divine punishment of these very wicked cities serves, through the rest of Scripture, as the preeminent paradigm of God's judgment on the last day (e.g., Deut 29:23; Is 1:9-10; 13:19; Jer 49:18; 50:40; Lam 4:6; Hos 11:8; Amos 4:11; Zeph 2:9; Lk 17:26-30; 2 Pet 2:5-9; Jude 6-7). Human justice must answer to divine justice, and God will call all people to account.

Second, human justice varies significantly from place to place in these narratives. The inhabitants of the cities in which the patriarchs sojourn are nonbelievers, but they are not all alike. On the positive side is the city of Gerar under King Abimelech. Things are not perfect here, but this city shows a basic concern for justice that at times surpasses the concern shown by the covenant people (Gen 20), as we discuss below. On the negative side is Sodom. This city commits heinous acts and shows utter disregard for justice (Gen 19:1-11). Other places that host the patriarchs are neither as just as Gerar nor as depraved as Sodom. Shechem, for example, winks at its prince's rape of a young girl (Jacob's daughter Dinah), yet shows some interest in making amends through intermarriage and establishing cordial economic ties with Jacob's family (Gen 34).

It is interesting to note that the patriarchs deal with different cities in different ways, depending on the cities' concern for justice. They resolve disputes openly and enter into covenants with the decent people of Gerar (Gen 21:22-34), avoid dealing with Sodom (Gen 14:21-24), and negotiate with Shechem without mutual trust (Gen 34:8-24). These narratives suggest that there may not be one single model for Christians to follow as they seek to live in a variety of civil societies. While they must always seek to love their neighbors and submit to lawful authorities, the extent to which they can participate in and contribute to the legal life of their communities may well differ depending on time and place, and require wise judgment about particular circumstances. Christians engaged in legal affairs, and the lawyers who represent them, do well to remain "wise as serpents and innocent as doves" (Mt 10:16).

A third feature of these narratives relevant for human law is the fact that nonbelievers sometimes show greater concern for justice than believers do. Genesis 20 provides the prime example. Abraham tricks Abimelech into the wicked act of taking Abraham's wife, Sarah, into his house. Conversely, Abimelech repents upon hearing what he has unknowingly done, gives Abraham a fair chance to defend himself and then sends him away unharmed. God had great interest in his covenant people learning the ways of "righteousness and justice" (Gen 18:19), but this did not automatically translate into moral and legal superiority. These stories provide a sobering reminder for Christians today. Christians (including Christian lawyers) frequently fall short of the ideals they promote, sometimes in public and embarrassing ways. Whatever advantage Christians have for knowing the ways of justice, through Scripture and the power of the gospel, non-Christians frequently outshine them in their conduct. Christians do well to be humble and to avoid demonizing others.

Fourth, these narratives contribute to our understanding of human law by presuming the existence of a universally knowable moral standard that ought to bind human interaction. When the patriarchs have legal disputes with their pagan neighbors, they do not appeal to a parochial moral standard known only through special revelation, but they presume (as their pagan neighbors often do also) a standard that is accessible to all. The presence of the "fear of God" in a particular locale, for example, is proof that justice can be attained in that place (Gen 20:11; 42:18). Similarly, there are certain things that "ought not to be done" that believer and pagan alike know should be shunned (Gen 20:9; 34:7). Though it would take more space than available here to argue the case, these appeals to a common and universally known (though not universally practiced!) moral standard provide evidence for the existence of some sort of natural law. However Christians may develop a theory of natural law, the existence of a universal moral standard has many potential implications for how they approach legal life in a diverse society.

A fifth point that we note from these narratives is the intriguing fact that so many of the social and legal disputes concern issues of sex and marriage and how to treat the stranger. Disputes arose because Abraham and Isaac pretended their wives were their sisters (Gen 12; 20; 26). A key part of the evidence against Sodom was its citizens' pursuit of homosexual gang rape. There was constant conflict between the wives within polygamous marriages. Shechem and Jacob came into conflict when Shechem raped Dinah and then asked for her hand in marriage. Scripture presents the family as foundational for human society, and the Noahic covenant indicates that "to be fruitful and multiply" (Gen 9:1, 7) is of central importance for God's ongoing preservation of the human community. In the present day, when sex is so often politicized and the nature of marriage is a bitterly contested legal issue, Genesis suggests that human law needs to give serious attention to such questions. God created marriage for human good, and law ought to help direct people to this good. Many problems arise in Genesis when human beings (sometimes the patriarchs themselves) pursue their own visions of good sexual and family relations, in contrast to God's.

Another hot contemporary issue addressed in these narratives is how to treat the stranger. When an alien enters a community, what can he or she expect from its residents, and what can the community expect of the alien? Though Genesis 19 and 20 certainly do not provide concrete guidance for immigration policy, it is striking how the relatively righteous city of Gerar is distinguished by its respect for Abraham, the alien among them, and how the condemned city of Sodom demonstrated its wickedness by violent threats against aliens within its walls. How people treat those who are different from them seems to be a fundamental test of their righteousness. In the present day, when issues of immigration and the place of (especially illegal) immigrants are widely debated in many societies, these Genesis narratives confirm the importance of such matters and provide much grist for reflection.

Finally, these narratives promote the idea of social organization by means of covenanting. In the previous section, we suggested that God's decision to preserve the human social order by means of (the Noahic) covenant may provide a model for the way that human beings are to order their particular societies. In Genesis 21 and 26 Abraham and Isaac, respectively, make covenants with a pagan city with which they have close relations. The patriarchs had a history of sometimes friendly, sometimes strained relations with Gerar, and in order to avoid future disputes they enter into oath-bound arrangements deemed beneficial to both parties. While these bilateral human covenants are not exactly analogous to God's unilaterally imposed Noahic covenant, the actions of the patriarchs and their neighbors do seem to reflect the action of the God in whose image they were created. In the Noahic covenant God ordained that justice be done on earth, yet he delegated the performance of that task to human beings, precisely as his image bearers (Gen 9:6). God did not establish just one valid form of government or legal organization but left the particulars to human wisdom, imagination and experimentation. God wills human creativity to mirror his own. In this context, developing political and legal systems by means of consensual covenants among the people, rather than by the coercive imposition of the ideas of the powerful, is attractive. Genesis suggests that the idea of social covenants, popular among many Western thinkers and political leaders in recent centuries, has a solid theological basis.[24]

Conclusion

In light of our brief tour through Genesis, let us revisit some of the fundamental questions raised in the introduction concerning the enterprise of civil law. On the issue of authority, the book of Genesis reveals a Creator who exercises supreme authority over the universe he made. This Creator enters into covenants through which he delegates a degree of governing authority to humans. In the worldview reflected in Genesis, at least some of those who rule in the human community can rightfully claim authority derived from the Creator. The book of Genesis does not give detailed guidance for resolving conflicts when different groups of humans make competing claims to govern, but it helps us understand why such conflicts arise and offers useful tools for mediating them, including the idea of covenants as a basis for organizing social life and the knowledge that all who contend for dominion will ultimately answer to the justice of God.

With respect to the nature of the good life, we see God drawing authoritative distinctions between good and evil, recognizing the good accomplished at each stage of creation, but declaring it "not good" for man to be alone. Disaster falls, however, when Adam and Eve reject God's assessment of the good life in favor of autonomous moral reasoning, eating of "the tree of the knowledge of good and evil." In terms of what makes for a good community, Genesis presents a picture of utopia—the Garden of Eden before the fall—as well as a number of dystopias, including the city of Cain in the days of Lamech, the prediluvian earth filled with violence, the cities of Sodom and Gomorrah, and even the domestic disharmony in the patriarchal families.

---

[24]For significant exploration of this theme, see David Novak, *The Jewish Social Contract: An Essay in Political Theology* (Princeton, NJ: Princeton University Press, 2005).

In its teaching concerning the image of God and through its description of the causes and consequences of our fall into sin, the book of Genesis helps us begin to answer questions about the nature of humans and the implications for governing institutions. Our creation in the image of God—the lawgiver—accounts for our tendency to gravitate toward law as a means of ordering the social world, while our fallen nature explains why law so often seems a dissatisfying means of social organization. The tension between the image of God and the fall into sin suggests that the civil law will remain valuable and necessary so long as the earth endures, but counsels against investing inordinate hope in the good that law can accomplish. Human government is an important institution, without which many would experience greater misery than they currently endure, but the civil authorities will neither take us back to the Garden of Eden nor move us forward to the City of God.

The *talionic* justice observed in Genesis may also moderate our aspirations for human government. At the very least, the ideal of retributive justice suggests the need for a proportionality limitation on punishments imposed by the civil authorities. More profoundly, however, it seems clear that the thoroughgoing divine justice reflected in Genesis lies beyond the capacity of human government. Since civil government cannot fully achieve justice in the biblical sense, it must stake out a more manageable set of objectives within the scope of its limited resources. "Lines must be drawn not between good and bad but between bad and worse—and also between that which is practically possible and that which isn't."[25]

Acknowledging the limits of human government might seem discouraging to citizens of this world. But those who live as aliens and strangers here need not despair over the weakness of the earthly city, for we look forward to "the holy city, new Jerusalem, coming down out of heaven from God, prepared as a bride adorned for her husband" (Rev 21:2). That is where humanity will once again gain access to the tree of life, with leaves prepared "for the healing of the nations" (Rev 22:2). Only in the new Jerusalem will humans see the face of God and reign with him forever and ever (Rev 22:4-5).

---

[25]William Stuntz, "Christian Legal Theory," *Harvard Law Review* 116 (2000): 1735.

2

LAW AND POLITICAL ORDER

Israel's Constitutional History

William S. Brewbaker III and V. Philips Long

Introduction

This chapter traces Israel's forms of government and also provides an overview of the Old Testament's history of Israel—from the patriarchs, through enslavement in and liberation from Egypt, the giving of the Mosaic law and the rule of judges and kings, to Israel's subjugation in and return from Babylon. The three chapters that follow address three sources of insight on civil law that emerge during this history: the Mosaic law, the Wisdom literature and the Prophets.

The aim of this chapter is to mine roughly one thousand years of Israel's history beginning with the exodus (c. 1450–1250 B.C.)[1] and ending in the late postexilic period (c. 450 B.C.) for insights into civil law. Even excluding, as we do, the material covered by Exodus 19–40, Leviticus, Numbers and Deuteronomy[2] (e.g., the Mosaic covenant and the giving of the law at Mount Sinai, the immediate breach of both, the wilderness wandering, the tabernacle, and the journey to the edge of the Promised Land), there is a lot to talk

---

[1]We will not here address the arguments surrounding the contested issue of the date of the exodus, though we do find the biblical and indirect extrabiblical evidence supportive of the event itself. See, for instance, James Karl Hoffmeier, *Israel in Egypt: The Evidence for the Authenticity of the Exodus Tradition* (New York: Oxford University Press, 1997).

[2]These books of the Bible and the Mosaic law are addressed in this volume in chapter three.

about. Between the exodus and the return to Jerusalem, the most significant events for our purposes are the death of Moses, followed by a succession of leaders that includes (more or less) faithful or unfaithful judges, priests and kings; the entry into the Promised Land; the building of the temple; wars with foreign kingdoms and between Israelite kinsmen; God's seeming abandonment, in the Babylonian captivity, of his promise to establish the throne of David; and the return from exile when Babylon falls to Persia.

The vast scope of the material to be covered is not the only challenge facing us. Even assuming, as we do, that the biblical narrative fairly portrays what happened in Palestine in the period under consideration,[3] substantial difficulties remain for those seeking lessons from Israel's history concerning the nature, function and scope of civil laws generally. To begin with, we are dealing with texts that are only partially prescriptive. On occasion the narrator gives us a God's-eye view of one event or another and its significance, but often we are simply left with a record of what happened and are required to parse out its implications for ourselves. The mere fact that Israel had a particular law or political institution at one time or another, or that Israel or its leaders took a particular action, is not necessarily a divine endorsement of that law or institution or action as best for all places and times, or even for the particular moment in the narrative. Indeed, Israel has, during this period, a wide variety of political institutions and practices, none of which seems to have been adequate to deal successfully with its fundamental problems. Moreover, the Old Testament has proven susceptible to misuse as a political sourcebook. At the lowest ebb, perhaps, have been efforts to transpose the practices of especially good or bad figures in Israel's history to new political contexts in an effort to legitimate or demonize rulers of the later era.[4] For example, as Christopher Hill notes, "Milton used the fact that Jehu killed his rightful king at the bidding of a prophet to argue that 'it was not permissible

---

[3]For a defense of this view, see generally Iain Provan, V. Philips Long and Tremper Longman III, *A Biblical History of Israel* (Louisville, KY: Westminster John Knox, 2003).

[4]This pattern of argument was apparently prevalent in seventeenth-century English sermons. See generally Christopher Hill, *The English Bible and the Seventeenth Century Revolution* (New York: Penguin, 1993). Thus, for example, a Puritan bishop argued that just as "the Lord . . . fought for Hezekiah and Jerusalem[, he] will also fight for her Majesty [Queen Elizabeth] and this realm against Sennacherib and the Spaniard" (ibid., p. 67, quoting M[iles] Smith, Sermons 108-11 [1632]). A royalist bishop cited Jeremiah's admonition to submit to Nebuchadnezzar in Jeremiah 27:5-6 as authority against resistance to monarchy in general (ibid., p. 107). Similar examples abound.

and good to put a tyrant to death because God commanded it, but rather God commanded it because it was permissible and good."[5]

The stories with which we are dealing have been employed not only in support of revered democratic institutions such as popular sovereignty, the rule of law and separation of powers, but also in support of Marxist revolution, regicide and the conquest of Native American tribal lands. The danger is, as Oliver O'Donovan points out, that Scripture will be used after the fashion of "a commonplace book or a dictionary of quotations."[6]

Our aim in the present chapter is to deal primarily with what lawyers might call the day-to-day constitutional law of Israel. By this we do not mean to claim the ground of our fellow contributors whose task it is to discuss the Mosaic law and covenant, which have been frequently characterized as something like a constitution for the polity of Israel.[7] Instead, our attention will be focused mostly on the institutions that attend the operation of Israelite polity over the span of Israel's biblical history—especially the question of whether this portion of the Scriptures has anything to say about the preferred institutional forms of government and how various institutions should relate to one another. So as not to neglect entirely other themes presented prominently in the text, we will also briefly discuss the exodus, holy war and the motif of exile.

THE EXODUS

Israel's transition from extended family to nation arguably begins in Egypt, following the flight of Jacob's family from Canaan to live there under the protection of the cast-off younger brother, Joseph (Gen 37–50). Over many generations, the people of Israel in Egypt multiply greatly. Trouble begins

---

[5]Ibid., pp. 67-68.

[6]Oliver O'Donovan, *The Desire of the Nations: Rediscovering the Roots of Political Theology* (Cambridge: Cambridge University Press, 1996). "To dip into Israel's experience at one point—let it be the Exodus, the promise of *shalom*, the jubilee laws, or, with Thomas Cranmer at the coronation of Edward VI, the reign of Josiah of Judah—and to take out a single disconnected image or theme from it is to treat the history of God's reign like a commonplace book or a dictionary of quotations" (ibid., p. 27). See also, "If the Scriptures are to be read as a proclamation, not merely as a mine for random sociological analogies dug out from the ancient world, then a unifying conceptual structure is necessary that will connect political themes with the history of salvation as a whole" (ibid., p. 22).

[7]See generally J. G. McConville, *God and Earthly Power: An Old Testament Political Theology, Genesis-Kings* (London: T & T Clark, 2006), especially pp. 85-88.

when there arises a pharaoh "who did not know Joseph" (Ex 1:8)[8] and who is determined to deal with the growing Israelite population by a campaign of subjugation and genocide. Having begun to fulfill his promise of posterity to Abraham through the twelve sons of Jacob and having sustained Jacob's family through Joseph's providential elevation in Pharaoh's service, God continues by elevating another of Abraham's descendants to high position in Egypt. This time Moses, raised in Pharaoh's very household, will be used by God to deliver Israel from Egyptian oppression.

The exodus is rightly regarded as a central event in salvation history and is repeatedly invoked by Yahweh as the mark of his *ḥesed* love to Israel.[9] The question for subsequent commentators has been in what sense, precisely, the exodus is central. On the surface, a number of important themes appear to be operating simultaneously. Among them are God's earthly answer to the call of a groaning and oppressed people, his commitment to the promise he made to Abraham, and deliverance from sin and death. Which one, if any, deserves privileged status?

Liberation theologians find God's deliverance of the poor from their oppressors to be the central concern of the exodus narrative.[10] In the hands of some contemporary interpreters, the exodus narrative has become, among other things, a mandate for the rejection of private property and of certain liberal institutions such as the "rule of law," on the ground that they legit-

---

[8]Unless otherwise noted, Scripture quotations in this chapter are from the ESV.

[9]See Exodus 20:2; Leviticus 11:45; 22:33; 25:38; Numbers 15:41; Deuteronomy 5:6; Psalm 81:10; Isaiah 43:3; Hosea 12:9; 13:4. See S. Croatto, "The Socio-historical and Hermeneutical Relevance of the Exodus," in *Exodus—A Lasting Paradigm*, ed. Bas van Iersel and Anton Weiler (Edinburgh: T & T Clark, 1987), p. 127. See quotation of Croatto in Richard Bauckham, *God and the Crisis of Freedom: Biblical and Contemporary Perspectives* (Louisville: Westminster John Knox, 2002), p. 9, n. 4: "The very name of the God of Israel is indissolubly bound up with the exodus experience of oppression-liberation."

Yahweh is Israel's special covenant name for God. *Ḥesed* is a semantically rich term in Hebrew for which precise English equivalents are not available. Translators have attempted to capture something of its significance by creating English compounds such as "loving-kindness." At its heart are notions of covenant loyalty and relational fidelity.

[10]See, e.g, Gustavo Gutiérrez, *A Theology of Liberation: History, Politics, and Salvation,* ed. and trans. Sister Caridad Inda and John Eagleson (Maryknoll, NY: Orbis, 1988), pp. 86-89. Gutiérrez views liberation from oppression as paradigmatic because of the close link between creation and salvation: "Creation is presented in the Bible, not as a stage previous to salvation, but as part of the salvific process" (ibid., p. 87, citing Eph 1:3-5). He continues: "The creation of the world initiates history, the human struggle, and the salvific adventure of Yahweh. . . . [Creation] is the work of a God who saves and acts in history; since humankind is the center of creation, it is integrated into the history which is being built by human efforts" (ibid., p. 87).

imize a fundamentally unjust capitalist order and are inconsistent with God's special concern for the poor.[11] In their view, the "spiritual" meaning of the book of Exodus and other accounts of God's liberating interventions in Scripture have been privileged over their political and social meanings primarily because the Bible has been interpreted in accordance with the interests of the institutional church, which is part of the established order.[12]

The economic and political plight of the Israelites is clearly an important focus of the narrative. The story has barely begun when we learn that the rulers of Egypt have

> set taskmasters over them to afflict them with heavy burdens. They built for Pharaoh store cities, Pithom and Raamses. But the more they were oppressed, the more they multiplied and the more they spread abroad. And the Egyptians were in dread of the people of Israel. So they ruthlessly made the people of Israel work as slaves and made their lives bitter with hard service, in mortar and brick, and in all kinds of work in the field. In all their work they ruthlessly made them work as slaves. (Ex 1:11-14)[13]

And, of course, the story will get worse before it gets better. Pharaoh's response to Moses and Aaron's first request for the Israelites' release is to make it harder for the workers to meet their daily quota of bricks by taking away their straw and then to beat them when they fail to meet the quota. God acknowledges that he is hearing not only the cry of "my people" ("my firstborn son," Ex 4:22), but also the cry of his people in the midst of their oppression:

> Then the LORD said, "I have surely seen the affliction of my people who are in Egypt and have heard their cry because of their taskmasters. I know their sufferings, and I have come down to deliver them out of the hand of the Egyptians and to bring them up out of that land to a good and broad land, a land

---

[11]See Charles Villa-Vicencio, "Liberation and Reconstruction: The Unfinished Agenda," in *The Cambridge Companion to Liberation Theology,* ed. Christopher Rowland, 2nd ed. (Cambridge: Cambridge University Press, 2007), pp. 183, 186-89 (surveying prominent liberation theologians' preferences for socialism over capitalism or "third way" options); and Tom Moylan, "Denunciation/Annunciation: The Radical Methodology of Liberation Theology," *Cultural Critique* 20 (Winter 1991–1992): 33-64.

[12]See Gutiérrez, *Theology of Liberation,* pp. 34-38. Cf. Clodovis Boff, *Theology and Praxis: Epistemological Foundations,* trans. Robert R. Barr (Maryknoll, NY: Orbis, 1987), pp. 10-12.

[13]Cf. Gutiérrez, *Theology of Liberation,* p. 88 (noting these conditions and describing the liberation of Israel as a "political action").

flowing with milk and honey, to the place of the Canaanites, the Hittites, the
Amorites, the Perizzites, the Hivites, and the Jebusites. And now, behold, the
cry of the people of Israel has come to me, and I have also seen the oppression
with which the Egyptians oppress them. Come, I will send you to Pharaoh
that you may bring my people, the children of Israel, out of Egypt." (Ex 3:7-10)

Moreover, it is clear not only that God's concern about their oppression is
part of the motivation for his action, but also that official remembrances of
the event commanded by Yahweh recall both Israel's status as chosen people
and their status as oppressed.[14]

Nevertheless, it is also true that it is the affliction of "my people" that
God has seen, and that he has "come down to . . . bring them up . . . to a
good and broad land . . . flowing with milk and honey." God is hearing not
just anyone's oppressed cry, but rather the cry of his "firstborn son," which
makes problematic the notion that the exodus is merely a generic inter-
vention on behalf of oppressed people generally. Finally, it is not Israel's
oppressed status that marks out the boundaries of God's mercy when the
decisive plague is finally inflicted, but rather the blood of the sacrificial
lamb on the doorpost.[15] The plague against the firstborn is not merely a
power play on God's behalf designed to compel the recalcitrant Egyptian
ruler; it is a judgment "on all the gods of Egypt" (Ex 12:12), the blood on the
doorpost perhaps also containing a hint of sacrificial propitiation for sin.

EXODUS, ISRAEL AND HUMANITY

The exodus story and the subsequent conquest of the Promised Land raise
profound questions about the relationship between Israel and the rest of the
world, and God's relationship to both. Gordon McConville argues persua-
sively that the exodus is a story not merely for and about Israel but for and
about the whole world. According to McConville, it represents a continu-
ation of the Genesis creation narrative, which "begins simply with humanity."[16]

Israel is chosen not for its own sake but for the larger purposes of
showing forth God's glory in the world, of being a blessing to all the nations

---

[14]See Ronald J. Sider, "An Evangelical Theology of Liberation," *Christian Century*, March 19, 1980,
pp. 314-18 (citing Ex 13:11-16; Deut 26:5-8).
[15]Nor is the plague limited to the oppressor class of Egypt. See Exodus 12:29: "At midnight the LORD
struck down all the firstborn in the land of Egypt, from the firstborn of Pharaoh who sat on his
throne to the firstborn of the captive who was in the dungeon, and all the firstborn of the livestock."
[16]McConville, *God and Earthly Power*, p. 36.

of the world both in its demonstration of the benefits of following the only true God (see, e.g., Deut 4:6) and in being the root from which springs the fulfillment of the covenants in Christ (see Rom 9:4-5). McConville explains,

> Israel is at once with, separate from, and for other nations. It is *with* them in that it shares with them its place in God's created order, and also the fundamental institution of law. It is *separate from* them in the sense that it is separated from both Egypt and Canaan, at the beginning and end of its journey into land. This separation has religious, moral and political aspects. And it is *for* them, in the sense that it is called to display to them what a nation might be like under the one God Yahweh.[17]

It is not Israel, but "humanity, as such, [that bears] the 'image of God' ([Gen] 1.26), shoulders the 'royal' responsibility of God's vicegerent on earth, and has dominion over the creation ([Gen] 1.28)."[18] Although the balance of Genesis is focused on God's chosen people, there is a "divine purpose for the whole world,"[19] not just Israel, and humanity as a whole is to imitate the LORD (that is, Yahweh), "the judge of all the earth," in ruling with justice and righteousness.[20]

On McConville's reading, the subjection of Israel to slavery in Egypt is a "creation conflict" in which Pharaoh's treatment of Israel is directly at odds with God's good purposes. Pharaoh is determined to dominate the world rather than to exercise dominion in accordance with the LORD's justice; Israel, likewise, is to labor on Pharaoh's behalf rather than worshiping and serving God alone. Pharaoh is expressly concerned to prevent Israel from "be[ing] fruitful and multiply[ing]" (Gen 1:28); he is determined to prevent God's fulfillment of his promise to give Israel possession of the Promised Land. Like those at Babel, he is determined to prevent the dispersion of humanity in order that his grand projects not be threatened. Israel's eventual worship at the tabernacle is "a precise antithesis to the allegiance extracted from it forcibly by Pharaoh."[21] Indeed, "in its synthesis of constructive work, worship, and rest, [the] Exodus [narrative] offers a revolutionary antithesis

---

[17]Ibid., p. 31 (emphasis original).
[18]Ibid., p. 36.
[19]Ibid.
[20]Ibid., pp. 48-49.
[21]Ibid., p. 54. For additional discussion of Genesis 1 and the image of God in this volume, see "The Image of God" in chapter one.

to Pharaoh's degradation and enslavement of humanity."[22] God's deliverance of the Israelites is both execution of just judgment and deliverance of a chosen people. We need not choose among the text's connections to God's covenant loyalty to Israel, believers' exoneration from sin on account of the blood of the Lamb and divine opposition to human oppression.[23]

HOLY WAR

The exodus and Israel's subsequent conquest of the Promised Land raise longstanding questions about holy war. How can the destruction of Israel's enemies be squared with Israel's call to show forth God's glory in the world and to be a blessing to all the nations (Gen 22:18)? How can Israel be viewed as a blessing when it is commanded by God to "drive . . . out" those nations that inhabit the Promised Land, to "devote them to complete destruction" and even to "save alive nothing that breathes" (Ex 23:31; Deut 20:16-18)?

Israel's history does not justify violence as a means of furthering contemporary religious objectives.[24] Even without the clarity of Jesus' teaching that we are to love our enemies and turn the other cheek,[25] the account of Israel's history in the Old Testament provides no justification for such conduct. Moreover, properly understood, there is no conflict between the accounts of holy war in the Old Testament and Israel's call to be a blessing to the nations. As with the exodus, the Canaan narratives make clear that God is determined both to show forth his justice in the world and to use Israel for its salvation.

Four features of Israel's military activity may be singled out in support of these claims. First, when the Canaanites are defeated, it is not merely in order to clear the way for Israelite occupation of their land. As God makes

---

[22]Ibid.

[23]See Bauckham, God and the Crisis of Freedom, p. 9: "The point of the exodus is not freedom in the sense of self-determination, but service, the service of the loving, redeeming, and delivering God of Israel, rather than the state and its proud king" (quoting J. D. Levenson, "Exodus and Liberation," Horizons in Biblical Theology 13 [1991]: 152 [emphasis in original]).

[24]For more developed accounts of this issue, see generally Tremper Longman III and Daniel G. Reid, God Is a Warrior (Grand Rapids: Zondervan, 1995), pp. 31-60; C. S. Cowles, Eugene Merrill, Daniel Gard and Tremper Longman III, Show Them No Mercy: 4 Views on God and Canaanite Genocide, ed. Stanley N. Gundry (Grand Rapids: Zondervan, 2003).

[25]See Matthew 5:44 and Luke 6:27-35; see also Matthew 26:52-54: "Then Jesus said to him, 'Put your sword back into its place. For all who take the sword will perish by the sword. Do you think that I cannot appeal to my Father, and he will at once send me more than twelve legions of angels? But how then should the Scriptures be fulfilled, that it must be so?'" For additional discussion in this volume on Jesus' command that we love our enemies, see "Law as a Means of Loving One's Neighbor" in chapter six.

clear to Abram in Genesis 15, his provisions for Israel's material resources are made in the context of just judgments rendered against their oppressors.[26] God tells Abram that Egypt will afflict Abram's offspring for four hundred years, "but [God] will bring judgment on the nation that they serve, and afterward they shall come out with great possessions" (Gen 15:14). God not only uses the plagues of judgment to liberate Israel, but also allows Israel to "plunder the Egyptians" (Ex 3:22), as the Egyptians voluntarily part with their silver and gold. As for the populations living in the Promised Land, the text suggests that, at the time God speaks to Abram, extermination of the Amorites, one of the main tribes living in Canaan, would have been inappropriate because their "iniquity . . . is not yet complete" (Gen 15:16). Rather than punish the Amorites prematurely, God decrees that the Israelites must wait until "the fourth generation" to inherit the land that has been promised.

Second, Israel itself is also subject to severe judgment for its own disobedience to God. In Deuteronomy, God emphasizes that it is not because of Israel's righteousness that the people will receive the land, but "because of the wickedness of these nations the LORD your God is driving them out from before you, and that he may confirm the word that the LORD swore to your fathers, to Abraham, to Isaac, and to Jacob" (Deut 9:5). Leviticus 18:2 states that the former inhabitants of the Promised Land made the land unclean, "so that [God] punished its iniquity, and the land vomited out its inhabitants." Israel is warned not to commit the same sins, "lest the land vomit you out when you make it unclean, as it vomited out the nation that was before you" (Lev 18:28). Later, of course, this is exactly what happens, when Israel is sent away into exile in suffering that rivals the suffering experienced by the Canaanites.[27]

Third, the command to exterminate Israel's enemies applies only to wars fought within the borders of the Promised Land, and this fact is connected with Israel's calling to be a nation in covenant with God from whom the world's salvation will come. In the ordinary case, Israel (which was never to embark on military action without divine authorization)[28] was to offer terms

---

[26]Remarkably, the Israelites are to do justice even to the fruit trees surrounding a besieged city. Only trees that do not bear fruit may be cut down for use as siege works. See Deuteronomy 20:19-20: "Are the trees in the field human, that they should be besieged by you?"

[27]Indeed, Lamentations suggests that "the chastisement of the daughter of my people has been greater than the punishment of Sodom" (Lam 4:6).

[28]See Longman and Reid, *God Is a Warrior*, pp. 33-34.

of peace before fighting against any city, and to kill no one if the terms were accepted (Deut 20:10-11). Even if there were no surrender, only men were to be put to death (Deut 20:12-14). Only in the case of cities within the Promised Land was the entire population to be wiped out, and this was because of God's judgment against the culture (as previously noted) and also because of the likelihood (confirmed by later events) that the inhabitants would "teach you to do according to all their abominable practices that they have done for their gods, and so you sin against the LORD your God" (Deut 20:18). Canaanites, such as Rahab, known not to pose such a threat could apparently be spared notwithstanding the command to destroy all inhabitants (Josh 6:17).

Finally, strange as this may sound to modern ears, Israel's wars—insofar as they were waged in direct obedience to God's commands—were acts of worship, but they are not capable of being repeated outside of ancient Israel's specific theocratic context. Not only was Israel never to fight without specific divine authorization, the most important warrior in Israel's battles was God himself. Because the appropriate human response to God's presence is worship, God's specific presence with Israel introduced a liturgical element into Israel's military action. As Tremper Longman and Daniel Reid have documented, these elements are evident in the nation's preparations for war, which include sacrifices and other acts of consecration, as well as the law governing ritual cleanness in the war camp. Likewise, Israel's conduct of the military operations is inexplicable outside the context of divine worship. The armies of Israel march into battle singing God's praises behind the ark of the covenant, which symbolized the very presence of God. The fighting itself involved the otherwise baffling strategy of regarding "a large army and superior weapons technology [as] a liability."[29] Israel's human military weakness, which occasionally reaches comic proportions, allows God's mighty works on its behalf to be on full display. Victory in battle occasioned the composition of hymns and the offering of the spoils of war to God.[30]

Although one may observe in the Crusades and elsewhere regrettable examples of Christians waging war out of a religious motivation, Israel's history provides no support for such a practice. Once Israel's theocracy ceased to exist, it became inconceivable that the prerequisites for waging holy war described above could be met. Jesus' advent as the divine warrior

---

[29]Ibid., p. 37.
[30]See generally ibid., pp. 32-46.

who "defeated the powers and authorities not by killing but by dying,"[31] not surprisingly shifted the locus of most Christian debate about war to the question of whether followers of Jesus were required to be pacifists and, if not, the limited circumstances in which killing in war might be morally permissible.[32] Israel's military history has, accordingly, been of relatively little significance in guiding Christian reflection about when armed conflict is appropriate. One can, however, find instances in which specific features of Israel's military history have been invoked as authority for the ways in which war should be conducted once it has been initiated.[33]

ISRAEL THE NATION

Israel's arrival in the Promised Land represented a dramatic change in the political life of God's people. Abraham's descendants numbered only seventy when they fled to Egypt to avoid the famine (Ex 1:5). At that point, they might best have been described as an extended family; God's promise to make a great nation of Abraham and to give him land from the "river of Egypt" (Gen 15:18) to the Euphrates was still just a promise. By the time they left Egypt, the population of Israel had greatly increased (Num 1:45-46), and the fulfillment of the divine promise of nationhood seemed imminent.[34] A new set of opportunities and challenges presented itself. Israel needed political, military and religious leaders, institutions it had not previously required.

Some of these institutions were provided even before Israel entered the

---

[31]Tremper Longman III, "The Case for Spiritual Continuity," in *Show Them No Mercy: 4 Views on God and Canaanite Genocide*, ed. Stanley N. Gundry (Grand Rapids: Zondervan, 2003), p. 181.

[32]But see John Howard Yoder, "On Not Being in Charge," in *The Jewish-Christian Schism Revisited*, ed. Michael G. Cartwright and Peter Ochs (Grand Rapids: Eerdmans, 2003). "It is one of the marks of our culture's anti-Judaic heritage that the pacifism of the early Christians is routinely understood as having taken off from scratch from a few words, or a few deeds, of Jesus, when, as a matter of fact it was part of the common Jewish legacy which Jesus and the apostles shared with their non-messianic contemporaries" (ibid., p. 170).

[33]See, e.g., Hugo Grotius, *The Rights of War and Peace* (1625), trans. John Morrice (1738), ed. Richard Tuck from the edition by Jean Barbeyrac (Indianapolis: Liberty Fund, 2005), 3.5.2 (citing Deut 7:5 for the principle that sacred objects are not exempt from the law of the spoils of war); ibid., 3.6.1 (citing Josh 22:8 with respect to the appropriate division of the spoils of war); but cf. ibid., 3.4.9 (refusing to cite Israel's slaughter of Canaanite women and children in support of the lawfulness of injuring women and children on the ground that "it was the special Act of GOD, whose Right over Men is far greater, than, that of Men over Beasts").

[34]Estimating the actual number of those departing Egypt is a controversial affair; see, e.g., C. J. Humphreys, "The Number of People in the Exodus from Egypt: Decoding Mathematically the Very Large Numbers in Numbers I and XXVI," *Vetus Testamentum* 48, no. 2 (1998): 196-213. For a brief discussion, see Provan, Long and Longman, *Biblical History of Israel*, pp. 130-31.

Promised Land. Moses initially served as a single leader who sought God on Israel's behalf, proclaimed God's word to Israel and to Pharaoh, judged the causes of Israel's citizens and led them into battle. Even before Israel reached the Promised Land, Jethro advised Moses to appoint additional judges to handle the "small matters" that arose among the people (Ex 18:13-27). Once God had led Israel out of Egypt, he entered into covenant with them at Sinai and gave them his law. All that remained was for them to enter and take the Promised Land.

JOSHUA, JUDGES, MONARCHY AND SUCCESSION:
AFTER MOSES, WHAT?

Deuteronomy ends, and Joshua begins, with the succession of Joshua as the new leader of Israel. God himself "commissions" Joshua (Deut 31:14, 23; Josh 1:1-9),[35] but there are hints from the beginning that Joshua will not entirely replace Moses.[36] To be sure, Joshua is the new military leader of Israel, and there are striking resemblances between him and Moses.[37] Nevertheless, in some of his most important political actions Joshua is seen acting in concert with tribal leaders and even in subordination to Eleazar the high priest, Aaron's successor.[38]

Of potentially greater significance than any one person's role, however, is the question of what shape the Israelite polity will finally assume. The question has been thought important because, assuming it could be shown that God ordained particular types of institutions for Israel, those institutions might deserve pride of place in political society more generally. As noted, episodes in Israel's biblical history have been cited as authority on all sides of constitutional debates in the West—for and against monarchy, for and against constitutionalism, for and against separation of powers, for and against the right of rebellion against tyrants, and so on. In the Anglo-American tradition, in particular, certain aspects of Israel's history have

---

[35]Joshua has previously been commissioned by Moses at God's directive. See Numbers 27:12-23.

[36]Deuteronomy 34:10-12; see also McConville, *God and Earthly Power*, p. 106, citing C. Schäfer-Lichtenberger, *Josua und Salomo: Eine Studie zu Autorität und Legitimität des Nachfolgers im Alten Testament* (Vetus Testamentum Supplements, 58; Leiden: E. J. Brill, 1995); O'Donovan, *Desire of the Nations*, p. 52.

[37]See McConville, *God and Earthly Power*, pp. 105-6 (noting that, like Moses, Joshua "leads Israel across a body of water," leads them "in conquest and distribution of land," "receives personal assurances from Yahweh" and "is entitled to the allegiance of all the tribes").

[38]See ibid., pp. 106-7.

been thought to fit neatly with liberal institutions generally: the condemnation of monarchy in 1 Samuel 8,[39] the limitation of monarchy by God's law in Deuteronomy 17:14-20 as implemented by Josiah (2 Kings 22–23), the apparent primacy of the judiciary as opposed to the executive or legislature in the book of Judges, and separation of powers in Deuteronomy 16–18, among others. In each instance, biblical authority has been marshaled on the other side of the question as well.

A number of possible explanations could be offered for the discouraging inconclusiveness of political theology based on Israel's history. Perhaps the biblical text has generated so much heat and so little light because texts themselves are intrinsically indeterminate and are thus merely the field on which political debates mask themselves as intellectual controversies with no possibility for "objective" interpretation. Another possibility is that there is disagreement because the texts themselves do not speak with one voice. Some of the biblical history books, for example, seem to favor monarchy; others seem to oppose it—again, depending supposedly on the interests and context of the particular writers and editors involved. While this is certainly a theoretical possibility, it runs counter to most canonical understandings of Scripture.[40] A third possibility is that interpretive disagreements result from the fact that it is the fate of the texts themselves, though they speak clearly, to be interpreted by fallen and fallible human beings. On this account, Israel's history may be, for example, demonstrably pro- or anti-monarchical, but disagreement is intractable because some (or all!) of the participants in the debate are unable or unwilling to read the text as they should. A final possibility is that the texts contain mixed messages on the question of political institutions because, although different political institutions have different strengths and weaknesses in various contexts, the Bible's goal is not to endorse a single set of political arrangements as best for all places and times. The latter position is the one most consistent with the bulk of the Christian tradition, and we are in full agreement with it. Nevertheless, we will also argue that the biblical account of Israel's history offers important insights for readers who are interested in matters related to politics and law.

---

[39]To be precise, it is not monarchy per se that is condemned in 1 Samuel 8, but rather a demand for monarchy that entails rejection of Yahweh's own rule (1 Sam 8:7).

[40]A *canonical* reading of Scripture resists assuming incoherence or inconsistency in the texts until every effort has been made to discover how the texts cohere.

In our view, focusing solely on the question of institutional form (as if all monarchies, all aristocracies and all democracies are equivalent) may actually obscure what the Bible has to teach about political ordering. Indeed, Israel's history has much to say about the need for political order, the appropriate limitations on that order and the dangers of investing earthly rule in human hands. Israel's recurrent political failures suggest both that government must be strong enough to provide the background order without which freedom is impossible and also that according such power to sinful rulers is a dangerous proposition. In the longer horizon, Israel's history sets the stage for the promised and longed-for kingship of the Son of David.

One need not look far to understand why many biblical commentators have seen what they took to be divine endorsement of or opposition to particular institutional arrangements. One of the best-known passages in this respect is 1 Samuel 8. In this familiar story, Israel asks for "a king to judge us like all the nations" (1 Sam 8:5).[41] God tells Samuel that in making this request the Israelites "have not rejected you, but they have rejected me from being king over them" (1 Sam 8:7). Samuel then issues his warning about the ways of Israel's future king:

> He said, "These will be the ways of the king who will reign over you: he will take your sons and appoint them to his chariots and to be his horsemen and to run before his chariots. And he will appoint for himself commanders of thousands and commanders of fifties, and some to plow his ground and to reap his harvest, and to make his implements of war and the equipment of his chariots. He will take your daughters to be perfumers and cooks and bakers. He will take the best of your fields and vineyards and olive orchards and give them to his servants. He will take the tenth of your grain and of your vineyards and give it to his officers and to his servants. He will take your male servants and female servants and the best of your young men and your donkeys, and put them to his work. He will take the tenth of your flocks, and you shall be his slaves. And in that day you will cry out because of your king, whom you have chosen for yourselves, but the LORD will not answer you in that day."

---

[41]What is the reader to make of such a request? "Of particular significance is the notice in [1 Sam] 7:12 that 'thus far the LORD has helped us.' That Israel's elders should so quickly—in narrative time at least—demand 'a king to govern us, like other nations' ([1 Sam] 8:5) strikes the attentive reader as a foreboding development" (Provan, Long and Longman, *Biblical History of Israel*, p. 207).

> But the people refused to obey the voice of Samuel. And they said, "No! But there shall be a king over us, that we also may be like all the nations, and that our king may judge us and go out before us and fight our battles." (1 Sam 8:11-20)

It is not hard to see why monarchy's opponents have seized upon Samuel's denunciation. Samuel's speech not only comes on the heels of God's characterization of the people's demand for a king as a rejection of his authority but also is made in response to God's charge to Samuel to "warn [the people] and show them the ways of the king who shall reign over them" (1 Sam 8:9). Nevertheless, the passage cannot ultimately support such a categorical reading.

To understand why, it is necessary to go both forward and backward in Israel's history. God tells Abram when he is chosen that "kings will come from [Abram]" and his wife Sarah (Gen 17:6, 16). The promise is repeated to Jacob (Gen 35:11), who uses royal imagery in blessing his son Judah (Gen 45:10; see also Num 24:7, 17-19). In addition, Deuteronomy 17 expressly permits kingship, though it regulates the identity and prerogatives of the king, and also requires the king to give attention to God's law (Deut 17:14-20). These facts pose a formidable obstacle to the idea that kingship is per se a rejection of God's authority.

Exactly how the apparent condemnation of monarchy in 1 Samuel 8 can be reconciled with Deuteronomy's authorization of it has been the subject of considerable interpretive dispute. Eric Nelson identifies at least six interpretations that have been important in Christian understandings of biblical teaching concerning monarchy.[42] Two understandings predominated prior to the Reformation. One argued that Israel's sin was to "select[] kings who did not meet the criteria established by God in the Deuteronomy passage."[43] The second emphasized God's providence in the ordination of rulers; on this view, Israel's rejection of Samuel was, in effect, a rejection of God's providence in putting Samuel in authority.[44] In neither case is 1 Samuel 8 understood as a critique of monarchy per se.

A third interpretation likewise sees the demand for a king as rebellion against God's will, but focuses on the form of rule rather than the identity

---

[42]Eric Nelson, *The Hebrew Republic: Jewish Sources and the Transformation of European Political Thought* (Cambridge, MA: Harvard University Press, 2010), pp. 23-56.

[43]Ibid., p. 28. Nelson attributes this view to John of Salisbury, Aquinas and Erasmus.

[44]Ibid., pp. 28-29. Nelson notes that this reading was adopted by Calvin and, not surprisingly, by monarchists like Jean Bodin.

of the ruler: unlike the other nations, Israel had no earthly king, but its earthly polity nevertheless had a heavenly king—namely, God. Following the first-century A.D. Jewish historian Josephus, the sixteenth-century Protestant Reformer Theodore Beza argued that Israel's demand for a human king was, in effect, a rejection of the theocracy established by God, and not merely a rejection of Samuel. On this view, monarchy may well have been appropriate for other nations, but not for Israel.[45] A fourth interpretation faulted the manner of the Israelites' request for a king—in particular, their grumbling about Samuel—rather than the request itself.[46]

Nelson argues that, with the European discovery of Jewish rabbinic sources in the wake of the Reformation, the debate over the relationship between Deuteronomy 17 and 1 Samuel 8 was "dramatically reorganized."[47] Some rabbinic scholars held that monarchy was obligatory for Israel, and eventually this argument was adopted in support of the view that monarchy was obligatory for other states too.[48] On the other side, however, John Milton and others marshaled competing rabbinic sources to argue, for the first time in the Western Christian tradition, that monarchy amounted to idolatry and thus was not only bad for Israel but for other states as well.[49]

In our opinion, the traditional view that Scripture neither endorses nor proscribes monarchy in general (or any other form of government) best fits with the constellation of Old Testament passages treating the matter. The biblical text is opposed only (and consistently) to a kind of monarchy that resists divine rule. The evidence suggests that God all along anticipated giving Israel a king but that the Hebrew king was to be a vicegerent of the Great King, not a king "like all the nations" (1 Sam 8:5).

Judges

The alternative to monarchy in the Old Testament was rule by the judges. During the judges' reign, God was Israel's sole "king," and the judges exercised both military and judicial functions under God's declared law. The account of the judges' reign, while perhaps not a full-throated endorsement of monarchy, presents an account of Israel's life under the judges that shows

[45]Ibid., pp. 30-31.
[46]Ibid., pp. 34-35. Nelson attributes a view not unlike this to Grotius (see esp. p. 35).
[47]Ibid., p. 31.
[48]Ibid., p. 35.
[49]Ibid., pp. 37-50.

a pattern of continuing apostasy and failure and suggests that Israel would do well to have a (good) king.

The refrain in Judges—"In those days Israel had no king; everyone did what was right in his own eyes" (Judg 17:6; 18:1; 19:1; 21:25)[50]—is usually taken to be an endorsement of the monarchy.[51] At a minimum, it is a recognition of the need for stronger political authority. Indeed, the refrain's appearance in the final verse of the book may well be taken to set the stage for the subsequent narrative in 1 and 2 Samuel (the next books in the Hebrew Bible),[52] in which the monarchy (and eventually the reign of King David) is established.

On the other hand, there are also passages in Judges that suggest profound unease about the appropriateness of monarchy for Israel. Gideon refuses to be made a hereditary monarch, rebuking the "men of Israel" who made the request: "I will not rule over you, and my son will not rule over you; the LORD will rule over you" (Judg 8:23).[53] Even more striking is Jotham's fable in Judges 9:7-15. In the fable, the olive tree, the fig tree and the vine all refuse the requests of the other trees to reign over them because they are occupied with more noble matters. Only the despised bramble accepts the request and threatens to send out fire that will "devour the cedars of Lebanon." Although Martin Buber has called the fable "the strongest anti-monarchical poem of world literature,"[54] it is not clear whether the fable is anti-monarchy or merely anti-Abimelech. Clearly Abimelech is a "bramble," but must that be said of kings in general?[55]

More to the point is the question of what constitutes Israel's fundamental problem. Is it lack of concentrated leadership or disobedience to the LORD? The first section of the book (Judg 1:1–2:5) suggests quite clearly that it is the latter. After rehearsing the various tribes' failures to take the Promised Land, we hear the angel of the Lord saying "'you shall make no covenant with the inhabitants of this land; you shall break down their altars.' But you have not

---

[50]The phrase "everyone did what was right in his own eyes" is omitted in Judges 18:1 and 19:1.

[51]See Bruce K. Waltke with Charles Yu, *An Old Testament Theology: An Exegetical, Canonical and Thematic Approach* (Grand Rapids: Zondervan, 2007), pp. 685-86.

[52]We refer here to the Hebrew ordering of the Old Testament canon. In the English ordering, the book of Ruth stands between Judges and 1 and 2 Samuel.

[53]For an argument that the story of Gideon is not antimonarchical, see Waltke and Chu, *Old Testament Theology*, pp. 683-84.

[54]Martin Buber, *Kingship of God*, 3rd ed. (New York: Harper & Row, 1967), p. 75; quoted in McConville, *God and Earthly Power*, p. 125.

[55]See Waltke, *Old Testament Theology*, pp. 684-85.

obeyed my voice" (Judg 2:2). The consequence? God "will not drive them out
before you, but they shall become thorns in your sides, and their gods shall
be a snare to you" (Judg 2:3). The balance of the book is most plausibly read
as a repeated cycle of Israel's disobedience, followed by the threat of annihi-
lation from an outside conqueror, followed by Israel's cry to God, followed
by God's raising up a judge-deliverer who saves them from their enemies,
followed by a repetition of the cycle (Judg 2:16-23). The theme of Judges is
thus arguably less the need for a powerful monarch than God's faithfulness
to his people in the midst of their unfaithfulness to him. The judges themselves, for the most part,[56] are unworthy of any sustained allegiance from the
people. Rather, the narrative presents them as flawed and fallible (and occasionally even comic) figures. Judges may signal that monarchy is on the
way, but will monarchy be the answer to Israel's problems?

This question is squarely confronted in 1 and 2 Samuel, where we observe
the rise of the monarchy and see it in operation, culminating in David's ac-
cession to the throne. From the start, the monarchy does not appear promising. To start with, the beginning of 1 Samuel is a "microscopic scrutiny of
dynasticism,"[57] a usual feature of monarchy. God raises up Samuel to be a
faithful priest after he has rejected Eli's household because of the unfaithfulness of Eli and his sons Hophni and Phinehas (1 Sam 2:12-36). Nevertheless, Israel's demand for a king is fomented by the question of who will
succeed Samuel. Although the Lord tells Samuel that the real reason Israel's
elders demanded a king was their rejection of God, the stated reason for the
demand is that Samuel's sons "did not walk in his ways but turned aside
after gain. They took bribes and perverted justice" (1 Sam 8:3).

SAUL

From there we encounter Samuel's warning about monarchs, which is followed by the down-and-up-and-down kingship of Saul. From the beginning, however, it is clear that even if God is ultimately content for Israel
to have a king, the monarchy is not intended to be like that of other nations. One indication of this is found in the words used to describe the
kings in the accounts of their anointing by Samuel. Although Israel asks
for a "king" (*melek*), God tells Samuel to anoint Saul "prince" or "designee"

---

[56]A notable exception is Deborah. See Judges 4–5.
[57]See McConville, *God and Earthly Power,* p. 134.

(*nāgîd*) (1 Sam 9:16), a term Samuel will repeat with respect to the anointing of Saul (1 Sam 10:1) and David (1 Sam 13:14) and elsewhere.[58] Like the rest of Israel, the king is subject to God's law, a fact that is underscored by the existence of the law specifically governing the exercise of kingship (1 Sam 10:25; cf. Deut 17:14-20). Finally, in Samuel's anointing of the kings,[59] as well as in subsequent depictions, the point is repeatedly made that the kingship belongs to the LORD, not to the king. The promise of succession and prosperity in a dynastic line is conditional. It is the LORD who gives the land rest from its enemies and who establishes the king in the land or, as we shall see, tears the kingdom away from heirs apparent and eventually tears Israel away from the land. Stability is not guaranteed by the right institutional structure but, at least in Israel's case, results from God's vindication of a ruler and people who live in covenant faithfulness to him.[60]

The fact that monarchy alone cannot lead to Israel's peace and prosperity is quickly illustrated in the story of Saul. The story appears initially to be one of poetic justice—God's giving the Israelites exactly what they said they wanted. Saul is the embodiment of the worldly kingship Israel desires, but almost from the beginning it seems that he is not up to the task. God sends him to Samuel by way of a less-than-glamorous assignment (retrieving his father's lost donkeys), during which Saul shows a lack of leadership and perception.[61] When, despite his obtuseness, Saul nevertheless encounters Samuel and is anointed, he falters in the starting gate.[62] That is, he fails to "do what [his] hand finds to do" (1 Sam 10:7), which in the light of 1 Samuel 10:5 and the subsequent action of his son Jonathan in 1 Samuel 13:3 should have been to attack the Philistine garrison in Gibeah-Elohim. When Saul's inaction threatens to derail his rise to power, Samuel convenes an assembly

---

[58]See ibid., pp. 137-38.

[59]See ibid., p. 139.

[60]The Elisha cycle is another indication of the subjection of the kingship to Yahweh. See ibid., p. 155, citing Jacques Ellul, *The Politics of God and the Politics of Man,* trans. and ed. Geoffrey W. Bromiley (Grand Rapids: Eerdmans, 1972), pp. 23-40.

[61]The text suggests that the new king of Israel is not the leader of even this minor expedition. The servant suggests the course of action that ultimately leads to the recovery of the donkeys, and even provides the "quarter of a shekel" to pay the "prophet" to assist them in locating the lost animals (1 Sam 9:5-10).

[62]See V. Philips Long, *The Reign and Rejection of King Saul: A Case for Literary and Theological Coherence* (Atlanta: Scholars Press, 1989), chap. 2 and passim; more recently and more briefly in V. Philips Long, *The Art of Biblical History* (Grand Rapids: Zondervan, 1994), pp. 214-17; and in Provan, Long and Longman, *Biblical History of Israel,* pp. 211-14.

in Mizpah and casts lots to discover publicly whom God has chosen (1 Sam 10:17-21). When the lot falls on Saul, he is found "hiding among the baggage" (1 Sam 10:22). It begins to appear that perhaps Saul's sole qualifications for the job are his good looks and the fact that he is "head and shoulders taller than any man in Israel" (1 Sam 9:2). Eventually, when the Ammonites threaten the citizens of Jabesh-gilead and Saul hears of it, the "Spirit of God rushe[s] upon Saul" (1 Sam 11:6), and the previously passive man musters and leads a large contingent of Israelites into battle against the Ammonites. At this moment, it appears that God is with Saul and his monarchy. In the aftermath of this event, the kingdom is renewed at Gilgal, and Samuel confirms that even though Israel has sinned in asking for a king, "the LORD has set [Saul] over [them]" (1 Sam 12:13). He then cautions that if Israel "will fear the LORD and serve him and obey his voice and not rebel against the commandment of the LORD, and if both you and the king who reigns over you will follow the LORD your God, it will be well" (1 Sam 12:14). At this point, Saul's kingship looks somewhat promising, at least as long as he and the people continue to fear, serve and obey God.

Immediately after Saul's confirmation as king,[63] however, God finds it necessary to reject Saul's kingship on the basis of a series of failures on Saul's part, beginning in the aftermath of Jonathan's assault on the Philistine garrison at Geba, which led to the Israelites' hiding themselves "in rocks and in tombs and in cisterns" (1 Sam 13:6), followed by Saul's disobedient sacrifice in Samuel's absence, Jonathan's victory over the Philistines and Saul's rash vow that leads

---

[63]One cannot be entirely sure how much time passes between the events recorded in 1 Samuel 12 and in 1 Samuel 13. In terms of the narrative, however, Saul is rejected by the Lord almost immediately upon his confirmation as king. See Provan, Long and Longman, *Biblical History of Israel*, p. 210, describing a three-stage process of taking power in early Israel—"designation, demonstration and confirmation." Having failed to do what lay at hand at the time of his anointing (1 Sam 10:5, 7), Saul nevertheless does offer something of a demonstration of his abilities in his defeat of the Ammonites and is confirmed by the people in the renewal of the kingdom in 1 Samuel 11:14-15. After Samuel's warnings in a Samuel 12, however, the next event is Saul's failure to await Samuel's arrival in Gilgal (as instructed in 1 Sam 10:8), and as a consequence his kingship is not established by God.

Building on the work of Long in *Reign and Rejection of King Saul*, Provan, Long and Longman argue that Saul is never more than partially confirmed as king. Saul's first task was to take the Philistine garrison at Gibeath-Elohim, which he fails to do (and which Jonathan eventually takes in 1 Sam 13). He is then redesignated in the lot-casting incident in 1 Samuel 10:17-27, so that the defeat of the Ammonites is a "substitute demonstration" of his fitness to be king. The final confirmation never occurs because of Saul's refusal to wait for Samuel in 1 Samuel 13:4-15 (*Biblical History of Israel*, pp. 210-14).

the people into sin because of their hunger (and nearly leads him to kill his son Jonathan) (1 Sam 13–14). Although the bulk of the narrative focuses on these events, Saul's military accomplishments are briefly acknowledged in 1 Samuel 14:47-52, only to be followed by the painful episode in which Saul vanquishes the Amalekites but fails to follow God's command to "devote them to destruction," leading to Saul's second rejection and the telling statement that "the LORD regretted that he had made Saul king over Israel" (1 Sam 15:35). From this point on, Saul becomes an unambiguously tragic figure—personally tormented, militarily ineffective, jealous of David to the point of murder and consulting a medium rather than the Lord before dying in defeat along with his sons.

DAVID

If Saul is, from the beginning, an ambiguous embodiment of the institution of kingship, the same cannot be said of his successor, King David. The first reference to David is to a king whom God has chosen and who is a "man after God's own heart" (presumably in contrast to the values of the people embodied by Saul). Moreover, the presentation of David between his anointing (1 Sam 16) and his adultery with Bathsheba (2 Sam 11) is one of great, if not completely unqualified,[64] success: David slays Goliath; soothes the king with his music; passes by two chances to take the life of Saul, "the LORD's anointed"; unites Israel in victory over the Philistines; returns the ark to Jerusalem; and is given "rest from his enemies" (2 Sam 7:1).

One can, perhaps, begin to see the unraveling of David's kingship in his desire to build the temple for God. This would have been a customary way for ancient Near Eastern rulers to celebrate good fortune, and may be an indication that David is on the verge of becoming a "king like all the other nations."[65] In any event, God will have none of it; it is not David who will build a house for God, but God who has been building, and will continue to build, a house (dynasty) for David. The next few chapters portray David

---

[64]Some of the low points in the initial, generally positive, phase of David's kingship include his feigned insanity while in the Philistine kingdom (1 Sam 21), his encounter with Nabal (1 Sam 25) and his extermination of the inhabitants of the villages while in exile in Gath (1 Sam 27). Some commentators have argued that even the first part of David's story may not be as unambiguously good as it has usually been taken to be. See McConville, *God and Earthly Power,* pp. 140-41 (summarizing arguments).

[65]On temple building and its motivations among ancient Near Eastern monarchs generally, see V. Philips Long, "2 Samuel," in *Zondervan Illustrated Bible Backgrounds Commentary: Old Testament,* ed. John H. Walton (Grand Rapids: Zondervan, 2009), 2:441-42 (*ad* 2 Sam 7:1).

in a favorable light, cataloging his military victories and recounting his kindness to Saul's son Mephibosheth.

The turning point in the David story is, however, his adultery with Bathsheba and his orchestration of the murder of her husband, Uriah the Hittite. From this point on, even though God may build David a house that will last forever, as Nathan prophesies, "the sword shall never depart from [it]" (2 Sam 12:10). Although the balance of David's story has its occasional bright spot, his kingdom is thereafter consumed by fratricide and civil war, and David once again finds himself hiding in the wilderness in fear for his life. The so-called appendix to 2 Samuel (2 Sam 21–24) leaves a mixed final judgment on David. On one hand, there are accounts of David's military prowess and psalms of praise to God. These, however, are sandwiched between two episodes of judgment, the latter of which is particularly striking insofar as it suggests David's obsession with his own power rather than his reliance on, and gratitude for, God's deliverance.[66] David may have been a good king whose early years brought great blessing upon Israel, but the latter portion of his career brings tragedy, and even plague.

SOLOMON

We can see a similar pattern in Solomon's reign—a promising start followed by an unhappy ending, even one that portends the realization of the very qualities of kingship about which Samuel warned Israel in 1 Samuel 8.[67] Although God gives Solomon wisdom to rule wisely, the temple is built and Israel seems to flourish, McConville points out that this picture

> is mocked by a range of factors: the application of "wisdom" to the murder of enemies, the construction of a military machine, the securing of power by means of alliance, national wealth in the service of the king's own grandeur at the expense of the citizens' freedom of action, and a chosen place intended for communal worship by the tribes of Israel now becomes the capital of a centralized and self-protecting state.[68]

---

[66]See McConville, *God and Earthly Power*, pp. 145-47.
[67]The seeds of the latter years are visible even in the early stages, with the needs of the royal household taking priority over the well-being of the people. See Iain W. Provan, *1 and 2 Kings*, New International Biblical Commentary (Peabody, MA: Hendrickson, 1993); see also McConville, *God and Earthly Power*, p. 152.
[68]McConville, *God and Earthly Power*, p. 153.

By the end of the story, Solomon's apostasy is in full view, and the kingdom is to be "torn away" from his son Rehoboam. We can see more clearly the origins of Solomon's downfall and his failure to abide by God's law for the king. He is lured into idol worship by his accumulation of many wives, and, at Rehoboam's succession, we see evidence of Israel's complaint against the heavy burdens of forced labor he has been imposing on the people. The kingdom is divided, and there follows a succession of good and bad kings that culminates in exile.

JOSIAH

If attacks on the institution of monarchy in the style of the surrounding nations find as their *locus classicus* Samuel's denunciation of kingship in 1 Samuel 8, King Josiah's repentance in 2 Kings 22 is perhaps the most unambiguous account of godly monarchy. Already in the process of repairing the temple, Josiah learns of the (apparently until-now mislaid) Book of the Law and has it read to him. In response, he repents, and, even though God has pronounced judgment on Israel (though not on Josiah), he proceeds to have the law read to the people, to renew the covenant, to eradicate the pagan temples in the kingdom and to restore the celebration of Passover. Although Josiah is perhaps the best example of a king ruling under God's law, so great has been Israel's sin that he is defeated in battle. Here, perhaps, is the most striking signal that institutional form cannot guarantee national prosperity. Even when the king has been obedient, the people's disloyalty to the covenant Lord leads to their exile.[69]

Israel's history suggests that the nation's primary problem is not whether it is operating under the appropriate set of political institutions; rather, it is whether Israel is heeding the voice of the Lord or turning aside to walk after other gods. Israel experiences times of divine blessing under several different political arrangements—the rule of Moses the warrior/prophet/lawgiver, of Deborah the judge and of David the king—and equally suffers under judges, under kings and finally under foreign powers. If Israel's vocation is to show forth the righteousness and justice of God in the world and so to be a blessing to all the nations, the primary political issue raised by its recorded history "is not so much whether any particular form of rule is recommended, but in

---

[69]The statement in the text should not be taken to imply that nations with godly people and rulers should necessarily expect prosperity. Israel, however, was entitled to make that assumption on the basis of God's specific promise. See, e.g., 1 Samuel 12:14.

what way humans can bear the responsibility of rule at all."[70] To be sure, Israel's destiny is ultimately to be ruled by Jesus, the Son of David, but the history of the earthly Davidic line is less an endorsement of earthly monarchy than a pointed statement of the human need for a true and better king.

This conclusion may disappoint readers interested in mining the Bible for prescriptions that might shape contemporary law and politics, but it is nevertheless significant. The Bible's suggestion that the fundamental political question facing Israel is whether it will obey the LORD—not whether it has a king—is a stark departure from modern presuppositions that peace or political stability can be achieved structurally by implementing the right political or economic arrangements. Israel's special status as the LORD's covenant people undermines to some extent conclusions about generic "nationhood" and kingship that might be drawn from Israel's experience.

Even so, the fact that Israel's history reduces the nation's political institutions to a secondary status does not mean that the biblical texts are entirely indifferent to the form of earthly political arrangements. Two of the most important texts we have encountered, 1 Samuel 8 and Deuteronomy 17, offer complementary perspectives about kingship—the former a warning about the characteristic perversions[71] of the institution and the latter a code apparently designed to help forestall those perversions.

THE KINGSHIP CODE

The kingship code of Deuteronomy 17 is, in our view, best read to frame the subsequent history so that "the historical books that follow . . . narrate one among many possible 'histories'" and so that "an element of measure and critique is built into the structure."[72] On this reading, the Bible provides norms for kingship (although monarchy is only a permissible and not a mandatory form of government for Israel), and the subsequent history of Israel is the story of the failure, by and large, of Israel's rulers to obey God's law, just as Israel in general has been unable to keep the law.[73]

---

[70]McConville, *God and Earthly Power*, p. 134.

[71]We are indebted to David Skeel for suggesting this term.

[72]J. Gordon McConville, "Law and Monarchy in the Old Testament," in *A Royal Priesthood? The Use of the Bible Ethically and Politically, a Dialogue with Oliver O'Donovan*, ed. Craig Bartholomew, Jonathan Chaplin, Robert Song and Al Wolters (Grand Rapids: Zondervan, 2002), pp. 69, 83.

[73]An alternative reading, adopted by O'Donovan, is the obverse of the one we endorse and is related to source-critical theories that connect Deuteronomy's composition with the reign of Josiah. On this reading, Deuteronomy is not a backdrop against which the entire royal history may be critically

In fact, Deuteronomy 17 and 1 Samuel 8 may be seen as a shorthand survey of the primary ways in which the temptations of pride, wealth, sex and military power could be predicted to affect a king. (The language of the texts suggests that the disapproved practices had become the norm for Israel's neighbors.) In modern terms, Israel's monarchy is not absolute but constituted under law, and the law is designed to restrain the predictable negative consequences of kingship. Under the Deuteronomic law, Israel's king is not a god but a "brother" (Deut 17:15).[74] The expected privileges of neighboring kings—horses, wives and wealth—are to be denied him (Deut 17:16-17). And the king himself is to be one under authority; he is to

> learn to fear the LORD his God by keeping all the words of [the] law and [the] statutes, and doing them, that his heart may not be lifted up above his brothers, and that he may not turn aside from the commandment, either to the right hand or to the left, so that he may continue long in his kingdom, he and his children, in Israel. (Deut 17:19-20)[75]

The primary institutional response to the problem of self-interested rule is that the king is not to be autonomous but is bound to rule in accordance with God's law, including his specific instructions as delivered by prophets such as Samuel and Nathan.

It is hard to imagine how the law could emphasize this more strongly than in its insistence that when the king "sits on the throne of his kingdom, he shall write for himself in a book a copy of this law approved by the Levitical priests" (Deut 17:18). The king may not be selective about what he copies, but is accountable to the priests. Moreover, "it shall be with him, and he shall read in it all the days of his life" (Deut 17:19) so that (1) "he may learn to fear the LORD his God by keeping . . . the law" (Deut 17:19), (2) so

---

read, but is rather part of a larger synthesis of the accumulated wisdom and history of Israel. See O'Donovan, *Desire of the Nations,* pp. 30-81. In its critique of the excesses of kingship and its emphasis of the king's obedience to the law, Deuteronomy serves as a justification for the Josianic reforms but, by the same token, cannot be plausibly read as a dramatic limitation on kingly power. See Oliver O'Donovan, "Response to Gordon McConville," in *A Royal Priesthood? The Use of the Bible Ethically and Politically, a Dialogue with Oliver O'Donovan,* ed. Craig Bartholomew, Jonathan Chaplin, Robert Song and Al Wolters (Grand Rapids: Zondervan, 2002), pp. 89-90.

[74]See Bauckham, *God and the Crisis of Freedom,* p. 174: Israel's king "is a brother set over his brothers and sisters, but still a brother, and forbidden any of the ways in which rulers exalt themselves over and entrench their power over their subjects. His rule becomes tyranny the moment he forgets that the horizontal relationship of brother/sisterhood is primary, and kingship secondary."

[75]See McConville, "Law and Monarchy in the Old Testament," p. 76.

that he does not become proud in relation to his fellow Hebrews (Deut 17:20), (3) so that he does not forget the commandments and go his own way and (4) "so that he may continue long in his kingdom" (Deut 17:20).

The insistence that Israel's king should rule in accordance with God's law rather than legislate in accordance with his own autonomous judgments, along with other features of Israel's history,[76] have suggested to Oliver O'Donovan and Joan Lockwood O'Donovan that political authority should be seen as "primarily juridical" as opposed to "primarily directive and administrative."[77] In this vision, the ruler's role is not to engage in social ordering that produces a "body politic [that is] self-sufficient in all things requisite for the good life of its members,"[78] but rather to "adjudicat[e] . . . right and wrong on the basis of received communal understandings of divine and natural law."[79] On this account, the ruler's vocation is reactive rather than directive; it is to intervene to prevent and punish oppression and reward righteous conduct and to leave its members free, within the confines of God's law, to respond to God's call in accordance with their own conscience.[80]

APPOINTMENT AND SUCCESSION

Although the claim that the Bible supports a modern conception of separation of powers is the subject of dispute,[81] structural features of the Israelite polity as envisioned in Deuteronomy clearly do place significant limitations on the powers of the king. To begin with, one of the most striking features of

---

[76]See, e.g., O'Donovan, *Desire of the Nations,* pp. 37-39 (grounding vision of government as "judgment" in Old Testament passages).

[77]See Oliver O'Donovan, "Government as Judgment," in Oliver O'Donovan and Joan Lockwood O'Donovan, *Bonds of Imperfection: Christian Politics, Past and Present* (Grand Rapids: Eerdmans, 2004), pp. 207-24; O'Donovan, *Desire of the Nations,* pp. 37-40; Oliver O'Donovan, *The Ways of Judgment: The Bampton Lectures, 2003* (Grand Rapids: Eerdmans, 2005), pp. 3-12; and Joan Lockwood O'Donovan, "Subsidiarity and Political Authority in Theological Perspective," in O'Donovan and Lockwood O'Donovan, *Bonds of Imperfection,* p. 227.

[78]Joan Lockwood O'Donovan, "Subsidiarity and Political Authority in Theological Perspective," p. 243.

[79]Ibid., p. 228. See also O'Donovan, *Desire of the Nations,* pp. 37-39.

[80]See, e.g., John Witte's discussion of Milton's political thought in John Witte Jr., *The Reformation of Rights: Law, Religion, and Human Rights in Early Modern Calvinism* (New York: Cambridge University Press, 2007), pp. 209-75.

[81]See O'Donovan, *Desire of the Nations,* p. 65 (arguing for unitary government with a distribution of functions); but see McConville, "Law and Monarchy in the Old Testament," pp. 76-77; Jonathan Chaplin, "Political Eschatology and Responsible Government: Oliver O'Donovan's 'Christian Liberalism,'" in *A Royal Priesthood? The Use of the Bible Ethically and Politically, a Dialogue with Oliver O'Donovan,* ed. Craig Bartholomew, Jonathan Chaplin, Robert Song and Al Wolters (Grand Rapids: Zondervan, 2002), pp. 265, 292-95.

Deuteronomy 17 is that, taken in its larger context, the passage is almost entirely negative. As McConville says, "while a king is permitted, he has no essential role."[82] The law of kingship is set within a larger section (Deut 16:18–18:22) that distributes authority within Israel among several officials, of which the king is only one, and is, in fact, the only office holder whose position is permissive and not mandatory.[83] Moreover, there is no clear authorization for dynastic rule; on its face, the text would seem to suggest that hereditary succession is a possible choice for God and the people to make, but it is not a requirement. The text merely gives Israel permission to "set a king over [itself] whom the LORD your God shall choose" (Deut 17:15).

Not only is the decision whether to have a king to be made by the people, but the people, not the king, assume important roles of authority at other decisive moments, appointing their own judges and affirming together in solemn assemblies their status as the LORD's people and their obligation to submit to his law.[84]

The narratives concerning the appointment and succession of monarchs in the historical books also present a surprisingly complex picture of the distribution of authority in Israel.[85] The paradigmatic Israelite monarch, King David, was appointed by God (and anointed by Samuel) but is later also "anointed . . . king over Israel" (2 Sam 5:3) through a series of covenants that includes the "tribes of Israel" and the "elders of Israel" (2 Sam 5:1-5).[86]

In passages like these, which depict Israel as a society of dispersed authority brought together in covenant, biblical commentators and political theorists have found implications that go well beyond the question of hereditary monarchical succession. We have already alluded to the modern concept of separation of powers, but other important concepts emerge as well. In the hands of Reformed theorists such as the enormously influential Johannes Al-

---

[82]McConville, "Law and Monarchy in the Old Testament," p. 76.

[83]See Deuteronomy 16:18-19 (providing for judges), Deut 18:1-8 (priests) and Deut 17:8-13 (a high court); see McConville, *God and Earthly Power,* pp. 76-77.

[84]See Deuteronomy 1:13, 4:9-14, 16:18, 27:9-16 and 29:1; see also McConville, "Law and Monarchy in the Old Testament," p. 77.

[85]Cf. Provan, Long and Longman, *Biblical History of Israel,* p. 210 (discussing the three-stage process of taking power in early Israel—"designation, demonstration and confirmation").

[86]See also 1 Chron 11:3, 2 Chron 23:1-3, 1 Kings 1:34-40 and 2 Kings 23:1-3. See also Glenn A. Moots, *Politics Reformed: The Anglo-American Legacy of Covenant Theology* (Columbia, MO: University of Missouri Press, 2010), pp. 27-28, arguing that "without the formation of these perpetual covenants between the tribes and the monarch, civil authority was in doubt," and comparing Solomon and Rehoboam in this respect.

thusius, for example, Israel's path to nationhood is depicted as an organic procession from "the marital household of Abraham and Sarah to the extended families of Isaac and Jacob, then to the twelve tribes founded by Jacob's twelve children, then to the towns and cities led by Joshua and the later Judges, and finally to a single nation of Israel ruled by kings."[87] At each point along the way, Althusius finds "a 'consensual covenant' between the rulers and the people, with God presiding as third-party governor and guarantor."[88]

Israel's covenantal political framework has been cited in support of a number of important liberal political developments. The fact that Israel's kings, though chosen by God, were confirmed in covenant with the people, has been seen as recognition of a natural right of popular sovereignty.[89] From the idea of popular sovereignty mediated by covenant, it was a short step to limited government—both on the theory that leaders received their power from a (presumably not unlimited) delegation of power from the covenanting people[90] and because rulers were bound by the covenant obligations they assumed (in the case of Israel's rulers, to rule according to God's law). Moreover, the persistence of tribal identity even after Israel's constitution as a nation provides a model for a constitutional structure whereby "lower" units and officials within the political order retain their integrity even in the face of higher authorities.[91]

EXILE

Like the exodus and the monarchy, the exile of Israel into Babylonian captivity has been a central theme in Christian reflection about politics. First and foremost, the exile provides a marked contrast to the Israelite theocracy that preceded it, confronting the exiles with an entirely new set of political questions. Instead of asking, for example, how political rule can be faithfully carried out, the question is what it means to live faithfully when somebody else is in charge.[92] The object of this chapter—to consider what the Bible might teach us about the civil law—is more closely connected to the former question than to the latter, which might be said to concern the ethics of citizenship.

---

[87]Witte, *Reformation of Rights*, p. 188.
[88]Ibid.
[89]See ibid., p. 189.
[90]See ibid.
[91]See Moots, *Politics Reformed*, p. 28: "King David's covenant with tribal leaders . . . demonstrates the principle of federalism wherein a network of covenanted polities and jurisdictions forms a nation rather than one central authority governing a people and forming a nation."
[92]Cf. Yoder, "On Not Being in Charge."

When the captives faced the challenge of living as political outsiders, Jeremiah admonished them to "seek the welfare of the city where I have sent you into exile, and pray to the LORD on its behalf, for in its welfare you will find your welfare" (Jer 29:7). Seeking the welfare of the city "did not mean merely that [the Jews] hoped and prayed to be granted social tranquility and saved from persecution."[93] Esther, Nehemiah and Daniel held critical roles of influence in the alien culture and continue to serve as models for Christian political and cultural involvement.[94] As Yoder notes: "Not being in charge of the civil order is sometimes a more strategic way to be important for its survival or its flourishing than to fight over or for the throne."[95] Influence in the courts of worldly rulers can nevertheless be problematic, however, as the negative presentation of empire in Daniel attests.[96]

Once exiled, Israel lost its status as nation in the conventional sense. Even after the return, it remained more or less a subjugated people.[97] Strictly speaking, a politically powerless Israel can generate no more models of earthly political rule intended to vindicate the creation order and no more civil laws, the wisdom of which is intended to make the Gentiles marvel (Deut 4:6). Nevertheless, Israel's focus on maintaining its identity as a worshiping community had tangible political consequences. After the exile, Israel was no longer a merely geographic or ethnic community (if it ever was);[98] rather, "the spiritual commitment to I AM unites true Israel," and it "includes 'all who separated themselves from the neighboring peoples for the sake of the Law of God' (Neh. 10:28; cf. v. 29[30]) and excludes those who are descendants of the ancestors but refuse to identify with the congregation of returnees (Ezra 10:7-8)."[99] Maintaining this identity resulted in a

---

[93]Ibid., p. 172.

[94]See, e.g., Wayne Grudem, *Politics According to the Bible: A Comprehensive Resource for Understanding Modern Political Issues in Light of Scripture* (Grand Rapids: Zondervan, 2010), pp. 42, 58-59, 67, 79, 80-88; and David VanDrunen, *Living in God's Two Kingdoms: A Biblical Vision for Christianity and Culture* (Wheaton, IL: Crossway, 2010), p. 96.

[95]Yoder, "On Not Being in Charge," p. 172.

[96]See O'Donovan, *Desire of the Nations*, p. 87. For further discussion of the issue of empire in Daniel in the present volume, see chapter nine.

[97]For a survey of literature on the question of whether Israel was still in exile even after the return to Jerusalem, see Craig A. Evans, "Jesus and the Continuing Exile of Jerusalem," in *Jesus & the Restoration of Israel: A Critical Assessment of N. T. Wright's Jesus and the Victory of God*, ed. Carey C. Newman (Downers Grove, IL: InterVarsity Press, 1999), pp. 77-100.

[98]See McConville, *God and Earthly Power*, pp. 69-71.

[99]Waltke, *Old Testament Theology*, pp. 797-98.

number of institutions that would later serve as important models for the
Christian church, especially the synagogue, the role of the Torah in defining
the community, and the rabbinate.[100] While the Jews were politically subordinate to their earthly rulers, they nevertheless maintained their own laws
and courts,[101] providing an early model for the presence of competing jurisdictions and legal standards within a single polity.

Despite their adjustment to Israel's changed political condition, the exiles
would not have thought that the state of affairs in which they found themselves was, in any sense, normal. Had not God promised that David's descendants would reign on the throne of Israel forever? Given that promise, the
obvious expectation was that God would restore the theocracy at some point,
permit the rebuilding of the city and the temple, and restore political rule to
Israel. Oliver O'Donovan summarizes the exilic expectations as including (1)
the gathering of the scattered Jews and the conversion of the world to the
worship of God, (2) the healing of the divide between the northern and
southern kingdoms and (3) the restoration of the Davidic monarchy.[102]

At this point, Israel's contribution to legal and political thought, picked
up explicitly in the New Testament, is its insistence that, as with Pharaoh's
rule in Egypt, neither its exile nor its subjugation to alien powers will ultimately survive. As O'Donovan argues:

> To treat the coexistence of Israel and Babylon as a permanent ordinance was,
> in effect to accept the emperor's own assessment of himself, to bow down
> before his image of gold. To arm itself against that temptation Israel must,
> once again, heed prophecy, alert for the culmination of Yhwh's purposes in
> which the Ancient of Days will entrust his Kingdom to a son of man, who
> should also represent the people of the saints of the Most High.[103]

CONCLUSION

The relevance of the specifics of ancient Israel's institutional arrangements
for modern times is rightly the subject of debate. Israel's history, however, is

---

[100]See Yoder, "On Not Being in Charge," p. 171. See also David Novak, "Law and Religion in Judaism," in *Christianity and Law: An Introduction,* ed. John Witte Jr. and Frank S. Alexander (New
York: Cambridge University Press, 2008), pp. 33-52.
[101]See, e.g., the repeated references to the presence of elders in Ezekiel. See, e.g., Ezekiel 7:26; 8:1,
11-12; 9:6; 14:1; 20:1, 3; and 27:9.
[102]See O'Donovan, *Desire of the Nations,* p. 84.
[103]Ibid., p. 88.

told from a point of view that is in large measure at odds with contemporary approaches to politics. To be sure, attention is given to the construction of workable institutional structures. Nevertheless, the foundational assumption of much contemporary constitutional theory—that humans are capable of engineering a just state structure that can achieve lasting stability by reconciling the competing claims of individuals and groups—is hardly at the forefront of the narrative. The story of Israel presupposes that God is the Lord of history and that stability or, better yet, blessing and prosperity, are under his righteous control.

3

CRIMINAL AND CIVIL LAW
IN THE TORAH

The Mosaic Law in Christian Perspective

David Skeel and Tremper Longman III

INTRODUCTION

Scholars who wish to trace the implications of Scripture for contemporary law frequently must look for lessons and hints in passages that lack any explicit legal content. Not so with the final four books of the Pentateuch: Exodus, Leviticus, Numbers and Deuteronomy. These books are full of law. When Jesus speaks of the law and the prophets, the law he has in mind is these books, which contain nearly all the Mosaic law.

Christians and Christian churches come to the regulations in these books at several removes. God gave the law to a particular community—Israel—for a particular place. Its regulations included not only criminal and civil law but also requirements for their worship. For Christians, many of the laws no longer apply, and others do not apply in the same way, as a result of the new covenant inaugurated by Christ's life, death and resurrection.

As we explore the implications of the Mosaic law for contemporary secular law, we therefore must proceed gingerly. The issues we will be considering have vexed theologians and the church for centuries. We cannot claim to resolve them definitively, much less offer a simple blueprint of the implications of the Mosaic law for particular issues, controversial or otherwise. But we believe that serious attention to these four books would force many Christians to rethink radically their understanding of the role and emphasis of secular law.

In the discussion that follows, we first place the Mosaic law in covenantal and New Testament perspective. We then briefly summarize the regulations in each of the four books under consideration. After noting some of the distinctive characteristics of the laws, we explore their implications for contemporary criminal law; economic and commercial law; and marriage, divorce and sexuality.

The Law in Its Context

Old Testament context. In the Old Testament, the law is situated in a literary and theological context. In the first place, law is covenantal. The covenant is a legal metaphor for God's relationship with Israel. In the past half-century, due to comparisons with ancient Near Eastern texts, it has become increasingly clear that the word generally translated "covenant" in English texts (in Hebrew *běrît*) is more specifically described as a treaty. God, the great king, enters into a treaty with his subject people.

In ancient Near Eastern treaties and in biblical covenants, law follows historical prologue. The historical prologue rehearses the beneficial actions that the great king has performed on behalf of the vassal. After the historical review, the great king presents the law that he expects the vassal to obey. In other words, law does not create the relationship, but rather is in response to the previous actions of the sovereign. The law is then followed by sanctions or blessings and curses that follow obedience or disobedience.

The book of Deuteronomy presents Moses' final sermon to the Israelites before he dies and they enter into the Promised Land. The form of this sermon roughly follows that of a covenant/treaty document since he is exhorting them to reaffirm that relationship established at Sinai (Ex 19–24), which is today known as the Sinaitic or Mosaic covenant. Here we see the law (Deut 4–26) following the historical prologue (Deut 1:9–3:27) and preceding the blessings and the curses (Deut 27–28).[1]

---

[1]The other elements of a covenant/treaty are also found in Deuteronomy, including the introduction of the parties (Deut 1:1-5) and the mention of witnesses (Deut 30:19-20). For a fuller explanation, see Meredith G. Kline, *Treaty of the Great King: The Covenant Structure of Deuteronomy, Studies and*

The placement of the law after the historical review is of important theological significance, reminding Israel that law does not establish relationship with God. On the contrary, God's gracious redemption precedes law, and obeying law is a way of expressing gratitude to God. That grace precedes law is concisely illustrated by the fact that the Ten Commandments themselves are preceded by a short historical prologue: "I am the LORD your God, who brought you out of Egypt, out of the house of slavery" (Ex 20:2).[2]

However, the fact that the law is followed by blessings and curses also indicates that obedience maintains the divine-human relationship. If Israel disobeys the law, then the curses of the law come into effect.

The second important matter of context to bear in mind to begin a study of the Old Testament law has to do with the relationship between the Ten Commandments and the case law—that is, the application of legal principles to particular contexts. The Ten Commandments articulate general ethical principles, while the case law applies those principles to specific cases according to the sociological and redemptive-historical situation of Israel. An example is the case law that states, "When you build a new house, make a parapet around your roof so you may not bring the guilt of bloodshed on your house, if someone falls from the roof" (Deut 22:8). This case law takes the principle enunciated by the sixth commandment: "You shall not murder" (Deut 5:17; see also Ex 20:13) and applies it to Israelite residential architecture. After all, in ancient Israel the roof was a living space, and an unprotected roof meant that people could easily fall and be injured or die.

A third important feature of Old Testament law, especially when considered from the perspective of the New Testament church, is that it is addressed to Israel, which is a nation. That is, the people of God have the form of a nation (in contrast to the present time when the people of God are drawn from many different nations). This transition from the Old to the New Testament will affect how the Old Testament law is appropriated today.

New Testament context. The frame for Christian consideration of the Mosaic law comes from Jesus' familiar admonition in the Sermon on the Mount. "Do not think that I have come to abolish the Law or the Prophets,"

Commentary (Grand Rapids: Eerdmans, 1963); K. A. Kitchen, "The Fall and Rise of Covenant, Law and Treaty," *Tyndale Bulletin* 40 (1989): 118-35; and Dennis J. McCarthy, *Old Testament Covenant: A Survey of Current Opinions,* 2nd ed. (Rome: Pontifical Biblical Institute, 1978).

[2]Unless otherwise indicated, all Scripture quotations in this chapter are from the NIV 1984.

Jesus said. "I have not come to abolish them but to fulfill them. I tell you the truth, until heaven and earth disappear, not the smallest letter, not the least stroke of a pen will by any means, disappear from the Law until everything is accomplished" (Mt 5:17-18).[3] The terms of Jesus's embrace of the law—he will "not abolish" and he will "fulfill"—rule out two stances toward the Mosaic law that have sometimes proven tempting for Christians.[4] Christians cannot ignore the law, but neither can they simply assume its direct, unfiltered relevance to contemporary concerns. In its most egregious form, the first error is known as Marcionism, after a heretical second-century theologian who insisted that the Old Testament was altogether superseded by Christ and had no further relevance. An example of the second, less common error is theonomy, a small but much-discussed theological irruption whose advocates called for the direct application of Old Testament law in a biblically centered American polity.[5]

Christ's words not only warn us against either ignoring Old Testament law or applying it in unfiltered fashion. They also characterize the fulfillment of the law as ongoing, a process that Christ has begun but that will continue until "everything is accomplished." To understand what this may mean for contemporary secular law, we begin by identifying some of the focal points, the foundational principles, of the Mosaic law. While others may characterize the principles that underlie the Mosaic law differently, we focus here on three general themes that run through these books and provide the foundation for the law.[6]

First is the nature of God himself. God is the creator of all things and is completely holy. Although God stands apart from the creation, he is not aloof from it. He has chosen a people for himself and is in relationship with them. "I, the LORD, am holy and have set you apart from the nations to be my own," he says in Leviticus 20:26. Elsewhere in the Old Testament,

---

[3]For further discussion in this volume of this statement by Jesus, see "The Kingdom of God, Law and the Heart" in chapter six.

[4]In Ephesians 2:15, Paul describes Jesus as "abolishing the law of commandments and ordinances," but he is speaking of the replacement of the old framework with our justification through Christ, not pronouncing on the question of whether any of the law's principles are still relevant.

[5]Rousas John Rushdoony, *The Institutes of Biblical Law: A Chalcedon Study* (Nutley, NJ: Craig Press, 1973); and Greg L. Bahnsen, *Theonomy in Christian Ethics* (Nutley, NJ: Craig Press, 1977).

[6]Our three themes are loosely patterned on a framework developed by Christopher Wright. Wright refers to them as "paradigms," apparently to assure flexibility in application. Christopher J. H. Wright, *Old Testament Ethics for the People of God* (Downers Grove, IL: InterVarsity Press, 2004).

Israel is frequently described as God's bride,[7] or as God's child. The books that compose the Mosaic law admonish Israel to imitate God, as when Israel is instructed to care for the sojourner. "Love those who are aliens," Israel is told, "for you yourselves were aliens in the land of Egypt" until God rescued them (Deut 10:19).

Second is the unique nature of the community for which the Mosaic law was given. The Israel of the Mosaic law is God's chosen people, a nation set apart for himself. They are called to be holy both in their purity and in their separateness from other nations. Their distinctiveness is reflected in God's command that they eschew the practices of the nations around them and that they eat only those foods that are designated as "clean" (as for example, in Lev 11, which distinguishes clean and unclean foods in detail). God promises to reward Israel's obedience by showering it with blessings. If Israel disobeys, on the other hand, it will be cursed. The community is responsible for the behavior of its members and will itself be punished for tolerating lawlessness in its midst. In Leviticus, for instance, God threatens, as the culmination of a stream of horrific punishments for disobedience, to "scatter you among the nations," and "draw out my sword and pursue you," so that "your land will be laid waste, and your cities will lie in ruins" (Lev 26:33).

The third theme is the land. The Mosaic law is framed in anticipation of Israel's entrance into the Promised Land, and the land is a central concern of the legal framework. Of particular importance are the facts that Israel did not obtain the land through its own prowess or strength and that its ownership of the land is not absolute. Borrowing from modern American property concepts, we might call Israel's interest in the land an obedience-estate. Much as a person who holds a life estate in property owns the property for as long as she lives, after which it reverts to the original owner, Israel was entitled to live peacefully on the land and to enjoy its fruits for as long as the Israelites remained faithful to God. But disobedience would terminate Israel's estate.

The double nature of Israel's ownership—the land was a gift from God, but God remained its ultimate owner—is woven deeply into the Mosaic law. It underscores Israel's dependence on God and underwrites the law's concerns that the people imitate the holiness of their holy God and that they

---

[7] Usually implied when Israel is depicted as an adulterous wife (Ezek 16; 23; Hos 1; 3); however, see Jeremiah 2:1-3.

show the kind of care for aliens and the vulnerable in their midst that God showed for the Israelites when they were oppressed in Egypt.[8]

We subsume in these three themes several major concerns of the Mosaic law that could easily be treated as additional themes. We have not yet mentioned, for instance, the detailed instruction on the dimensions of the tabernacle, the sacrifices and the responsibilities of the priests in overseeing the sacrifices. The tabernacle and sacrifices lie at the heart of Israel's relationship with God, testifying to God's holiness and defining the community that Israel was called to be. We will consider them in that context—as the sinews that hold the community together and link it to God.

THE MOSAIC LAW: A BRIEF OVERVIEW

With the larger themes as a backdrop, we turn now to the law itself. We will begin with a brief survey of the four books under consideration before analyzing the overall structure of the Mosaic law in more detail.

Exodus 20 opens with this majestic statement: "And God spoke all these words." Starting with the Ten Commandments, later described as the "ten words," the second half of Exodus is devoted almost entirely to legal regulation. Exodus 20 concludes with an admonition against making gold or silver idols. Exodus 21 begins with a series of regulations about the treatment of slaves, punishments or payments for injuries in a fight or for striking a slave, and restitutionary payments for injuries to someone else's animals. In contemporary terms, the first group of laws might be characterized as general civil regulation, the next as a mixture of criminal law and tort, and the last as tort law. The regulation continues (in Ex 22) with a series of tort laws involving damage to a neighbor's property or animals; more criminal laws; and admonitions (to be enforced not by Israel but by God) not to mistreat sojourners, widows or orphans, not to charge interest on loans to the poor, and not to neglect the obligation to offer their firstfruits (whether it be children, animals or crops) to God. Exodus 23 instructs Israel to let the land lie fallow every seventh year, commands rest for all on the sabbath and calls for three annual feasts.

Exodus 25–31 provides detailed instructions for the ark of the covenant and other elements of the tabernacle, which was to be the focal point of Is-

---

[8]Wright, *Old Testament Ethics*, emphasizes these attributes of the land.

rael's camp, their worship and God's presence during the years in the wilderness. While Moses is on Mount Sinai receiving these instructions, Aaron responds (in Ex 32) to the people's insistence that they be given idols "who will go before us" by making a golden calf for them to worship. Infuriated when he returns to an orgy of dancing before the golden calf, Moses destroys the two tablets on which God has engraved the Ten Commandments, and God sends a plague. Moses subsequently persuades God to lift the plague and at God's command makes two new tablets to replace the two he had destroyed (Ex 34). After the startling disobedience of the golden calf incident, which threatened Israel's very relationship with God, Exodus 35–40 recounts in tender detail Israel's construction of the tabernacle and the priestly garments. After this faithful fulfillment of God's instructions, the glory of God fills the tabernacle at the conclusion of Exodus.

Leviticus picks up where Exodus left off, with the tabernacle newly constructed and filled with the glory of God. Leviticus 1–10 outlines the sacrifices that Israel is to offer to God. Holiness, a central concern of the sacrificial system, is the dominant theme of the regulations that follow. Leviticus 11 details the dietary laws that distinguish Israel from other nations, listing the "clean" animals, which Israel is permitted to eat, and the "unclean" ones, which are off-limits. Leviticus 12–16 prescribes processes of purification for a woman who has just given birth, a person with a skin disease, a house with mildew, and menstrual and semen discharges. Leviticus 17–18 prohibits Israel from eating blood and from sexual relations with close relatives. Leviticus 19 opens with the instruction to "Be holy, because I the LORD your God, am holy," and outlines an eclectic series of obligations—to leave the edges of their fields unharvested, for the benefit of the poor or sojourner; not to lie or steal; not to do injustice in court; not to eat blood or sell a daughter as a prostitute; to honor the elderly; and to use just weights. Leviticus 20 is primarily concerned with the punishments for violating these obligations— prescribing death for those who sacrifice a child or commit adultery with a neighbor's wife, and instructing that those who turn to wizards or have sex with a sister be cut off from the people. Leviticus 21–23 prescribes the holiness obligations of priests and establishes the appointed feasts in the priestly calendar, starting with the weekly sabbath and Passover.

The case of a woman (whose mother was an Israelite and father an Egyptian) who blasphemed God is recounted in Leviticus 24, along with

God's instruction to Moses that the blasphemer be stoned by the entire congregation. This is followed by the instruction that anyone who takes a human life must be put to death, and the eye-for-an-eye principle of punishment known as *lex talionis.*

The regulations that follow (in Lev 25) are devoted to the release of those bound by debt and the restoration of property to its original owner. Every seventh year is to be a sabbath year of rest for the land; the fiftieth year is to be the year of jubilee. The jubilee regulations instruct God's people once again to rest the land, provide for redemption of any property that has been sold by an Israelite who becomes poor, call for support of a poor fellow Israelite and invite redemption of an Israelite who has been sold into servitude. "Even if he is not redeemed in any of these ways," the regulations conclude, "he and his children are to be released in the Year of Jubilee, for the Isrealites belong to me as servants" (Lev 25:54-55). Leviticus concludes with the promise of blessings for obedience and punishment for disobedience (Lev 26), and detailed regulation of vows of gifts to the Lord (Lev 27).

In Numbers, which recounts Israel's subsequent wanderings in the wilderness, the additions to the Mosaic law are more scattered. Among the notable additions are the establishment of a ritual that allows for the consecration of non-Levites (Num 6) and an elaborate test to determine whether a jealous husband's wife has committed adultery.[9] God also instructs Moses to appoint seventy elders to help bear the burden of overseeing the people. Another section prescribes sacrifices to atone for unintentional sins and recounts Moses' ruling that a man who gathered sticks in violation of the sabbath must be stoned by the congregation.[10] Numbers distinguishes between murder and unintentional killing, establishing six cities of refuge to provide safety for unintentional manslayers from vengeance-seeking family members. Murderers must be put to death, and they cannot be ransomed (Num 35:31-32).[11] (In the view of some scholars, this prohibition of ransom for murder implies, by negative inference, that other punishments could be and were substituted for the death penalty with crimes other than murder.[12])

---

[9]Numbers 5:5-7 (restitution); 5:11-31 (test for adultery).

[10]Numbers 15:22-31 (unintentional sins); 15:32-36 (sabbath-breaker executed).

[11]Proverbs 6:34-35 also implies that the offended husband could substitute a fine for the death penalty but would likely not be inclined to do so because of his anger.

[12]See, for example, Walter C. Kaiser Jr., *Toward Old Testament Ethics* (Grand Rapids: Zondervan, 1983), p. 73.

Framed as Moses' final sermon as he nears death and Israel prepares to enter the Promised Land, Deuteronomy retells the events of the three previous books, including God's giving of the Ten Commandments. As in Leviticus, legal regulations run through much of the book (Deut 4–26), often elaborated or articulated differently from the earlier books. Unlike the emphasis on holiness in Leviticus, Deuteronomy does not explicitly announce a prevailing theme or themes. But its heart, even more than in Exodus, is the Ten Commandments. The extensive regulatory instructions that come after the Ten Commandments may in fact entail a working out of some of the implications of each of the commandments,[13] a fact true of all the case law.

Deuteronomy devotes particular attention to the mechanisms of administering justice. Moses instructs the people to appoint judges and officers in each town, which suggests that judging was largely local. If a case were particularly difficult, however, the local officials are instructed to take it to the Levitical priests and central judge. In addition, every king must read the law every day and keep it, so that "his heart may not be lifted up above his brothers" (Deut 17:18-20).

Deuteronomy 20–25 sets forth a long sequence of regulations, many of which are given in narrative form, apparently as case studies, and few of which are accompanied by explicit punishments. Deuteronomy 20 excuses from military service men who have built a new house, have recently planted a vineyard, are betrothed or are fearful of battle. Many of the laws concern cleanness and uncleanness, marriage, sexual morality, and protection of the poor and needy from economic oppression.

Moses concludes his address with an assurance of blessings if Israel obeys the laws, warnings of the curses for disobedience, a public reading of the law, his farewell song and a final blessing on the tribes of Israel.

A FEW ATTRIBUTES OF THE MOSAIC LAW

The centrality of the Ten Commandments is perhaps the most striking feature of these four books of the Mosaic law. Indeed, as explained above, all the case law is derived from them. Literally given on a mountain, the

---

[13]For scholarly interpretation in these terms, see, for example, John H. Walton, "Deuteronomy: An Exposition in the Spirit of the Law," *Grace Theological Journal* 8 (1987): 213-25. The classic modern work in this vein is Stephen A. Kaufman, "The Structure of the Deuteronomic Law," *Maarav* 1/2 (1978–1979): 105-58.

commandments seem to rise above the rest of the regulatory landscape, providing the framework for God's covenantal relationship with his people. It is tempting to compare the Ten Commandments to a constitution, and the remaining regulations to the laws that are enacted after a constitution is in place. The analogy must be used carefully. Old Testament ethics courses, particularly in theologically conservative seminaries, sometimes foreground the Ten Commandments so heavily that other dimensions of the Mosaic law disappear. But the Ten Commandments clearly are the touchstone for the regulations as a whole.

Another striking and similarly well-known attribute of the Mosaic laws is their mixture of religious and civil regulations. In modern Western legal traditions, religion and civil obligations occupy separate domains, except in the few fraught areas where they overlap. The Mosaic laws govern both domains—regulating worship as well as criminal law, family law and torts—although the particular regulations are generally kept separate.

A third noteworthy attribute is the form the regulations take. The Ten Commandments are direct, absolute and incontestable. To use the theological term, they are *apodictic*. From the first commandment ("you shall have no other gods before me") to the last ("you shall not covet"), the commandments are both literally and figuratively set in stone.

Commands in the law outside the Ten Commandments function more like case studies designed to be applied by analogy to other contexts. Here the theological term is *casuistic*. One of the Deuteronomic laws states, for instance, "When you make your neighbor a loan of any sort, you shall not go into his house to collect his pledge" (Deut 24:10). This law seems intended to protect a debtor's dignity and invites extension to contexts other than the debtor's home, and perhaps to other kinds of transactions as well.[14]

The distinction must be handled with care. Apodictic regulations may reach beyond their immediate, literal context. We have already noted, for example, that the entire Deuteronomic code (indeed all the case laws) can be seen as extending and applying the principles of the Ten Commandments. But the form of the commands is different. The extension of an apodictic command is like the ripples of a stone thrown into a pond, expanding outward, whereas

---

[14]A Talmudic scholar would question our use of principles to understand the Mosaic law, arguing that it is designed to be understood casuistically. See, e.g., Chaim Saiman, "Jesus' Legal Theory—A Rabbinic Reading," *Journal of Law and Religion* 23 (2007): 97.

casuistic reasoning asks whether two distinct things are meaningfully similar. Paul reasons casuistically, for instance, when he cites the command against muzzling an ox that is treading grain as evidence that preachers are entitled to be supported by God's people (1 Tim 5:17-18; 1 Cor 9:3-10).

A fourth element is the relationship between particular laws and the remedies attached to them. Some laws do not provide for any explicit remedy. The law (Ex 21:2-11) mandating that Hebrew slaves be released in the seventh year unless they commit to remain with their master does not prescribe a punishment for violation; presumably, a slave could sue for freedom if he were held for more than six years, but this is nowhere stated in the text. Other laws have very specific criminal or civil penalties. The same sequence of laws in Exodus states that "Anyone who kidnaps another and sells him . . . must be put to death" (Ex 21:16) and that one who steals an ox or sheep "must pay back five head of cattle for the ox, and four sheep for the sheep" (Ex 22:1).

Of particular interest here is the large number of commands that do not have a remedy but include a phrase emphasizing why Israel should honor the command. "Do not oppress an alien," one regulation begins. "You yourselves know how it feels to be aliens, because you were aliens in Egypt" (Ex 23:9). This explanation—or "motive phrase"—highlights a distinction between formal law and moral suasion that we will return to below.

As should be evident even in the handful of examples we have used in this section, the three themes identified earlier run through all the Mosaic law: God is the creator, he is holy and he expects holiness from his people. Israel is a unique community that has been set apart as God's people; the regulation of this community is designed to promote its holiness and proper devotion to God. The land is the community's proper home, and its regulation reflects the qualities God has and expects from his people, such as justice and care for sojourners and the poor and oppressed.

Lessons for Contemporary Issues

To apply the Mosaic laws to contemporary issues, Christians must come to grips with the implications of Jesus' having come not to abolish the law but to fulfill it. Jesus' sacrifice removes the need for the sacrificial system, for instance, as the book of Hebrews explains at length. But elsewhere the law retains its force, and the principles of law may remain fully relevant even where its specifics have been superseded.

Dating back at least to medieval theology, the traditional approach distinguishes among three kinds of law—moral, civil and ceremonial. Because the civil and ceremonial law applied to Israel as a nation, these laws were deemed not to be binding on Christians. Moral laws, such as the Ten Commandments, by contrast, are permanent and fully binding (with the possible exception of the fourth commandment concerning the sabbath, which seems to be a ceremonial law; see also Col 2:16-17).

The traditional typology neatly simplifies the question of how to apply the Mosaic law after Christ, and it can be defended as a general shorthand. But it is an undependable guide to the application of many parts of the Mosaic law, especially if employed indiscriminately. According to Deuteronomy 24:6, for instance, "Do not take a pair of millstones—not even the upper one—as security for a debt, because that would be taking man's livelihood as security." This looks like a civil law, with particular application to economic relations in Israel, which might suggest that it has been superseded by Christ. But the regulation surely has an important moral dimension as well. A loan that is secured by a debtor's millstone would put the debtor's livelihood at risk in the event he was unable to repay. From this perspective, the regulation implicates a creditor's moral responsibilities in credit transactions. As this illustration suggests, the traditional division will not carry us far in our application of the Mosaic law to the contemporary secular law.

In the discussion that follows, we will attempt to draw out some of the implications of the Mosaic law in a more nuanced fashion. In each of three areas—criminal law; economic and commercial regulation; and marriage, divorce and sexuality—we first situate the regulations of the Mosaic law in the context of the three principles we outlined at the outset, analyzing how the rules might have applied in Israel and what the significance of the laws seems to have been. Only after putting the regulations into this larger context do we reflect on the relevance for contemporary law.

Criminal law. Much of the Mosaic law is criminal in nature. As often noted, the death penalty is called for as a punishment for offenses ranging from murder to blasphemy and a child's disobedience to his parents. Intent is a central concern of the law—as reflected, for instance, in the cities of refuge provided to protect unintentional killers—although unintentional injuries also are treated as crimes. The Mosaic law seems to contemplate that trials will be conducted locally, and it shows particular concern for the nature of the evidence produced, ordinarily requiring the testimony of at least two witnesses (Num 35:30).

The context of the criminal law is Israel's unique relationship with God as his chosen people. The law reflects God's holiness and his expectation that his people will be holy too. The criminal law therefore covers every aspect of life, including worship, and the penalties are designed both to punish individual wrongdoing and to promote the well-being of the community. This last point bears emphasis. The emphasis on individual responsibility is evidenced in the laws themselves, and in the command in Deuteronomy that "fathers shall not be put to death for their children, nor children put to death for their fathers; each is to die for his own sin" (Deut 24:16). At the same time, the criminal law was not solely concerned with individual responsibility. The call for the community to execute wrongdoers, for instance, underscores that criminal offenses are offenses against the community.

One other oft-noted theme of the criminal laws requires clarification. A key principle of the criminal law—alluded to by Jesus himself—is the eye-for-an-eye principle known as *lex talionis*. (As has often been pointed out, in its historical context *lex talionis* was a comparatively lenient standard that limited retaliation.)[15] The *lex talionis* most clearly governs unconsented-to physical harms to another person, such as an assault or murder. Its application to other crimes—such as blasphemy, sabbath breaking or homosexual intercourse—is less evident.

The land features in the criminal law framework both directly and as a metaphor for the law's commitment to providing as much protection for the poor or sojourner as for more affluent community members. The cities of refuge provide a zone of safety for those who have unintentionally killed someone. The perpetrators of intentional crimes, on the other hand, are excluded from the camp and from the land. As a metaphor, the laws concerning the land model God's concern for justice and for the holiness of the community.

The most obvious effect of Christ's coming is to transform the nature of the covenant community. The community's focus shifts away from the land and nation to Christ and the church, and to the hearts of the believers

---

[15]David VanDrunen, "Natural Law, the *Lex Talionis*, and the Power of the Sword," *Liberty University Law Review* 2 (Spring 2008): 945-67. For additional discussion of the *lex talionis* in this volume, see "The Covenant with Noah" in chapter one and "God's Moral Law, the Mosaic Law and Legislation" in chapter six.

themselves. This also severs the link between the community of worship and the apparatus of the state. The extent of the separation, however, should not be overstated. Israel's subjugation by Rome had already created a division between the governing authority and the community of God's people. And Rome would later embrace the church, reuniting church and state. But the transformation brought by Christ complicates the use of the criminal law to police matters of worship. Not only is the church urged to handle grievances internally, as when Paul chastises the Corinthians for suing one another in secular courts (1 Cor 6:1-8),[16] but it becomes much less evident that secular law should be used to prosecute those who blaspheme God or break the sabbath, given that secular law must apply both to Christians and to those who do not identify themselves with Christ.

Two attributes of the criminal prohibitions in the Mosaic law seem especially relevant in a contemporary context. The first is the scope of criminal enforcement. Because Israel was a much more tightly knit community than is a modern nation like the United States, the range of misbehavior that could plausibly be policed through criminal law was far broader. The law does indeed speak to a very wide range of behavior—not just the core principles of the Ten Commandments but the broad spirit of those principles. Yet in many cases, God, not Israel, is the one who will enforce the prohibitions, as we noted earlier. The formal punishments that the Mosaic law instructs Israel to mete out are, as in modern law, almost invariably reserved for clear actions, rather than simply thoughts. Overall, the range of offenses that are subject to formal criminal punishment is surprisingly narrow. Contemporary discomfort with the harshness of the Mosaic law's penalties can make it easy to overlook this. In our view, the limited scope of formal criminal punishment in the Mosaic law has important implications for the proper role of criminal law in a contemporary secular society. It suggests that the state cannot, and should not be expected to, police every form of misbehavior.[17]

The second attribute, mentioned earlier, is the emphasis on local enforcement. At some points in Israel's history, centralized enforcement would

---

[16]For further discussion of 1 Corinthians 6 in this volume, see "Civil Litigation in 1 Corintians 6:1-11" in chapter eight.

[17]For an argument that criminal law must play a "double game," restraining the sins of the citizenry without sweeping so broadly that it invites discriminatory enforcement by police and prosecutors, see David A. Skeel Jr. and William J. Stuntz, "Christianity and the (Modest) Rule of Law," *University of Pennsylvania Journal of Constitutional Law* 8 (2006): 809-30.

have been quite plausible. And the shift to a monarchy did produce a central-
izing tendency. But the model for enforcement of all but the most difficult
cases was community-based judging, modeled on the pattern of village elders
sitting at the town gate. The shift away from community-based policing and
justice in the contemporary United States stands in notable contrast to this
biblical pattern.[18]

Economics and commercial law. The economic and commercial regulations of the Mosaic law are, like the criminal law, closely linked to God's
concern for justice, and foreground even more heavily the emphasis on
caring for the poor and the sojourner as God cared for his people during
their servitude in Egypt. The central role of the land in this framework calls
for particular care as we tease out implications for contemporary law.

The economic regulations of the Mosaic law are framed by reminders that
Israel's ownership of the land is conditioned on their obedience, and that
they are like aliens and sojourners. Rather than being entitled to the entire
produce of their acreage, each Israelite family must leave the edges unharvested for the benefit of those in need. Israelites are expected to make
interest-free loans to fellow Israelites who are in need, and they must release
those who are in servitude for debt in the seventh year. The climax of these
regulations is the jubilee outlined in Leviticus 25. In the fiftieth year, debtors
must be released from their servitude, and land that an original owner has
sold must be returned to its owner. This last requirement ensured (so long as
the jubilee was honored—2 Chron 36:21 implies that it was not observed
very often) that Israelite families retained the land of their original inheritance and that it did not all end up in the hands of a few giant landowners.

Jesus draws heavily on the Mosaic law's economic regulations even as he
transforms them. When he announces the year of the Lord's favor, invoking
the great promise from Isaiah that the year of the Lord's favor has come,
Jesus is, most scholars agree, proclaiming a jubilee (Lk 4:17-20, quoting Is
61:1-2).[19] And the salvation he offers—with its forgiveness and promise of
restoration—is framed in terms of redemption from debt. The economic
language attests to the continued relevance of the economic regulations.
But the new covenant in Christ changes the context in two respects. The

---

[18]The sad consequences of this shift are a central theme of Bill Stuntz's work. See William J. Stuntz,
  The Collapse of American Criminal Justice (Cambridge, MA: Harvard University Press, 2011).
[19]E.g., Wright, *Old Testament Ethics*, p. 206.

first is that the distinction between Israel and other nations no longer holds in the same way. Christians are called to pay special care to those in the church (as when Jesus says that a cup of cold water given to the least of us ministers to Jesus himself), as the economic regulations directed Israelites to do with their brothers, but Christians also are called to view those beyond their community as their neighbors[20] and to make disciples of all nations.[21]

Second, the details of the Mosaic law's economic regulations reflect the finite amount of land in Israel—which created conditions that economists refer to as "zero sum." An increase in the amount of land owned by one family meant that another family had less, in an economy in which most economic production required land. The jubilee was designed to correct the imbalances that families' disparate fortunes would inevitably create. To determine the jubilee's contemporary implications, we need to take into account the radical changes in context.

Even the most careful scholars often leap from the jubilee to current conditions without fully considering these distinctions. Christopher Wright, whose work has deeply informed our own, writes that "the principles and objectives" of the jubilee "are certainly not irrelevant to welfare legislation or indeed any legislation with socio-economic implications. And indeed, taken to a wider level still," he continues: "The jubilee speaks volumes to the massive issue of international debt. Not for nothing was the worldwide campaign to see an ending of the intolerable and interminable debts of impoverished nations called Jubilee 2000."[22]

This sweeping application comes after a careful analysis of the context of the biblical jubilee. While we agree that Jubilee 2000 was an admirable campaign, and that debt burdens continue to be a pressing issue (especially but not only in the developing world), it is important to recognize how far from the original context international debt relief is.[23] The campaign is aimed at nations, both as debtors and creditors, not individual families. To be sure, its enthusiasts believe that debt release will improve the lives of individual families. But this often may not be the case. Releasing the obligations of a highly indebted nation may simply benefit an oppressive regime or existing elites.

---

[20]See, for example, Luke 10:25-37 (parable of the good Samaritan).
[21]Matthew 10:42 (cup of cold water) and Matthew 28:19 (command to make disciples of all nations).
[22]Wright, *Old Testament Ethics*, p. 208.
[23]Wright does frame the extension of jubilee principles to debt relief as a "paradigmatic" application of the original principles. But it is essential to carefully trace the extension, even if it is acknowledged to be something other than a one-to-one correspondence.

The call for debt relief also prompts the question, what next? Is the debt relief campaign a one-time event, or should developing world obligations never be enforceable? The jubilee itself might seem to invite periodic debt remission—perhaps canceling debts every seven or fifty years, as in the Mosaic law. But here the context is especially important. The seven-year period imposed a time limit on human servitude—limiting it to a time period that is substantial but not overwhelming—and the same period for loans to struggling Israelites. Seven years would not have made sense for the repatriation of scarce land to families that had lost it because of the accumulation of land by the wealthy, and its loss by struggling families generally occurs over generations, not a few years. Fifty years is a much more apt timeline for reestablishing the original ownership patterns.

If one were looking for a time period for loans to developing countries, the appropriate period might well be somewhere between these periods— say twenty or twenty-five years, long enough, the reasoning might go, for the proceeds to be invested or squandered and the consequences to have become clear. A fixed schedule for debt relief would invite predictable responses by lenders: they would insist on higher interest rates and quicker repayment as the year of relief neared.

A twenty-year debt jubilee would therefore make it more costly for most nations to borrow funds for development, and might make it impossible for some. Although some might view the likely constraints on developing countries' access to loans as a price worth paying, the reduced access to funding surely would limit development. The United States depended heavily on foreign borrowing for development in the nineteenth century, as did other developed nations before it.[24]

While the precise terms of the jubilee do not translate well into debt relief and development, the underlying principles—that debt can become oppressive, and that provision for relief is essential—do. The jubilee movement itself has advocated bankruptcy as a mechanism for loosening the fetters of unsustainable debt, and the United Nations has implemented a limited program of targeted relief for "highly indebted poor countries." Each of these can be seen as reflecting the spirit of biblical treatment of debt.

---

[24]See, for example, Alan D. Morrison and William J. Wilhelm Jr., *Investment Banking: Institutions, Politics, and Law* (New York: Oxford University Press, 2007).

The same Mosaic law principles apply still more directly to the debt burdens of individual citizens. United States law has long provided bankruptcy relief for debtors who cannot repay their debts and also allows them to protect property that is seen as essential to their livelihood. Similar issues have arisen in debates over the regulation of credit cards. In 2009, the US Congress restricted the fees that credit card companies can impose and required them to give consumers longer to repay the monthly bill.[25]

In each of these areas—from an American consumer's credit card bill to a developing nation's debt burden—the guiding principles of the Mosaic law are clearer than their implications for specific regulation. Christians might disagree about whether a particular credit card law or bankruptcy reform is called for by the principles of the Mosaic law. But the Mosaic law recognizes both the importance of lending and the crushing effect that debt can have, and it is unabashedly paternalistic in its concern for the dignity of the poor. In our view, the general contours of US bankruptcy law, with its well-known emphasis on forgiving debts and giving the debtor a fresh start, are remarkably congruent with the Mosaic law.

Marriage, divorce and sexuality. The Mosaic laws on marriage and sexuality combine two qualities that seem, particularly for modern observers, to stand in considerable tension: concern for purity in Israelite's most intimate relations and accommodation to practices that are at odds with the moral principles of Scripture. The law demands fidelity in marriage and threatens severe punishments for adultery and other sexual sin. Yet the Mosaic law also permits divorce and polygamy.

This tension is not unique in the annals of Israel's relationship with God. God warned Israel against the dangers of establishing a monarchy like those of the surrounding nations. Yet not only did God accede to his people's demand for a king, he blessed the monarchs who were faithful and incorporated the Davidic line into his plan for restoration and salvation. From this perspective, divorce and polygamy are accommodations to human weakness and, with polygamy especially, to the norms of the Old Testament era.[26] The laws themselves (like the laws on slavery) are particularly concerned with the well-being of those who are at risk of oppression.

Jesus himself pointed out that divorce was permitted only because of the

---

[25]Credit Card Accountability Responsibility and Disclosure Act of 2009, 15 USC 1601.
[26]As Wright argues at length in *Old Testament Ethics*.

Israelites' weakness and announced God's expectation of a much higher standard for marriage. Man and wife "are no longer two but one flesh," Jesus said. "Therefore what God has joined together, let no one separate." A husband who divorced his wife for any reason other than adultery was himself committing adultery (Mt 19:3-9).

As with criminal law, the shift to a new covenant that is anchored not in a physical location but in the hearts of men and women foregrounds the distinction between the state's and the church's treatment of marriage. The history of this tension is long and complex, but the modern American intertwining of church and state oversight of marriage dates back to religious tensions in seventeenth-century England. Many dissenting Protestants insisted that marriage was a matter solely for the state because it was a contract between two people, and criticized the Anglican Church's inclusion of a marriage service in the Book of Common Prayer.[27]

One plausible conclusion—a conclusion reached by C. S. Lewis on divorce without directly considering the Mosaic law[28]—might be that Christian churches should promote biblical principles for marriage within their churches while abandoning efforts to influence secular regulation of marriage. This stance may be particularly attractive to those who are persuaded that Christians should disengage from politics in the United States, at least temporarily.[29] In its pure form, we think this conclusion goes too far. God is Lord over all creation, not just the church, and Jesus explicitly appealed to the creational order in his teaching on divorce (Mt 19). Because Christ's teachings are intended principally for the church, however, it also would be a mistake to assume that they should be directly incorporated into secular law.

The acid test of these principles at the time we write is gay marriage. In our view, gay marriage cannot be reconciled with the clear teaching of Scripture—both in the Mosaic law and in Christ's fulfillment of the law—that marriage must be between a man and a woman (e.g., Mt 19:4-6). Het-

---

[27]Horton Davies, *The Worship of the English Puritans* (Morgan, PA: Soli Deo Gloria Publications, 1997), p. 72.

[28]See, for example, C. S. Lewis, *Mere Christianity,* rev. ed. (1952; repr., New York: Simon & Schuster, 1996). Lewis, questioning Christian efforts to embody their understanding of marriage in the secular divorce laws, concludes: "There ought to be two distinct kinds of marriage: one governed by the State with rules enforced on all citizens, the other governed by the Church with rules enforced by her on her own members" (ibid., p. 102).

[29]See, for example, James Davison Hunter, *To Change the World: The Irony, Possibility and Tragedy of Christianity in the Late Modern World* (Oxford: Oxford University Press, 2010).

erosexual marriage is part of the creational order and is a central metaphor for God's relationship with his people. But the Mosaic law also suggests that blanket condemnation of existing cultural norms is not always the appropriate response and shows particular concern for the vulnerable. It is implicitly critical of but does not clearly condemn polygamy, for instance, perhaps for these reasons.[30] From this perspective, domestic-partnership laws may offer an alternative to either establishing gay marriage or resisting any legal accommodation to homosexual relationships. Provision for health and survivorship benefits for domestic partners can be seen as reflecting the humanitarian principles that lie at the heart of the Mosaic law.

The Mosaic law, as seen in a New Testament perspective, may have similar implications for divorce. In a culture as pluralistic as contemporary America, attempting to replicate in secular law the principles that govern divorce in Christian churches would create intractable enforcement dilemmas and a temptation to flout the law. When divorce is only allowed in cases of adultery, for instance, the state is forced to attempt to police adultery, and couples who wish to divorce may concoct sham sexual misdeeds. Provisions that require a waiting period before a couple can divorce, on the other hand, are more easily enforced. They may discourage some hasty divorces and nudge the secular law of divorce somewhat closer to biblical principles of marriage.[31]

CONCLUSION

We have found it helpful to begin by identifying three core principles that provide a foundation for the Mosaic law: God's nature as revealed in Scripture, the nature of Israel and the role of the land. Using these principles as our starting point, we have briefly explored the regulation of criminal law; economics and commercial law; and marriage, divorce and sexual purity. The general concerns of the law in these areas are much clearer than the precise implications for specific issues. We can state with

---

[30]See generally Wright, *Old Testament Ethics*, pp. 350-51: "In a society without much in the way of independent gainful employment for women, without welfare benefits for single, divorced or widowed women, and where childlessness was deepest shame, [an Israelite] might have argued that it was unquestionably better for every woman to be some man's wife, even if necessary in a polygamous marriage."

[31]For such a proposal, see Elizabeth Scott and Robert E. Scott, "Marriage as a Relational Contract," *Virginia Law Review* 84 (1998): 1225-1334.

confidence that the Mosaic law was concerned to protect the most vulnerable Israelites and to encourage marital faithfulness. We have attempted to suggest what this might mean in particular contexts such as credit card reform and divorce laws. While these specific implications will always be subject to debate even among Christians, we hope that identifying and exploring the core concerns may circumscribe the debate, at least a little, and may provide a way of thinking biblically about contemporary legal issues.

4

THE LAW OF LIFE

Law in the Wisdom Literature

Roger P. Alford and Leslie M. Alford

B IBLICAL WISDOM is the "ability to understand the world and be successful in it."[1] The pursuit of wisdom is the application of self-evident truth to life. It is discovering answers to fundamental questions of suffering, finitude, justice and order. Wisdom is both heavenly and earthly: the Lord is the author of wisdom, and through wisdom kings reign, communities flourish and the wise navigate the good life. This chapter will explore the depiction of law in the Psalms and Wisdom literature.

On the question of law, one finds a continuum in these books, with Proverbs at one end of the spectrum and Ecclesiastes at the other. Proverbs presents a picture of divine order, with the king anointed by God to do justice in the world. The book of Psalms presents a similar picture, though when this collection of songs was put into final form after the Babylonian exile, it expressed only a future hope of a Davidic king committed to God's law. Job moves further from Proverbs' ideal, with injustice in the world but a God who manifests himself to restore order. Ecclesiastes stands at the polar end of a continuum regarding the Wisdom literature's treatment of law.[2] Injustice reigns, humanity is indifferent and God is silent. Song of

---

[1]Matthew J. Goff, *The Worldly and Heavenly Wisdom of 4QInstruction* (Boston: Brill, 2003), p. 42.
[2]Martin A. Shields, *The End of Wisdom: A Reappraisal of the Historical and Canonical Function of Ecclesiastes* (Winona Lake, IN: Eisenbrauns, 2006), p. 37.

Solomon's focus is different from the rest of the Wisdom literature. It focuses on relational order, on love.[3] We describe these models as universal, covenantal, paradoxical, futilistic and relational. Depending on historical circumstances, each declaration is and can be the lived experience of God's people. Each presents a part of God's picture of law in this life.

PROVERBS

Proverbs is a guide to practical wisdom for daily living in the present life. The worldly vision in Proverbs is one of divine order, with God as the arbiter of right and wrong, demanding justice in the law courts, honesty in the marketplace, and generosity to the poor.[4] It was written

> that people may know wisdom and discipline,
> may understand words of intelligence;
> May receive training in wise conduct,
> in what is right, just and fair. (Prov 1:2-3)[5]

Under one theory, Proverbs was initially an instruction manual for bright, young, future Israelite government officials, written at a time when Israel was an emerging new nation, in political transition and historical ascendance. The development of royal administration required educated officials. Youth were to be trained to enter administrative positions in the kingdom, serving as professional courtiers, judges, teachers and government officials.[6] New leaders were needed in large numbers in Solomon's emerging administrative state, and royal schools trained youth in the path of practical wisdom.[7] What may have started as an instruction manual for officers in the royal kingdom became a guidebook for colonial government, and eventually a book of moral discernment taught in synagogues.[8]

Sages who instructed youth in this emerging administrative state were perhaps a distinct social group, along with priests and prophets. Sages served

---

[3] Although we have limited our analysis to five books, we recognize that other Wisdom and poetic literature exists in the Old Testament.

[4] E. W. Heaton, *Solomon's New Men: The Emergence of Ancient Israel as a National State* (London: Thames & Hudson, 1974), p. 123.

[5] Unless otherwise indicated, all Scripture quotations in this chapter are from the NAB.

[6] Leo G. Perdue, *The Sword and the Stylus: An Introduction to Wisdom in the Age of Empires* (Grand Rapids: Eerdmans, 2008), p. 100.

[7] Heaton, *Solomon's New Men*, pp. 122-26.

[8] Perdue, *Sword and the Stylus*, p. 100. For a critique of the royal-court theory of the origins of Proverbs, see Stuart Weeks, *Early Israelite Wisdom* (New York: Oxford University Press, 1994), chap. 3.

in the royal cabinet and as officers in various government positions.[9] It may be that, among other functions, these "sages in the wisdom schools educated youth in the law," recognizing that "some of them would become judges and lawyers."[10] The establishment of the early monarchy also required officials trained in international diplomacy and educated and socialized in the norms of public life.[11] "The wisdom literature is, for the most part, a product . . . of men of affairs in high places of state, and the literature . . . bears the marks of its close association with those who exercise the skills of statecraft."[12]

The book of Proverbs is replete with references to law and justice. Many of the subjects taught in law schools today are addressed in this book of Wisdom—indeed, the range is remarkable:

- Property: "Do not remove the ancient landmark that your ancestors set up." (Prov 22:28)

- Contracts: "False scales are an abomination to the LORD, but an honest weight, his delight." (Prov 11:1)

- Criminal law: "Crime is the entertainment of the fool; but wisdom is for the person of understanding." (Prov 10:23)

- Civil procedure: "Those who plead the case first seem to be in the right; then the opponent comes and cross-examines them." (Prov 18:17)

- Mediation: "The lot puts an end to disputes, and decides a controversy between the mighty." (Prov 18:18)

- Litigation: "The tillage of the poor yields abundant food, but possessions are swept away for lack of justice." (Prov 13:23)

- Evidence: "A trustworthy witness does not lie, but one who spouts lies makes a lying witness." (Prov 14:5)

- Remedies: "Discipline seems bad to those going astray; one who hates reproof will die." (Prov 15:10)

- Animal rights: "The just take care of their livestock, but the compassion of the wicked is cruel." (Prov 12:10)

---

[9]Perdue, *Sword and the Stylus,* pp. 105-6.
[10]Ibid., p. 107.
[11]Katharine J. Dell, *The Book of Proverbs in Social and Theological Context* (New York: Cambridge University Press, 2006), p. 69; Joseph Blenkinsopp, *Wisdom and Law in the Old Testament: The Ordering of Life in Israel and Early Judaism,* rev. ed. (New York: Oxford University Press, 1995), p. 5.
[12]William McKane, *Prophets and Wise Men* (Naperville, IL: Allenson, 1965), p. 44.

- Antitrust: "Whoever hoards grain, the people curse, but blessings are on the head of one who distributes it!" (Prov 11:26)
- Trusts and estates: "The good leave an inheritance to their children's children, but the wealth of the sinner is stored up for the just." (Prov 13:22)
- Legal ethics: "It is not for kings, Lemuel, not for kings to drink wine; strong drink is not for princes, Lest in drinking they forget what has been decreed, and violate the rights of any who are in need." (Prov 31:4-5)
- Taxation: "By justice a king builds up the land; but one who raises taxes tears it down." (Prov 29:4)
- Bankruptcy: "Do not be one of those who give their hand in pledge, those who become surety for debts; For if you are unable to pay, your bed will be taken from under you." (Prov 22:26-27)

Unlike the Torah (especially Exodus through Deuteronomy), Proverbs does not have the prolixity of a legal code. Instead, these sapiential teachings offer general principles that the counselor implements with wisdom. Proverbial sayings state the essence of laws, much like Hillel's reductionism of the Torah or Jesus Christ's articulation of the Golden Rule.[13] The great theological motif in Proverbs is the cosmic moral order. Natural law is part of the created order. In the beginning was wisdom; wisdom was the firstborn of God's creation and through wisdom all things were created (Prov 8:22-31; compare Jn 1:1-3). The divine order regulates both nature and society; God anoints kings, governs nations and determines events.[14] God gives wisdom, imparts knowledge, counsels the upright, shields the honest, guards the just, defends the poor and protects the pious (Prov 2:6-8; 23:22-23).

> The LORD has made everything for his own ends,
>   even the wicked for the evil day. (Prov 16:4)

Thus, Proverbs embraces a view of the state in which rulers are divinely anointed to serve the interests of justice and promote social order. Divine wisdom is imparted to "all the rulers of earth" (Prov 8:16), not simply the kings of Israel. Through divine wisdom, "kings reign, and rulers enact

[13]"That which is hateful to you, do not unto another: This is the whole Torah. The rest is commentary—Now go and learn it" (Hillel, Talmud, *Shabbat* 31a). "Do to others whatever you would have them do to you. This is the law and the prophets" (Mt 7:12). See Blenkinsopp, *Wisdom and Law*, p. 130.
[14]Perdue, *Sword and the Stylus*, p. 114.

justice" (Prov 8:15; see also Prov 21:1). Proverbs demands obedience to the king and, unlike the Old Testament prophets, counsels against rebellion or dissension toward the ruling authorities (Prov 24:21). Through divine wisdom,

> An oracle is upon the king's lips,
> > no judgment of his mouth is false. (Prov 16:10)

Proverbs generally presents a conservative and providential understanding of the political order, which often sounds quite different from the Prophets. Some church fathers rejected a literal interpretation of such a divine ordering of political rulers. In the fourth century, Jerome in a comment on Proverbs 21:1 ("A king's heart is channeled water in the hand of the LORD; God directs it where he pleases") argues that "king" here refers to "those who have control over sin." Jerome asked,

> Was the heart of Julian, the persecutor, in the hand of God? The heart of Saul, was it in the hand of God? . . . The heart of Ahab? Were the hearts of all the impious kings of Judah in the hand of God? Do you see that this verse does not admit of a literal interpretation?[15]

It would be an oversimplification, however, to suggest that the book of Proverbs is absolute in conjoining divine with political order, for other proverbs recognize that there are wicked rulers who destroy the nation through evil works (Prov 28:15, 28; 29:2). As one commentator puts it, such warnings provide a "much-needed corrective to . . . earlier veneration of government."[16] But there is no need to set some sayings of Proverbs against other sayings. The individual parts of the book, as *proverbs,* are meant to be read alongside each other, no individual proverbs giving the entire truth, but only one aspect of it, each of which needs to be qualified and filled out by others.[17]

It may be that Proverbs principally addresses the office rather than the officeholder. Governments acting pursuant to the rule of law are ordained institutions that, through divine wisdom and human discernment, are a blessing to the people. But a full understanding of the state allows for

---

[15]Jerome, *Homilies on the Psalms* 9, Fathers of the Church 48:67, in *Proverbs, Ecclesiastes, Song of Solomon,* ed. J. Robert Wright, Ancient Christian Commentary on Scripture, Old Testament 9 (Downers Grove, IL: InterVarsity Press, 2005), p. 135. Jerome's comment on Proverbs 21:1 occurred within his sermon on Psalm 137 (138).

[16]Christine Roy Yoder, *Proverbs* (Nashville: Abingdon, 2009), p. 265.

[17]For discussion in this volume of sections of the New Testament that present similar, seemingly contrasting views of the state, see "The State, Law and Empire" in chapter eight.

human sin, and when the wicked gain preeminence, the whole nation suffers. "By justice a king builds up the land" (Prov 29:4), but "when the wicked rule, the people groan" (Prov 29:2).

PSALMS

The book of Psalms rarely features the law explicitly, although there are allusions to it in the so-called Wisdom psalms.[18] While Wisdom literature is present in numerous Psalms,[19] the focus of this portion of our exploration will be limited to a small subset of Wisdom psalms, the three great Torah Psalms: Psalms 1, 19 and 119.

In Psalm 1 the message is one of legal piety. J. W. Rogerson and J. W. McKay argue that "the law" here includes more than simply the five books of Moses; it is God's teachings and instructions, the whole tradition of God's Word to humanity.[20] The placement of Psalms 1 and 2 together may suggest that Psalm 1 is actually a royal psalm, with the king of Israel the exemplar of one who obeys the law in the face of nations plotting to destroy the nation of Israel.[21] In this sense, the book of Psalms embraces an eschatological theocratic state, with the obedient king who delights in the law ruling as God's anointed one.[22] The righteous are called to trust in the Lord through devotion to his law, confident in the reign of the Lord notwithstanding the present earthly powers.[23]

Psalm 19 pairs the general revelation of the created order with the special revelation of God's law. The heavens tell the glory of the Lord; the law of the Lord is perfect and revives the soul. God is both universal and particular. He has been revealed through the glorious heavens and perfect law. From

---

[18]One skeptic has noted the widespread disagreement as to which psalms, if any, should be categorized as Wisdom psalms. See James Crenshaw, *The Psalms: An Introduction* (Grand Rapids: Eerdmans, 2001), pp. 87-95.

[19]See, e.g., Psalms 37; 49; 73; 112; 127; and 133; Hermann Gunkel, *Introduction to Psalms: The Genres of the Religious Lyric of Israel*, completed by Joachim Begrich, trans. James D. Nogalski (Macon, GA: Mercer University Press, 1998), pp. 295-96; Sigmund Mowinckel, *The Psalms in Israel's Worship*, 2 vols. (New York: Abingdon, 1962); Roger Whybray, "The Wisdom Psalms," in *Wisdom in Ancient Israel: Essays in Honour of J. A. Emerton*, ed. John Day, Robert P. Gordon and H. G. M. Williamson (New York: Cambridge University Press, 1995), p. 152.

[20]J. W. Rogerson and J. W. McKay, *Psalms 1-50* (Cambridge: Cambridge University Press, 1997), p. 16.

[21]Jamie A. Grant, *The King as Exemplar: The Function of Deuteronomy's Kingship Law in the Shaping of the Book of Psalms* (Boston: Brill, 2004), p. 284; Patrick Miller, *Israelite Religion and Biblical Theology: Collected Essays* (Sheffield: Sheffield Academic Press, 2000), pp. 273-77.

[22]Grant, *King as Exemplar*, pp. 69-70.

[23]James Luther Mays, "The Place of the Torah-Psalms in the Psalter," *Journal of Biblical Literature* 106 (1987): 12.

the cosmos one understands the nature and character of God, and from the law one understands how to live in fidelity to the Creator in community.

Psalm 119 is an acrostic psalm with twenty-two stanzas; each stanza, composed of eight verses, begins with a letter of the Hebrew alphabet in consecutive order. The stanzas extol the virtues of law, using at least eight different words for law—*law, testimony, ordinance, commandment, statute, precept, word* and *promise.*[24] The main purpose of Psalm 119 is "the glorification of the Law . . . [which] is the expression of the divine will; it is not the Law *per se,* that he loves . . . ; he loves the Law because it tells of God's will."[25] Martin Rozenberg and Bernard Zlotowitz argue that law in Psalm 119 is not limited to the Pentateuch, but rather the designation refers to all of God's teachings, the "sum total of God's instructions to Israel that make for the good and moral life."[26]

The Torah Psalms affirm the existence of natural law.[27] Careful study of this law will serve as "a lamp for my feet" and "a light for my path" (Ps 119:105). Many of the synonyms for *law* found in Psalms convey this understanding of natural law. "Precepts" are "implanted in the human heart, that is, are laws we obey because of an inner feeling of right and wrong."[28] By contrast, "statutes" are rules that lack an explanation, such that one's natural inclination would be to rebel against such laws.[29] Closely related to statutes are "commandments," which are truths that require faith; that is, they are not subject to rational analysis.[30] In between these extremes are "ordinances" or "judgments," which connote divine case law, and the study of God's rulings in history is required to understand the policies behind such decisions.[31] "Testimony" refers to God's work in history.[32] "Rules" suggest divine order in creation, that is, the laws of nature.[33] "Promises" or "word" refer

---

[24]Robert G. Bratcher and William D. Reyburn, *A Translator's Handbook on the Book of Psalms* (New York: United Bible Societies, 1991), p. 996.

[25]Ibid., p. 997.

[26]Martin S. Rozenberg and Bernard M. Zlotowitz, *The Book of Psalms: A New Translation and Commentary* (Northvale, NJ: Aronson, 1999), pp. 755, 771.

[27]For additional discussion of natural law in this volume, see "The Patriarch Narratives" in chapter one and "Romans 2:14-15: Natural Law and Empire" in chapter eight.

[28]Rozenberg and Zlotowitz, *Book of Psalms,* pp. 772, 774, 789 (discussing Ps 119:3, 15, 104).

[29]Ibid., pp. 772-73, 797 (discussing Ps 119:5, 8, 12, 155); Bratcher and Reyburn, *Translator's Handbook,* p. 1007 (discussing Ps 119:33).

[30]Ibid., pp. 782, 786, 788, 791 (discussing Ps 119:66, 86, 98, 115).

[31]Ibid., pp. 772, 784 (discussing Ps 119:7, 75); Bratcher and Reyburn, *Translator's Handbook,* pp. 996, 999, 1009 (discussing Ps 119:7, 39).

[32]Ibid., p. 771 (discussing Ps 119:2).

[33]Ibid., p. 786 (discussing Ps 119:91).

to God's covenant with his people, connoting God's pledge, protection and deliverance.[34] "Teachings" or "law" is the sum total of all God's instructions and the instrument of government for God's people.[35]

The choice of different terms to define the law, Grant believes, stresses the "fullness and diversity of divine revelation, accentuating the completeness with which the word of God addresses the life of the Old Testament believer."[36] God is active in the large and small, in creation and history, in divine and earthly law. Law, in all its varieties, is an expression of God's covenant with his people.[37]

The high place accorded to the law in these psalms subordinates the king to the law. While the kings of the ancient Near East were a law unto themselves, a Davidic king was not above the law. Gerald Gerbrandt says, "The king, although the supreme leader of Israel, [was] still subject to the covenant and its law, and in this respect on [an] equal footing with all other Israelites."[38] Kingship yielded to the law is the central message of the Torah Psalms. The king had limited powers. He was subject to the law and must be an exemplar of fidelity to the law. Grant suggests, "He is no different from all the others, his obligations are no different. If anything . . . the king is expected to excel in keeping the law as an example for the people."[39] The Torah Psalms teach us that there is a moral order ordained by God, and the divinely appointed king must be subject to that order.

JOB

Job does not address civil law per se. Rather, the book uses the law and legal metaphors to address the question of theodicy. The great problem of evil is examined through law. Law is not the object of the book, but it is the vehicle through which the problem of evil is addressed. Seen in this light, the book of Job is not about a test or a bet between Satan and God but is tragic drama involving the trial of Job, and ultimately the trial of God. Modern readers

---

[34]Ibid., p. 778 (discussing Ps 119:38); William Michael Soll, *Psalm 119: Matrix, Form, and Setting* (Washington, DC: Catholic Biblical Association of America, 1991), p. 39.

[35]Rozenberg and Zlotowitz, *Book of Psalms*, pp. 771, 790, 798 (discussing Ps 119:1, 105, 160); John Goldingay, *Psalms* (Grand Rapids: Baker Academic, 2008), 3:761; Soll, *Psalm 119*, p. 36.

[36]Grant, *King as Exemplar*, p. 159.

[37]Soll, *Psalm 119*, p. 45.

[38]Gerald Eddie Gerbrandt, *Kingship According to the Deuteronomistic History* (Atlanta: Scholars Press, 1986), p. 148.

[39]Grant, *King as Exemplar*, p. 220.

may miss the legal narrative that runs throughout Job because of translation errors or their ignorance of the administration of justice in the Old
Testament and the ancient Near East. But recent scholarship suggests a legal
backdrop for the theodicy drama.[40] Recast in this light, the legal context
sheds interesting insights into the message of Job.

The trial of Job begins with the allegation that Job is "capable of committing blasphemy."[41] Blasphemy is a crime punishable by death (Lev
24:13-17). Satan, the adversary, accuses Job of the crime (Job 1:9-11; 2:4-5).[42]
In the ancient Near East, the accusation of a crime initiated legal
proceedings,[43] much like private prosecutions in modern history.[44] Job
subsequently loses everything. Only Job's wife is spared, and her recom-
mendation to Job is to curse God and die, precisely the crime Satan predicted Job would commit (Job 2:9). Job's suffering may constitute a formal
legal investigation of his culpability.[45]

Job's suffering may be part of pretrial investigation. In the ancient Near
East, a suspect accused of a crime could be subject to immediate pretrial
arrest, torture and penalty.[46] Satan's investigation of Job resulted in pretrial
loss of property and family, and severe mental and physical anguish. God
stayed his hand either because he had to recuse himself as a codefendant in

---

[40]See, e.g., F. Rachel Magdalene, *On the Scales of Righteousness: Neo-Babylonian Trial Law and the Book of Job* (Providence, RI: Brown Judaic Studies, 2007); Robert Sutherland, *Putting God on Trial: The Biblical Book of Job* (Victoria, Canada: Trafford, 2004); Michael Brennan Dick, "The Legal Metaphor in Job 31," in *Sitting with Job: Selected Studies on the Book of Job*, ed. Roy B. Zuck (Grand Rapids: Baker Book House, 1992), p. 321; Norman C. Habel, *The Book of Job: A Commentary* (Philadelphia: Westminster Press, 1985); J. J. M. Roberts, "Job's Summons to Yahweh: The Exploitation of a Legal Metaphor," *Restoration Quarterly* 16 (1973): 159.

[41]Magdalene, *On the Scales of Righteousness*, p. 100. Magdalene suggests that "the reason a faulty intention alone justifies God's trial and punishment of humanity is that God, from the point of view of the writers of the Hebrew Bible, can more easily determine the intentions of the human heart than humans can" (ibid., p. 111).

[42]See Magdalene, *On the Scales of Righteousness*, pp. 99-114.

[43]Ibid., pp. 66-75; Shalom E. Holtz, *Neo-Babylonian Court Procedure* (Boston: Brill, 2009), pp. 103-7.

[44]For an analysis of private prosecutors in modern history, see Daniel Klerman, "Settlement and the Decline of Private Prosecution in Thirteenth-Century England," *Law and History Review* 19 (2001): 1; Matthew S. Nichols, "No One Can Serve Two Masters: Arguments Against Private Prosecutors," *Capital Defense Journal* 13 (2001): 279; Joan E. Jacoby, *The American Prosecutor: A Search for Identity* (Lexington, MA: Lexington Books, 1980).

[45]Still others argue that Satan's accusation and Job's suffering are not part of a trial at all, but simply a setup for Job's trial against God's injustice. See Habel, *Book of Job*, pp. 54-57.

[46]Magadalene, *On the Scales of Righteousness*, pp. 75-77, 123 (discussing investigation in neo-Babylonian trial law and citing Gen 39:14, 17, 20; 20:2; 37:14-16; 41:1 as biblical examples); Holtz, *Neo-Babylonian Court Procedure*, pp. 151-61.

Satan's accusation, or because God could not stop the proceedings without proving Satan's accusation to be correct.[47]

The surprising turn in the narrative is Job's decision to bring suit against God for his crimes. These alleged crimes include abuse of authority, injustice and disorder.[48] Job recognizes that the difficulties of bringing suit against God appear insurmountable.[49] God cannot be summoned or forced to appear in court (Job 9:3, 19), and there is no one who can adjudicate the claim (Job 9:32-33). Nonetheless, Job expresses his desire to "reason with God"; Job has "prepared [his] case"; and, though God will serve as both defendant and judge, Job says, "I know that I am in the right" (Job 13:3, 18).

Job defends himself by swearing an oath of innocence (Job 31). In the ancient Near East, an accused person could exculpate himself with an oath by invoking the name of God to confirm the veracity of his testimony. If the statement was false, the oath-taker was calling on God to curse him.[50] Such an oath proved the defendant's innocence.[51] Job swears to God that he has not (1) deceived others; (2) taken improper actions; (3) lusted after women; (4) failed to care for his servants; (5) withheld anything from orphans, widows or the poor; (6) forgotten to clothe the naked; (7) taken advantage of the helpless; (8) trusted in his riches; (9) rejoiced in his success; (10) worshiped the sun or the moon; (11) celebrated his enemies' misfortunes; (12) closed his house to the alien; or (13) concealed any of his transgressions (Job 31:5-34). In short, Job has fully complied with the spirit and the letter of the law.

Job concludes with a demand for a written indictment from his adversary so he can give an account of his innocence.

---

[47]Holtz, Neo-Babylonian Court Procedure, pp. 115-23.

[48]Magdalene, On the Scales of Righteousness, pp. 145, 157, 176.

[49]Habel, Book of Job, p. 55.

[50]See Habel, Book of Job, p. 433; Hans Jochen Boecker, Law and the Administration of Justice in the Old Testament and Ancient East (Minneapolis: Augsburg Fortress Publishing, 1980), p. 35 (citing Ex 22:8-11 ESV: "If the thief is not found, the owner of the house shall come near to God to show whether or not he has put his hand to his neighbor's property.... The case of both parties shall come before God.... If a man gives to his neighbor a donkey or an ox ... and it dies or is injured or is driven away, without anyone seeing it, an oath by the LORD shall be between them both to see whether or not he has put his hand to his neighbor's property. The owner shall accept the oath, and he shall not make restitution").

[51]See Boecker, Law and the Administration of Justice, p. 35; Magdalene, On the Scales of Righteousness, pp. 78-82. It is from such an oath that we swear "to tell the truth, the whole truth and nothing but the truth, so help me God."

> Oh, that I had one to hear my case:
> here is my signature: let the Almighty answer me!
> Let my accuser write out his indictment! (Job 31:35)

Under the law, Job's elaborate oath of innocence would exonerate him unless his adversary denies or confirms his claims. As Habel says, "If God remains silent, Job's oath proves his innocence and by implication makes God appear to be the guilty party."[52] God has been summoned to appear formally in court to respond to the allegation or to concede Job's innocence.[53]

The brash young Elihu comes forward as Job's second accuser and God's defender. As with Eliphaz, Bildad and Zophar in earlier chapters, Elihu defends God from Job's charges and presents himself as a witness to Job's crimes. Contrary to Job's indictment, Elihu argues that God is all-powerful, just and righteous (Job 34:17; 36:3, 5, 32; 37:23). Elihu asks Job who he is to say to God, "You have done wrong" (Job 36:23). God cannot be summoned; God does not appear before human beings in litigation (Job 34:23). His silence deserves no condemnation (Job 34:29; 37:19). He does not answer legal complaints.

> Surely God does not hear an empty cry. . . .
> How much less when you say that you do not see him,
> that the case is before him, and you are waiting for him! (Job 35:13-14 ESV)

With poetic irony, God then answers Job. But he comes not to accuse Job of crimes but rather to defend himself against Job's accusations. God provides a lengthy defense of the created order (Job 38–39). On what basis does Job question this divine governance?

> Will one who argues with the Almighty by corrected?
> Let him who would instruct God give answer! (Job 40:2)

In response to Job's allegations that the world is arbitrary and chaotic, God asks Job to "prove his capacity to understand the way the universe is governed before he will come before Job as an equal in court."[54] Job has no response and recognizes that his allegations of a world in disarray are unsustainable, or at least incapable of evidentiary proof (Job 40:3-5). God's second

---

[52]Habel, *Book of Job*, p. 431.
[53]Ibid., p. 439.
[54]Ibid., p. 549.

defense introduces the role of evil in the world. Behemoth and Leviathan symbolize the wicked forces at work in the world and in the universe.[55] Only God can subdue and control such chaos and power (Job 40:24; 41:1-2).[56] In the face of such arguments, Job repents of his suit against God (Job 42:1-6).

The narrative then shifts to the lawsuit against Job. God addresses the accusers—Eliphaz, Bildad and Zophar—and rejects their condemnation of Job. They have not spoken the truth, as Job has. God declares that Job is innocent of any crime, just as Job swore in his oath of innocence (Job 42:7-9). God sits in judgment on the false accusers, not the accused. God declares that the allegations against Job are false. Satan's great accusation, that Job would commit blasphemy if circumstances were bad enough, proved false. In good times and in bad, Job never cursed God.

The book closes with Job's vindication and restoration. His fortunes are double what they were before the lawsuit, a legal remedy customary in the ancient Near East and elsewhere in the Old Testament.[57]

Some of the more perplexing issues in the book of Job are seen in a fresh light when interpreted as a legal drama. The story takes on new meaning when one interprets Satan as a private prosecutor, God's absence as an instance of judicial recusal, Job's suffering as pretrial investigation, the speeches of Job's friends as the presentation of legal witnesses, Job's protestations as an oath of innocence, God's whirlwind appearance as a defense against a legal complaint, and Job's restoration as a post-trial remedy. Ancient civil law is the lens through which Job's theodicy can be understood.

ECCLESIASTES

Although Ecclesiastes addresses numerous subjects, concerns about government abuse stand out as a major theme. Ecclesiastes presents a lawless world of injustice, oppression and corruption. The Teacher, identified as the author of Ecclesiastes (Eccles 1:1),[58] highlights the specter of injustice. "In

---

[55]Ibid., p. 558.

[56]Ibid., pp. 564-68; Magdalene, *On the Scales of Righteousness*, pp. 255-56.

[57]Magdalene, *On the Scales of Righteousness*, pp. 89-90, 261, 265. See Genesis 43:12, 15; Exodus 22:3; and Isaiah 61:7.

[58]Historically, this teacher has been identified as Solomon, but the book's criticism of the king (see Eccles 5:8-9) calls this claim into question. See Craig G. Bartholomew, *Ecclesiastes* (Grand Rapids: Baker Academic, 2009), pp. 43-54; Thomas Krüger, *Qoheleth: A Commentary*, trans. O. C. Dean Jr., ed. Klaus Baltzer (Minneapolis: Fortress, 2004), p. 19; Tremper Longman III, *The Book of Ecclesiastes* (Grand Rapids: Eerdmans, 1998), pp. 2-9.

the judgment place I saw wickedness, and wickedness also in the seat of justice" (Eccles 3:16). In the administration of justice by elders at the city gates—the *situs* of the courts—there are only injustice and unrighteousness.

He then observes oppression. "I saw all the oppressions that take place under the sun: the tears of the victims with none to comfort them! From the hand of their oppressors comes violence, and there is none to comfort them!" (Eccles 4:1). Power is in the hands of the oppressor and the great masses cry out in pain, but nothing is ever done. So great is the oppression that he declares the dead to be more fortunate than the oppressed.

Finally, the Teacher presents a disturbing image of rampant government corruption. "If you see the poor oppressed in a district, and justice and rights denied, do not be surprised at such things; for one official is eyed by a higher one, and over them both are others higher still. The increase from the land is taken by all; the king himself profits from the fields" (Eccles 5:8-9 NIV). The problem is deep-seated and systemic—the low-level official who takes a bribe is protected by corrupt higher officials, and even the king is on the take.

The message of injustice, oppression and corruption is both historical and ahistorical. Some have suggested that its historical setting is the third century B.C., when Palestine was under Ptolemaic rule. In that context, the wealthy made great profits while the population lived in poverty.[59] But the concerns about lawlessness are not confined to one historical context, for the book presents a philosophical skepticism about whether anything can ever be done about government abuse. The message is that injustice and oppression are always with us, and it is vain to think that human effort can remove evil from the seat of power.

In its utter pessimism about the rule of law, Ecclesiastes stands alone in the Bible's Wisdom literature. We see no claim in Ecclesiastes that God appoints the king to rule over the people and no reason to hope for justice in the world. Governments come and go, and with every new leader there is great hope, but in the end they disappoint (Eccles 4:13-16).[60] The kingly

[59]Enrique Nardoni, *Rise Up, O Judge: A Study of Justice in the Biblical World*, trans. Seán Charles Martin (Peabody, MA: Hendrickson, 2004), p. 138; James L. Crenshaw, *Ecclesiastes: A Commentary* (Philadelphia: Westminster Press, 1987), pp. 49-50; Dave Bland, *Proverbs, Ecclesiastes and Song of Songs* (Joplin, MO: College Press, 2002), p. 341.
[60]Jacques Ellul, *The Reason for Being: A Meditation on Ecclesiastes*, trans. Joyce Main Hanks (Grand Rapids: Eerdmans, 1990), pp. 76-77.

power is absolute, and kings will ignore words of wisdom to pursue their own desires (Eccles 8:2-5).[61] As for God's role in the world, he is not the champion of the oppressed who will vindicate the poor and vanquish the unjust rulers.[62] Regarding the affairs of the world, God seems distant, indifferent and sometimes cruel.[63] All one can say with confidence is that one day God will judge the wicked and the good (Eccles 3:17).

If Ecclesiastes presents no rhyme or reason when it comes to God's law, it does reveal the emotional and mental distress many experience amidst life's confusions, tragedies and disappointments. In this way, God's poetic dimension leaves room for the soul who does not find resolution or peace of mind in this world. Room is left for unanswered questions to find a voice. The poetry of the Old Testament makes room for the skeptic and cynic, the hopeless and the confused, to find a place to lift their voices and lodge their complaint.

God's silent response in Ecclesiastes might be interpreted as a faithful waiting on his part rather than an abandonment—a waiting for those who are practicing their vocation, as followers of God's covenant love—to step in and do the authentic work of followers who are indelibly marked by the *imago Dei*. Can civil law imitate divine law in greater measure and, in so doing, actively work to level valleys of suffering and death where they exist?

If there is a positive aspect to Ecclesiastes's understanding of the law, it is in the epilogue. When all is said and done, what matters is that we fear God and keep his commandments (Eccles 12:13). He will finally bring judgment on the world, not in this life but the next (Eccles 12:14). While this world is lawless and life is ephemeral, honoring God by keeping his law is the only thing that matters in the end. But as for the world, it is vain to think that history has a linear progression. Creation groans in all its futility. It is a futility longing for a purpose, a purpose that the apostle Paul later recognized as part of Christ's salvation story. Paul recognized that creation itself was "subjected to futility," and he was waiting for the day when it would be set free from its bondage and corruption (Rom 8:19-20).[64] The kingdom of God is the Christian response to the futility of the lawless injustice, oppression and corruption of the social order.

---

[61]Bartholomew, *Ecclesiastes*, pp. 281-82.

[62]Leo G. Perdue, *Wisdom Literature: A Theological History* (Louisville, KY: Westminster John Knox, 2007), p. 199.

[63]Longman, *Book of Ecclesiastes*, p. 35.

[64]William P. Brown, *Ecclesiastes* (Louisville, KY: John Knox, 2000), pp. 124-25.

SONG OF SOLOMON

For centuries the Song of Solomon has been interpreted as an allegory of divine love. Jewish sages interpreted it as an allegory of God's love for Israel.[65] Rabbi Akiba underscored the sacredness of the Song of Solomon when he declared, "All the ages are not so worthy as the day on which the Song of Solomon was given to Israel. For all the scriptures are holy, but the Song of Songs is holiest of all."[66] At the time of the ancient church, Jews under the age of thirty were not allowed to read the book, not "on account of its dangers to juvenile imagination, but on account of the theological profundities which it presented . . . which required the maturity of age to be adequately appreciated."[67]

Christians interpreted the book as an allegory of Christ's love for his church, supplemented with New Testament passages that espouse bridal theology.[68] Bernard of Clairvaux said, "The cause of loving God is God, and the mode is to love without measure. . . . [T]he Word and the soul as . . . bridegroom and bride . . . have all things in common, have nothing which either claims, nothing in which the other has no share."[69] A third allegorical interpretation, adopted since Origen, is that of God's love for the human soul.[70]

While such allegorical interpretations are now disfavored by many biblical scholars, they have deep roots in Jewish and Christian understandings of the Song of Solomon and express in a profound way the biblical truth of God's deep love for his people.[71] Whether one interprets the duologue in the Song of Solomon as a private discourse between two lovers, metaphori-

---

[65]Tremper Longman III, *Proverbs–Isaiah*, rev. ed., Expositor's Bible Commentary 6 (Grand Rapids: Zondervan, 2009).

[66]Mishnah *Yadayim* 3:5.

[67]Albert Réville, *The Song of Songs* (London: Williams and Norgate, 1873), p. 3.

[68]The New Testament uses the analogy of groom and bride to describe Christ's relationship to the church—his commitment to her, his concern for her character, the intimate nature of the relationship and his love for her. See Matthew 9:15; John 3:29; 2 Corinthians 11:2; Ephesians 5:31-32; and Revelation 21:2.

[69]Andrew Harper, introduction to *The Song of Solomon: With Introduction and Notes* (1902) (Whitefish, MT: Kessinger Publishing, 2008), p. xliv.

[70]Origen, *The Song of Songs: Commentary and Homilies*, trans. and annotated by R. P. Lawson (Westminster, MD: Newman, 1957), p. 21; Tremper Longman III, *Song of Songs* (Grand Rapids: Eerdmans, 2001), pp. 28-30; Duane A. Garrett, *Proverbs, Ecclesiastes, Song of Songs* (Nashville: Broadman, 1993), p. 355; Andrew Harper, *The Song of Solomon: With Introduction and Notes* (Cambridge: Cambridge University Press, 1907), p. xli.

[71]Longman, *Song of Songs*, p. 58; J. Cheryl Exum, *Song of Songs: A Commentary* (Louisville, KY: Westminster John Knox, 2005), pp. 71-72.

cally as a discourse between God and his Consummate Bride or allegori-
cally, the confessions of love in the Song of Solomon are striking in their
exclusive attention and unbridled passion. This love relationship conveys
both a wholesale abandon between the lovers and a mutuality of passionate
discourse and yearning pursuit. When the bride proclaims, "Let him kiss
me with kisses of his mouth, for your love is better than wine" (Song 1:2),
Ambrose saw the soul panting for the "many kisses of the Word. . . . It is
with the kiss that lovers cleave to each other and gain possession of grace
that is within. . . . Through such a kiss the soul cleaves to God the Word."[72]
This radical love is characterized by a full-blown yield and mutual regard
between lovers. Their duologue radiates the heat of a love that knows no
doubt, no infidelity, no lack of trust. It is thoroughly and securely enveloped
in an unconditional, inviolable covenantal love bond.

Not surprisingly, those who have preached the traditional allegorical
meaning of the Song of Solomon have at times been suspected of antinomianism. For example, in the antinomian crisis in seventeenth-century New
England, some people raised this accusation against John Cotton, a prominent minister of the day, for his belief that assurance of salvation primarily
came objectively through the Spirit rather than subjectively through
works.[73] This view arose, at least in part, out of his exegesis of the Song of
Solomon: God was "a vibrant and affectionate lover, not an abstract, formidable judge."[74] So intent was God's pursuit of his bride in Cotton's thought
that the Massachusetts court feared Cotton's followers would, in John Win-
throp's words, "tend to slothfulness" and thereby undermine the commonwealth's efforts to maintain social order. If citizens passively embraced
God's loving pursuit, they would no longer recognize the need for arduous
spiritual regeneration, resulting in "great damage" to the commonwealth.[75]

Far from illustrating sloth, however, Song of Solomon's betrothed pair
pursues love passionately, even to the point of death:

[72]J. Robert Wright, ed., *Proverbs, Ecclesiastes, Song of Solomon,* Ancient Christian Commentary on
Scripture 9 (Downers Grove, IL: InterVarsity Press, 2005), p. 292.

[73]See Gregory Allen Selmon, "John Cotton: The Antinomian Calvinist" (PhD diss., Vanderbilt
University, 2008), http://etd.library.vanderbilt.edu/available/etd-03192008-144956/unrestricted/
JohnCottondissertation.pdf.

[74]Julie Sievers, "Refiguring the Song of Songs: John Cotton's 1655 Sermon and the Antinomian
Controversy," *New England Quarterly* 76 (2003): 73, 93.

[75]Ibid., p. 94.

> Set me as a seal upon your heart,
> as a seal upon your arm;
> For Love is strong as Death,
> longing is fierce as Sheol.
> Its arrows are arrows of fire,
> flames of the divine. (Song 8:6)

The image is one of single-minded devotion, an affirmative, positive jealousy reserved exclusively for the beloved.[76] It is a jealous love that will overcome death itself (Rom 8:38).

It may be that the love exemplified in Song of Solomon could undercut some forms of law. As God's love is social and personal in nature, human law understood merely in codified terms of incentive and obligation seems quite the opposite of love. But as Christ was to explain centuries after Song of Solomon, love is the very framework on which God's law hangs (Mt 22:35–40).[77] God's law is a manifestation of love.

SUMMARY

The Wisdom literature presents distinct perspectives on the question of the relationship between God and world order. These typologies may be described as *universal, covenantal, paradoxical, futilistic* and *relational*. Each typology represents a partial answer. There are historical and textual explanations for these typologies, but each answer echoes through the ages with sufficient frequency that they seem to be less the product of history than of the nature of the problem itself.[78]

Proverbs presents an assimilation of God and universal world order. The universal model presents a God active in the world to serve justice and promote social order. God anoints secular kings, and these kings judge their people with divine wisdom to promote the common good. "By me kings reign, and rulers enact justice; by me princes govern, and nobles, all the judges of the earth" (Prov 8:15-16). Through God all things are created, and through wisdom divine and world order unite in perfect harmony. "Secular theocracy" is possible through the mediation of wisdom. Through the pursuit and exercise of practical wisdom, world leaders fulfill the divine

---

[76]Longman, *Song of Songs*, p. 211.

[77]For further discussion of law as a manifestation of love in this volume, see chapter six.

[78]Cf. H. Richard Niebuhr, *Christ and Culture* (San Francisco: HarperSanFrancisco, 2001), p. 40.

will. They practice a governance and leadership that reflects fidelity to godly notions of just rule. Wisdom is found by all who genuinely seek her with fervent devotion (see Prov 1–3; 8; 9:1-6; 21:1-2).

The Torah Psalms present a covenantal model of Davidic kings dependent on fidelity to God's law for their success. Commitment to God's law is the ideal, and the restoration and maintenance of power and order in Israel depend on leaders who subordinate themselves to the law. Kings of the earth may rise up against the Lord and his anointed one, but God has installed his king, a king who delights in the law of the Lord and meditates on it day and night (Pss 1:2; 2:2-6). The Torah Psalms present a battle between the forces of evil in the world and the divinely anointed Davidic king who has the power to overcome the world, if only he would obey the law and rule with justice. The conviction that the Lord Jesus Christ is the true and perfect Davidic king provides Christians with profound hope that, despite all the injustice that continues in the world, one day he will establish perfect righteousness in all his creation.

Job presents a paradox between God's divine order and the apparent chaos of the world. In this paradoxical model, the world appears unjust in the face of righteous suffering and inexplicable evil. Nonetheless, God is just, and there is a divine order beyond human comprehension. Only when we stand face to face with God does the divine plan make sense. With our limited perspective we might discredit God's justice, but with perfect knowledge we would recognize that we have dealt with "things too marvelous for me, which I did not know" (Job 42:3) and that, in fact, God is all-powerful and that none of his purposes can be thwarted (Job 40:8; 42:2-3). The lawless disorder we observe in the world does not negate the reality of a divine order. God is put on trial, but in the end he reveals himself and is vindicated.

Ecclesiastes presents a futile world of injustice, oppression and corruption. In the futilistic model, God is divorced from the affairs of the world, and there is no explanation for the chaos of the world. The world is fallen, and it is vain to think that history progresses. The lawless world is unredeemed and unredeemable. Society is dysfunctional. The righteous honor God's law and wander as aliens in the world, waiting for deliverance from the vanity of life "under the sun" (Eccles 1:9).

Song of Solomon presents a relational model in which the law is fulfilled in love. Order is found in loving relationships—God's love for his people, spouses' love for one another, humanity's love for neighbor. The relational ideal presents a model of perfect harmony, where men and women love like angels, without the coercion that is inherent in human law. It is antinomian in the sense that the ethical impulse for proper living comes from within, rather than from outward sanctions or incentives. But, in fact, the vision painted by Song of Solomon is one that shows great respect for law. God's law is written in the human heart, and through ethical living in communion with God and in the spirit of that love, relationships are transformed. Divine law is ordered love that is bound by covenant between God (Bridegroom) and his people (Bride).

As the typologies discussed in this chapter make clear, the Wisdom literature does not present a singular response or approach to the question of the relationship between God's law, God's love and world order. The models presented here can be seen as complementary perspectives. Each typology taken by itself is inconclusive and unsatisfying. The relationship between divine and world order is more complicated and nuanced than any particular set of human paradigms can capture. Each typology presented here is admittedly partial in scope. Despite the incompleteness, the models present fundamental motifs that have explanatory power. We begin and end at the same point: God's law can be understood at its very heart as God's love.

Jesus was asked by a teacher of the law, "Which is the first of all the commandments?" His reply was twofold: "You shall love the Lord, your God, with all your heart, and with all your soul, and with all your mind" and "You shall love your neighbor as yourself. The whole law and the prophets depend on these two commandments" (Mt 5:37, 39).[79] God's law and God's love are clearly and inextricably intertwined (Mk 12:28-31). The Wisdom literature is linked to both aspects of Jesus' command, for it shows us how to live and how to live well in service to God and creature at one and the same time.

THE WISDOM LITERATURE AND CIVIL LAW

Finally, what does the Wisdom literature suggest for the civil law? First, the Wisdom literature reinforces the importance of the law. Proverbs repeatedly extols the virtue of civil law, while Ecclesiastes laments its absence. The book of Psalms suggests that all of Israel's law, including its civil law, was an expression of God's covenant with his people. Job suggests that knowledge of the law can even explain the inscrutable ways of God.

---

[79]Quoting Deuteronomy 6:5 and Leviticus 19:18.

Second, the Wisdom literature is unwavering in its commitment to the idea of divinely inspired natural law, where goodness, order and justice can be discerned through the exercise of practical wisdom. There is a category of universal norms that is applicable in all societies and at all times. These norms are sometimes presented at a high level of abstraction and other times at a concrete and particularized level. But the Wisdom literature leaves no doubt that these norms exist, should be pursued and can be applied.

Third, the Wisdom literature attaches vital importance to the role of law in society. Civil law is a vehicle to do justice in the world, to exercise wisdom and to promote social order. The office of government is part of God's plan to promote the rule of law in the world. Just rulers fulfill that plan, while unjust rulers undermine it. Government officials are condemned when they abuse power and praised when they properly exercise it. Lawyers and lawgivers are compelled to exercise practical wisdom and discernment in promulgating and enforcing the law. Citizens are compelled to show respect and deference to the office of government.

Finally, the Wisdom literature does not offer an immediate solution to the problem of injustice in the world. When government is corrupt or wicked, the people suffer and groan under its weight. There is a future promise that God will judge the unjust ruler. As for judgment in the present world, the Wisdom literature anticipates, but does not discuss, the other great office to promote the rule of law: the Prophets.

5

CRYING OUT FOR JUSTICE

CIVIL LAW AND THE PROPHETS

Barbara E. Armacost and Peter Enns

T HE TASK OF THIS CHAPTER is to explore the implications of the prophetic literature for contemporary law. Stated this way, the project suggests its own difficulties. The prophetic literature is directed primarily toward the nation of Israel, a theocratic monarchy. Its primary ethical and theological message is a call for Israel to return to its covenantal relationship with God: to turn from idolatry and back to obedience to God's commandments. No modern government is in a covenantal relationship with God. Indeed, it is part and parcel of the good news that no one people enjoys favored nation status, for Christ's authority now extends throughout the cosmos (Mt 28:18).[1] The question, then, is what do these ancient documents have to say that could be normative—or at least suggestive—for contemporary, primarily secular, legal systems? In the end, we believe the Prophets have something to contribute to the issue of modern law, but only by taking careful account of both the original context of the Prophetic Books and the fact that we are living at a time after which Jesus has already fulfilled the Law and the Prophets (Mt 5:17).

---

[1]An excellent treatment of the church's proper relationship to secular government is Michael J. Gorman, *Reading Revelation Responsibly: Uncivil Worship and Witness: Following the Lamb into the New Creation* (Eugene, OR: Cascade, 2011).

READING THE PROPHETS IN CONTEXT

Author, audience and setting. Prophetic literature is rooted in the activity of Israel's prophets, which is to say it either records, attests to or grows out of the ministries of Israel's prophets. This definition recognizes that what we call prophetic literature includes not only the words of the prophets themselves but also narratives and historical accounts about the lives and actions of the prophets and their contemporaries. It also includes some prophetic material that appears outside the canonical prophetic books, for example, the words of and stories surrounding Moses (referred to as a prophet in Deut 34:10) and the ministries of Israel's "nonwriting" prophets such as Elisha and Elijah.[2] Moreover, contemporary biblical scholars across the ideological spectrum generally accept that the prophetic books were not necessarily written, in their entirety, by the named author. Rather, the writings that make up the biblical canon are likely the culmination of a process in which scribes collected and arranged various discrete units of prophetic discourse, added their own interpretations, updated the prophecies to create new prophetic literature, and linked the prophetic writings to other parts of the canon, such as the Torah and the wisdom literature.[3] "Of these [elements]," says David Peterson, "the copious updating or contemporizing of prophetic words and traditions for a new generation seems to be the distinguishing feature of prophetic literature."[4]

This process ultimately resulted in our biblical canon of prophetic books: the three Major Prophets (Isaiah, Jeremiah and Ezekiel) and the twelve Minor Prophets (Hosea, Joel, Amos, Obadiah, Jonah, Micah, Nahum, Habakkuk, Zephaniah, Haggai, Zechariah and Malachi). While early biblical scholarship on the Prophets tried to identify the elemental building blocks of prophetic literature, namely, smaller oral units that were collected and arranged by later schools, more recently biblical scholars have sought to understand the ways in which entire prophetic books work as a unit. This

---

[2]See generally David L. Petersen, *Prophetic Literature: An Introduction* (Louisville: Westminster John Knox, 2002), pp. 215-36. "Nonwriting" is the conventional way of referring to those prophets who do not have books named after them. In this essay, we focus on the "writing prophets."

[3]In our view, as well as that of many others, recognition of such clear historical development in the writing of the prophetic books that led to their final form does not entail failure to respect those books as authoritative Scripture for the church.

[4]Petersen, *Prophetic Literature*, p. 35.

analysis has moved toward consideration of units larger than a single book, particularly with respect to reading the Minor Prophets together as the Book of the Twelve.[5]

Ancient Israel did not have prophets at every stage of its existence. Individuals who identified themselves as prophets and served as intermediaries between God and humanity began to appear around the time when Israel was first governed by a king (around 1040 B.C. under Saul). Prophetic activity continued through the divided monarchy, which began in 930 B.C. after Solomon's death and ended in 722 B.C. when the northern kingdom was conquered and deported by the Assyrians. Prophetic activity continued in the southern kingdom until the Babylonian exile (586 B.C.) and into the fifth century B.C. at least, as seen in the books of Haggai, Zechariah and Malachi. That the presence of prophetic activity in Israel was strongly identified with the period of kingly rule speaks to the need for such prophetic activity to hold kings accountable to God's law rather than being a law unto themselves (see Deut 17:14-20; 1 Sam 8:1-22).

While popular understandings of the prophets often assume that they spoke from a position outside the mainstream of Israelite society, this is only partly accurate. It is true that some of Israel's prophets were from the lower class and made their living from professions not connected with Israel's religious practices that were centered on the temple (e.g., Amos was a shepherd and tender of sycamore-fig trees; see Amos 1:1; 7:14-15). These prophets derived their authority from charismatic experience, and their followers tended to be from disadvantaged groups who found their calls for reform attractive. Many of Israel's prophets, however, were from the upper class and functioned near the circles of power. These prophets held offices—in the sense of playing a recognized role in Israel's religious structure—and they derived their power from their temple office (e.g., Jeremiah and Ezekiel). Some were on the temple payroll and some, such as Nathan, Isaiah and Haggai, had ready access to the king. Whether central to Israel's power

---

[5]For example, see James D. Nogalski, *Literary Precursors to the Book of the Twelve,* Beihefte zur Zeitschrift für die alttestamentliche Wissenschaft 217 (New York: De Gruyter, 1993); idem, *Redactional Processes in the Book of the Twelve,* Beihefte zur Zeitschrift für die alttestamentliche Wissenschaft 218 (Berlin: De Gruyter, 1993); James D. Nogalski and Marvin A. Sweeney, eds., *Reading and Hearing the Book of the Twelve,* Society of Biblical Literature Symposium Series 15 (Atlanta: Society of Biblical Literature, 2000).

structures or peripheral to them,[6] prophets were "intermediaries between the human and the divine worlds,"[7] including representing humans to God or God to humans, acting with the power of God in the world, envisioning the cosmic world, seeking God's counsel, and analyzing the actions and circumstances of human beings, particularly Israel's rulers.

That Israel's prophets often had access or close proximity to the king suggests their close connection to political power during much of ancient Israel's history. The prophets' message was directed primarily at Israel and its leaders, since covenant fidelity was normally the topic of discussion, but it also included "oracles against the nations" such as Jeremiah 46–51 and Amos's cryptic condemnation of Moab "because he burned, as if to lime, the bones of Edom's king" (Amos 2:1).[8] Because the focus was on covenant fidelity to Yahweh,[9] the prophetic prescriptions and condemnations often targeted structural, political, governmental and social issues rather than personal ones. The exchanges often took the form of a courtroom-style dispute, where the prophet, speaking for Yahweh, would bring an accusation against Israel's leaders. The prophets' message was not, however, only directed at kings and leaders; the responsibility to act with righteousness and justice in one's affairs was ultimately the responsibility of all.

All of this is to say that Israel's prophetic literature arose in various particular contexts for particular purposes. Although we do not wish to restrict the application of the prophetic word without cause, grappling with the historical particularity of the prophetic utterances should be a guide to help discourage application of the prophetic word to utterly dissimilar contexts, and to any modern context without due theological reflection.

The message of the Prophets. There is certainly no one message that characterizes all the Prophets. Each has its own emphasis, and each book should be read as a literary unit. That being said, there are themes that can be found throughout the prophetic writings as a genre. As intermediaries between Israel and its God, the Prophets present a message that em-

---

[6]On the notion of central and peripheral prophets, see Paul L. Redditt, *Introduction to the Prophets* (Grand Rapids: Eerdmans, 2008), p. 10. For a fuller treatment see Robert R. Wilson, *Prophecy and Society in Ancient Israel* (Philadelphia: Fortress, 1980).

[7]Petersen, *Prophetic Literature*, p. 7.

[8]Unless otherwise indicated, all Scripture quotations in this chapter are taken from the NIV 1984.

[9]*Yahweh* is the personal name of the God of Israel and is conventionally translated LORD (small caps) in English Bibles. The significance of the name as an expression of God's saving activity in the exodus is explained in Exodus 3:13-15 and 6:2-5.

bodies "the religious affirmations and theological norms of ancient Israel."[10] While it is impossible to identify a single prophetic theology or ethical perspective, the one theme that unifies the prophetic literature is that it must be read against its covenantal background: the Prophets' primary purpose was to call Israel back to obedience to the covenant obligations to which it had agreed at Sinai. On the mountain, God called Israel into a unique relationship with himself. He promised that if the people of Israel would obey the commandments he had given to Moses and worship the Lord God only, he would set them apart as a nation for his own possession (Ex 19:5-6).[11] He promised to bless them if they kept covenant with him and obeyed his laws but also warned the people that disobedience would result in punishment (see Deut 28).

The primary unifying theme of the prophetic literature, then, is the call to "return to God," with all that such a reorientation means for social relations.[12] (See Is 10:21; Hos 14:1; Amos 4:4-13.) The Prophets charge that the people of Israel had failed to honor their twin obligations—worship of Yahweh alone and obedience that mirrors God's holiness—by turning to other gods and breaking his commandments. The Prophets also reiterate the consequences associated with keeping (or failing to keep) these covenant obligations—blessings as the reward for obedience, curses and destruction as the sanction for disobedience, and restoration as the result of confession of sin and repentance.

Since Israel's prophetic activity developed in conjunction with the birth of the monarchy, one of the Prophets' common tasks is to answer the question, What does it mean for a king to function in an Israelite/Yahwistic setting? The prophetic message was not, however, only relevant to Israel's affairs; it also embodied an imperial perspective that recognized the cosmic sovereignty of Israel's God. While Jeremiah is the only prophet who is explicitly designated "prophet to the nations" (Jer 1:5, 10; see also the oracles against the nations in Jer 46–51), several other prophetic books contain collections of sayings and oracles addressed to nations other than Israel (e.g., Is 13–23; Ezek 25–32; Amos 1–2).

---

[10]Petersen, *Prophetic Literature*, p. 17.
[11]See "The Law in Its Context" in chapter three.
[12]See generally Bernard W. Anderson, *The Eighth Century Prophets: Amos, Hosea, Isaiah, Micah*, Proclamation Commentaries, ed. Foster R. McCurley (Philadelphia: Fortress, 1978), pp. 23-24.

Reflecting this dual perspective—of covenant and imperium—the prophetic literature contains two levels of norms: those that are directed to nations other than Israel (less common in prophetic literature) and those that are specific to God's covenant people. An example of the first is the first two chapters of Amos, which are addressed to Israel's neighbors and target conduct that all human beings would generally deem immoral: genocide (Amos 1:6, 9), violence against civilians (Amos 1:13) and acts of ritual desecration (Amos 2:1). In other passages, nations or their leaders are indicted for excessive pride ("You said in your heart, . . . 'I will make myself like the Most High'" [Is 14:13-15]) and excessive violence in wartime (Is 10:12-15).

The most prominent theological norm directed toward Israel is the obligation to worship the Lord God only and to eschew loyalty to any other deity. The norm of monotheism, which the Lord God commanded, includes not only the worship of one God but also the denial of the existence of any other gods.[13] The prophet Isaiah describes the images of other gods as laughable: immovable idols made of gold, wood or clay and unable to answer or rescue (Is 40:18-20; 44:10-19; 46:1-2, 5-7). By contrast, the God to whom Israel owes worship is the one who "has measured the waters in the hollow of his hand" (Is 40:12), who "brings princes to naught and reduces the rulers of this world to nothing" (Is 40:23), who "bring[s] prosperity and create[s] disaster" (Is 45:7), and who delivers, rescues and redeems his people (Is 40:28-31; 46:11-13).

Importantly, the prophetic call to "return to God" included not only right worship but also right living and, in particular, righteousness and justice in one's relationships. In the first chapter of Isaiah, God declares that worship and offerings are "meaningless" and "detestable" if rendered by those whose hands are "full of blood" (Is 1:11-15). He continues in Isaiah 1:16-17:

Take your evil deeds
   out of my sight!
Stop doing wrong,
   learn to do right!

---

[13]Biblical scholars routinely recognize that Israel was likely monolatrous during much, if not all, of its history leading up to the exile. To be distinguished from monotheism (the belief that only one god exists), monolatry means that only one god is to be worshiped without denying the existence of other gods.

Seek justice,
encourage the oppressed.
Defend the cause of the fatherless,
plead the case of the widow.

The reward for this kind of obedient worship is forgiveness of sin and prosperity for the nation (see Isa 1:18-19).

An essential element of what it means to live rightly and acceptably before
a holy God is the obligation to "seek justice" in social relationships.[14] The
classic formulation of this idea is found in Micah 6:8, where the prophet says:

He has showed you, O man, what is good.
And what does the LORD require of you?
To act justly and to love mercy
and to walk humbly with your God.

The word *justly* is translated from the Hebrew *mishpat*, which is founda-
tionally an attribute of God, "all true *mishpat* finding its source in God himself
and carrying with it *his demand*."[15] When the Bible talks about the *mishpat* of
God, it is not talking primarily of God's laws but of his just claims over his
creation, for example, his claim of authority or his prerogative to show mercy
(Is 30:18). In Micah 6:8 and similar passages, God calls his people to embody
the attribute of *mishpat*, meaning "rightness rooted in God's character," and
to employ *mishpat* in their dealings with one another.[16]

In the biblical sense, then, "to act justly" is not so much to obey commandments as it is for human beings to establish relationships with one
another that conform to the ideal of the covenant established by God.[17] In
order to understand the biblical notion of justice—and its close neighbor
righteousness—one must put aside the distinctly Western notion of justice
as simply behavior that conforms to an ethical or legal norm. Rather, justice
is the fulfillment of the obligations of particular relationships, for example,
ruler and citizens, citizens and resident aliens, parents and children. Each

---

[14]Redditt, *Introduction to the Prophets*, p. 359.
[15]R. Laird Harris, Gleason L. Archer Jr. and Bruce K. Waltke, eds., *Theological Wordbook of the Old
Testament* (Chicago: Moody Press, 1980), 2:949 (emphasis in original).
[16]Ibid.
[17]Bruce K. Waltke, *A Commentary on Micah* (Grand Rapids: Eerdmans, 2007), p. 391 (quoting
Bernard Renaud, *La formation du livre de Michée: tradition et actualisation,* Etudes bibliques
[Paris: Gabalda, 1977]).

relationship has its own particular responsibilities, and, importantly, all
human relationships are ultimately determined by relationship to God.
When these various relational obligations are fulfilled, then justice prevails
and there is *shalom*, a Hebrew word that means "peace" or "welfare."[18]

In light of this community-centered view of justice, the prophets reserved
their harshest criticism for those in Israel with riches, authority and power:
the rulers, judges, priests, employers and landlords. There is no *shalom*, the
prophets declared, because the leaders in Israel had used their power cor-
ruptly or for personal gain rather than to fulfill the obligations of social relationships (e.g., Amos 4:1-3; Mic 2:1-2; 3:9-11). The prophets were particularly
concerned with the plight of those who were most vulnerable and least able
to defend their own cause. The prophetic shorthand for this group is widows
and orphans, prisoners (or the oppressed), the poor, and the alien (e.g., Is
1:16-17; Zech 7:8-10). The unifying feature is that these individuals had little
wealth and virtually no political power. Importantly, the call to do justice is
rooted not only in the covenant relationship between God and Israel but
also more broadly in the holiness of God himself (e.g., Is 1:4).

While the prophetic books are full of messages of judgment and calls to
repentance, they also include a clear and prominent message of hope that
the nation of Israel will be restored and become a blessing to all the nations
(e.g., Is 2:2-4; 60:1-3). Israel's restoration is part of God's ultimate plan,
which is both cosmic and international in scope. This theme is prominent
in the book of Isaiah. Isaiah interprets events—good and bad—as part of
God's overarching plan (Is 25:1-2; 28:29), he chides Israel for trying to carry
out plans that are not the Lord's (Is 30:1-3), and he affirms God's promise to
fulfill his plan for both judgment and restoration, as reflected in the words
of his "messengers" (Is 44:26; 46:10). Isaiah predicts that after a time of
judgment there will be a new day for Israel: Jerusalem will be reestablished
as a place where an obedient Israel will flourish (Is 2:2-4; 54:11-17), ruled by
a king from the line of David (Is 9:2-7; 11:1). This kingdom will be a place
where peace, truth and nobility will reign and where evil men will no longer
have power (Is 32:1-8). The "Spirit of the LORD" will rest upon the king who
will reign on David's throne with wisdom, righteousness and justice (Is
11:2-9; 9:7). The prophecy also emphasizes that the king will bring justice

---

[18]See generally Anderson, *Eighth Century Prophets*, p. 43.

and righteousness by caring for the poor and vulnerable in the community. Isaiah ends with a beautiful picture of a land ruled by a just and righteous king (Is 11:6-9).[19]

In sum, while the prophetic message is diverse and each individual book has its own unique flavor, a key unifying theme of the prophetic literature is the call for Israel to return to the obligations enshrined in its covenant with God. Covenant fidelity on Israel's part requires proper and exclusive worship of the one God and justice with regard to the powerless members of society. These two themes are not unrelated, for justice to the poor and oppressed reflects the character of Israel's God. Indeed, it is by his own compassion that he delivered the Israelites from oppression in Egypt. The juxtaposition of these two themes hearkens back to Exodus 22:20-24.

> Whoever sacrifices to any god other than the LORD must be destroyed.
>
> Do not mistreat an alien or oppress him, for you were aliens in Egypt.
>
> Do not take advantage of a widow or an orphan. If you do and they cry out to me, I will certainly hear their cry. My anger will be aroused, and I will kill you with the sword; your wives will become widows and your children fatherless.

Not only are proper worship and proper treatment of the oppressed set side by side, but infractions in both areas are met with the same penalty of death. Moreover, injustice toward aliens and the oppressed will be met with alien invasion ("the sword") and Israel's own experience of oppression.

Jesus fulfilled the Law and Prophets. In order to read the prophetic literature properly, it is not enough to identify its meaning for the original Israelite audience. As believers in Jesus, we read the prophetic word from the vantage point of knowing how Israel's story comes to its climax: Jesus is the fulfillment of all the prophetic hopes for a restored nation of Israel that would be ruled by an obedient king and would be "a light for the Gentiles" (Is 49:6; see Acts 13:47). The prophets believed they were predicting the reign of a Davidic king who would restore to prominence the nation-state of Israel as both covenantally faithful and militarily strong. When one compares the history of Israel's earthly kings to the prophets' words, however, it seems clear that Israel never had a king who quite fulfilled this vision (al-

---

[19]Redditt sees this passage as a reversal of the effects of the disobedience of Adam and Eve (*Introduction to the Prophets*, p. 74).

though David's reign is seen as the template for the future reality). Rather, the "idealized rhetoric of royalty" that made its way into the prophetic writings remained an expectation about a future in which God would make a new covenant with his people and he, himself, would rule as their king, albeit through an ideal, covenantally faithful earthly ruler.[20]

According to Luke's Gospel, the birth of Jesus was hailed by Mary (Lk 1:46-56) and Zechariah (Lk 1:67-79) as the inauguration of Israel's redemption (i.e., liberation) from oppressive rulers (Lk 1:52, 71). Luke also records the words of the "righteous and devout" (Lk 2:25) man Simeon, who said of the child Jesus when he was presented at the temple in Jerusalem,

Sovereign Lord. . . .
My eyes have seen your salvation,
    which you have prepared in the sight of all people,
a light for revelation to the Gentiles
    and for glory to your people Israel. (Lk 2:29-32; see Is 42:6; 49:6)

Later, at the beginning of his ministry, Jesus specifically identified himself with the promise of Israel's restoration and declared his coming as its fulfillment. In his first recorded public speech, Jesus stood up in the temple, opened the scroll of the prophet Isaiah and read:

The Spirit of the Lord is on me,
    because he has anointed me
    to preach the good news to the poor.
He has sent me to proclaim freedom for the prisoners
    and recovery of sight for the blind,
to release the oppressed,
    to proclaim the year of the Lord's favor. (Lk 4:18-19)

Jesus is quoting from Isaiah 61:1-2, in which the speaker announces that salvation and restoration have come at last to the suffering people of Israel in Babylonian exile. In context, the messianic figure in Isaiah is pictured as a military-royal figure who would fight for restoration of Israel's national existence. But at the end of his reading of this passage, Jesus rolled up the scroll, sat down and declared, "Today this scripture is fulfilled in your hearing" (Lk 4:21).

---

[20]Petersen, *Prophetic Literature*, p. 93.

With these words, Jesus proclaimed that he is the culmination of all the prophetic hopes and promises of a Davidic king who would restore Israel and rule the nation with justice and righteousness.[21] Jesus' primary message was that, in him, God had inaugurated the kingdom of God and had begun his reign on earth. Jesus' ministry, death and resurrection marked him as the one through whom God's kingdom would be realized. And his ministry among the people was the first stage of the physical demonstration of what the new kingdom *already was* and *finally would be* (the next stage being inaugurated at his resurrection). In other words, when Jesus healed the sick, gave sight to the blind, cleansed the leper and raised the dead, he was offering foretastes of the kingdom of God, which is both a present reality and a future promise. The final chapter (when Jesus returns again) will be a new heaven and a new earth ruled by the last Davidic king, Jesus himself (Rev 21:3). In the consummated kingdom, all of creation will be "liberated from its bondage to decay" (Rom 8:21), and "there will be no more death or mourning or crying or pain" (Rev 21:4).[22] The consummated kingdom of God is the ultimate fulfillment of Israel's deepest prophetic longings, a beautiful, prosperous and peaceful land ruled by a just and righteous king (Is 11:7-9).

To say that Jesus "fulfilled" the Law and the Prophets (Mt 5:17) is not to say that the prophetic literature is no longer relevant. In fact, it is to say just the opposite. The purpose of the prophetic message was to call God's covenant people back to worship of the Lord and to obedience that mirrored his holiness. In its original context, the message was directed toward the nation of Israel, and the call to right living was paired with a call to return to covenant fidelity. According to the book of Hebrews, however, Jesus is the mediator of a new covenant, which is the fulfillment of the words of the prophet Jeremiah:

"The time is coming," declares the LORD,
> "when I will make a new covenant
with the house of Israel. . . .
I will put my law in their minds
> and write it on their hearts.

---

[21]To say that Jesus was the fulfillment of the Old Testament prophecies is not the same thing as saying that the prophets had Jesus in mind by their original words in context. Whatever they had in mind, Jesus saw himself (as did the New Testament writers) in the role described by the prophets. See Redditt, *Introduction to the Prophets*, p. 101.

[22]For further discussion of the consummated kingdom, see chapter nine in this volume.

I will be their God,

    and they will be my people. . . .

For I will forgive their wickedness

    and will remember their sins no more." (Jer 31:31, 33-34; Heb 10:16-17)

As subjects of the new covenant, God's people must continue to heed the prophetic call to worship the one true God through Jesus Christ and the call to an obedience that mirrors the holiness of God as revealed in the person and work of Jesus.

God requires *more*, not less, from his new covenant people, as Jesus made clear in the Sermon on the Mount (Mt 5:17-20). "Be perfect," Jesus said, "as your heavenly Father is perfect," invoking in prophetic style the character of God as the motivation and pattern for right living (Mt 5:48). When the Pharisees criticized him for eating with tax collectors and "sinners," Jesus sent them back to the Prophets to "learn what this means: 'I desire mercy, not sacrifice'" (Mt 9:13; Hos 6:6). When asked, "Which is the greatest commandment in the Law?" Jesus referred to the prophetic literature, responding that "all the Law and the Prophets" are summed up in two commandments: "Love the Lord your God with all your heart and with all your soul and with all your mind. . . . Love your neighbor as yourself" (Mt 22:34-40).

Significantly, by invoking Isaiah 61:1-2 to inaugurate his earthly ministry—proclaiming that he came to preach to the poor, free the prisoners, heal the blind and rescue the oppressed—Jesus defined his mission in language used by the prophets to capture God's concern for *mishpat* (justice). (See, e.g., Is 10:2; Zeph 3:19.) While the passage might be read metaphorically to refer solely to Jesus' work of salvation, his public ministry, in which he offered physical healing as well as forgiveness of sins, makes clear that God's ultimate work of redemption is a material as well as a spiritual restoration.[23] That Jesus situated himself within this prophetic tradition has important implications for the continuing relevance of the prophetic literature to identify what it means to live obediently as God's covenant people.[24]

Reading the Prophets in light of the new covenant. As demonstrated by our discussion thus far, a central theme of the prophetic literature, and one

---

[23]See generally N. T. Wright, *Surprised by Hope: Rethinking Heaven, the Resurrection, and the Mission of the Church,* 1st ed. (New York: HarperOne, 2008), pp. 198-205.

[24]For further discussion of the kingdom of God and Jesus as a fulfillment of the message of the prophets, see chapter six.

that has particular significance for law and legal institutions, is the prophetic call to seek justice (*mishpat*). Before suggesting some specific implications of the biblical norm of justice to modern law, we offer four summary points from the previous sections: First, justice in the biblical sense is fundamentally relational. It describes the duties owed in particular social relationships, particularly by those in positions of leadership, authority and power over vulnerable groups who cannot protect their own interests. While the obligation to act justly was originally embedded in the covenantal relationship between God and the nation of Israel, it is also grounded more broadly in the character of God himself. The prophets linked their description of a holy God at work in the world to an elaboration of what it meant to live in relationship with such a God (e.g., Is 1:4).[25] Moreover, when Jesus stood up in the temple and quoted the prophet Isaiah (Lk 4:18-19), he explicitly associated himself with this prophetic tradition, affirming that the obligation to do justice is as much a part of the new covenant as it was the old. Thus, the prophetic call to act justly in social relationships has enduring significance for God's people today.

Second, however, the original prophetic message was directed toward Israel as a nation, with the primary purpose of calling the whole people of Israel back to its covenantal obligations. Consequently, any application to modern law must acknowledge that God's people are no longer defined by national affiliation but are distinguished by faith in Jesus and are spread among many nations. While ultimately citizens of a heavenly kingdom,[26] however, followers of Jesus are called to mirror God's holiness as citizens of particular communities and nations. Thus, while the prophetic literature does not speak to modern nations, as nations, it has continuing relevance in shaping the social obligations of God's new covenant people.

Third, and related, we believe it would be improper to read the prophetic literature as containing promises or judgments applicable to current national or world circumstances. In particular, we reject a reading of the Prophets as providing a religious basis for the claim that God has granted to any modern nation a unique role in human history that is akin to the nation of Israel.[27] We also believe it is inappropriate for readers to claim that particular events—for

---

[25]Anderson, *Eighth Century Prophets*, p. 8.
[26]See in this volume "The Kingdom of God, Law and the Heart" in chapter six.
[27]For example, we reject a reading of the prophets as providing a basis for American exceptionalism—the idea that God has given America a unique, religiously grounded world mission.

example, terrorist attacks or natural disasters—are direct, divine judgments for a particular nation's sins or, conversely, that positive circumstances are evidence of God's special blessing. We do not believe that any one country can be viewed as having a one-to-one relationship with the prophetic word. That word is now refracted through the gospel, where nationalistic boundaries are obliterated and one people of God is formed that knows "neither Jew nor Greek" (Gal 3:28). The prophets, therefore, cannot be read directly as promising blessings or curses on modern nations for particular behavior.

This is not to say it is without consequence whether a nation's laws and legal institutions mirror God's justice, or whether governmental officials and ordinary citizens act justly in their dealings with one another. God's commandments are for our good, and failure to keep them exposes individuals, and the communities they live in, to the human consequences of sin. Conversely, when those in authority are wise and seek justice, the governed will prosper, and when God's people act justly in their social relationships, whole communities will benefit (Prov 11:10). When our institutions mirror eternal principles, they will do a better job of restraining sin and furthering human flourishing. But whether a particular nation suffers blessing or calamity is not a function of equating its national identity with that of ancient Israel. The free spread of the blessings of the gospel presumes that no one nation has privileged status but that "all authority in heaven and on earth" resides in the risen Christ (Mt 28:18).

Fourth, and finally, reading and applying the prophetic literature properly is not a monolithic exercise. Some parts will have more direct application than others. Some passages, for example judgments against particular nations for specific conduct, are historically situated, and thus any modern application will be more attenuated. Other parts, for example admonitions grounded in the character of God, have more direct and universal application.

LESSONS FOR CONTEMPORARY LAW: THE ENDURING CALL TO "SEEK JUSTICE"

In this part of our discussion we draw out in more detail some implications of the prophetic call to do justice for contemporary law and government. We flesh out four basic points. First, biblical justice is procedural as well as substantive. It requires fair and unbiased adjudication as well as fair and principled laws. Second, justice is largely relational and has particular claims on those who are in positions of power or authority over others. Third, biblical justice requires special attention to the way laws and legal institutions treat the most vulnerable individuals in our communities. Fourth, there is a sense in which modern lawyers should see themselves as having a prophetic role in their communities, either as insiders working for justice in law and legal institutions or as outsiders who bring to light injustice and call for its eradication. (We will first address points one and two together, then three and four in separate sections.)

Procedural justice and the abuse of power. Recall again that the prophets leveled their heaviest criticism on the leaders in Israel, including rulers, legislators, judges and landlords. Some of the prophets had the ear of the king himself, while others were outsiders who raised their voices against corruption and injustice by those in power. Either way, the prophets' primary focus was on relationships involving power over others. Legislators were indicted for enacting

> oppressive decrees,
>> to deprive the poor of their rights
>>> and withhold justice from the oppressed of my people,
>> making widows their prey
>>> and robbing the fatherless. (Is 10:1-2)

Corrupt and unjust judges were condemned because they "acquit the guilty for a bribe, but deny justice to the innocent" (Is 5:23). Powerful witnesses were called to account who

> with a word make a man out to be guilty,
>> who ensnare the defender in court
>> and with false testimony deprive the innocent of justice. (Is 29:21)

According to the prophets, the lack of *shalom* in the community resulted because those in authority used their power not for justice but to oppress the weak. Theologian Bernard Anderson explains:

> The wealthy used economic power to grind the poor into the dust; rulers used their position not to defend the fatherless and plead the case of the widow, but to enhance their own prestige; the courts were not functioning to obtain a rightful position for the weak and legally helpless; and the religious

leaders used their influence to support the establishment and to silence any
voice of conscience about the violence perpetrated in society.[28]

That the prophets focused not only on substantive law (e.g., legislators) but
also on enforcement and adjudication (e.g., executive officials and judges)
highlights an important distinction in modern conceptions of law: the distinction between *procedural* guarantees and *substantive* guarantees. To illustrate, in American law the due process clauses of the Fifth and Fourteenth
Amendments of the US Constitution are procedural guarantees. They forbid
the government to deprive an individual of life, liberty or property without
adequate process, which means the person must receive notice of the potential
deprivation and the opportunity to make her case before a neutral arbiter or
judge. The guarantee of due process is designed to ensure that governmental
officials cannot execute a person, restrain her liberty, or take her property
unless they can publicly demonstrate lawful reasons for doing so. By contrast,
the equal protection clause of the Fourteenth Amendment to the US Constitution is a substantive right, forbidding racial discrimination outright.[29]

The prophetic literature makes clear that procedural as well as substantive justice is necessary in order to achieve *mishpat.* There can be no
justice, say the prophets, if judges are taking bribes (e.g., Mic 3:11; 7:3), ac-
quitting the guilty and denying justice to the innocent (e.g., Is 5:23), and
depriving the poor of fairness in the courts (e.g., Amos 5:12). Similarly, injustice reigns when powerful individuals engage in extortion (e.g., Is 33:15)
and fail to defend the cause of the weak (Is 1:23). The injustice in Israel is in
stark contrast with the justice of a holy God: When God's rule is established
on earth, he will judge "righteously" and "settle disputes" for the nations
(Jer 11:20; Mic 4:3). He will "judge the needy, [and] with justice he will give
decisions for the poor of the earth" (Is 11:4).

These prophetic indictments underline the fact that fair and adequate procedures are essential for ensuring substantive rights. If constitutions or laws
guarantee particular rights but corrupt officials ignore them with impunity or
judges fail to enforce them, they are not worth the paper they are written on.

---

[28]Anderson, *Eighth Century Prophets,* p. 44.
[29]Theoretically, the government could discriminate based on race if it had a "compelling state
interest," but this test has been viewed as "strict in theory, but fatal in fact." For an extremely
rare example in which the US Supreme Court found a compelling interest, see Korematsu v.
United States, 323 U.S. 214 (1944) (finding constitutional the internment of Japanese Americans during World War II).

Without the "rule of law"[30]—meaning some mechanism for making sure that the law applies to everyone equally (including those in authority)—there can be no justice. In American law, the constitutional guarantee of fair process is itself enforceable in state and federal courts. A related feature of procedural protections in the United States and some other countries is what is called the "separation of powers," meaning that the executive power, the legislative power and the judicial power are enforced by independent departments of the government. This ensures, for example, that legislators can't make laws and then selectively enforce them against others. Conversely, executive officials are empowered to enforce the laws but only as provided in written statutes enacted by the legislature. And finally, judges adjudicating disputes are constrained by the requirements of statutory and case law. The separation of powers is designed to ensure that everyone, including governmental actors, is subject to the same rules and that officials in different branches of government will serve as checks on one another's power.

While the prophetic message should not be read to require Western-style legal institutions, biblical justice does require some neutral and independent adjudicatory mechanism to restrain those in power from acting arbitrarily or illegally. To do justice in the biblical sense is to make sure that people are not unlawfully deprived of basic societal benefits necessary for human flourishing, such as material goods, fair treatment, liberty, dignity and security from harm. If governmental officials can take these things away and there is no way to challenge or review their actions, there can be no *mishpat* (justice). Similarly, if powerful private individuals or entities can harm, rob or enslave the weak with impunity, there can be no justice.

According to Gary Haugen, founder of the International Justice Mission,[31] the most important human rights challenge of our day is to make sure that the poor actually receive the justice promised to them by their own laws. He notes that the modern human rights movement has made great strides to articulate and codify international standards on fundamental rights, and

---

[30]A full exploration of the meaning and requirements of the "rule of law" is beyond the scope of this chapter. In its most basic sense, however, the rule of law requires some form of independent adjudicatory mechanism that applies the law equally to everyone.

[31]We highlight the work of the International Justice Mission (IJM) because it is the largest (and one of the few) faith-based, international human rights organizations doing justice casework and public justice reform around the world. For a description of IJM's philosophy and work, see generally Gary Haugen, *Good News About Injustice: A Witness of Courage in a Hurting World*, 10th anniversary ed. (Downers Grove, IL: InterVarsity Press, 2009).

many developing countries have begun to enact legal reforms that embed these norms into their own domestic law. The next big challenge, however, is to help these countries create functioning public justice systems so that the laws on the books are actually enforced. "Without functioning public justice systems to deliver the protections of law to the poor," Haugen and Victor Boutros argue, "the legal reforms of the modern human rights movement rarely improve the lives of those who need them the most."[32] Haugen cites a United Nations study that concluded that three out of every five people on earth are not protected by their own justice systems.[33] The reasons for this state of affairs are numerous. In many countries police officers, investigators, prosecutors and judges are poorly trained and overworked. Even honest officials who aspire to uphold the law are often hampered by a lack of administrative support, limited resources and shoddy record keeping. In the worst cases, officials are corrupt, abusive or subject to bribery by powerful private citizens. Under such conditions, the powerful can rob and oppress the weak with impunity and the machinery of government becomes a mechanism for public and private authorities to quash dissent and fulfill their own corrupt and violent objectives.

In the first instance, the transformation of a country's public justice system requires building capacity and accountability in legal and governmental institutions, such as police departments, prosecutors' offices and courts.[34] The International Justice Mission has employed a model of "collaborative casework" to build local crime-fighting and judicial capacity by selecting particular geographic areas, focusing on a particular kind of abuse that is relatively uncontroversial (for example, sexual abuse of children), and enlisting local officials to investigate and prosecute the perpetrators.[35] Sometimes the problem is that there are simply too few trained professionals to investigate, prosecute and adjudicate cases. For example, some countries with histories of unrest or ethnic cleansing may have lost large numbers of their most educated and professional citizens. This may require

---

[32]Gary Haugen and Victor Boutros, "And Justice for All: Enforcing Human Rights for the World's Poor," *Foreign Affairs* 89 (May/June 2010): 51.
[33]Haugen, *Good News About Injustice* (citing Commission on Legal Empowerment of the Poor, *Making the Law Work for Everyone*, vol. 1 [New York: United Nations Development Programme, 2008], http://www.undp.org/content/undp/en/home/librarypage/democratic-governance/Lep/making-the-law-work-for-everyone---vol-i---english.html).
[34]Haugen and Boutros, "And Justice for All," p. 59.
[35]Ibid., p. 61.

a long-term plan for educating a new generation of police officers, lawyers and judges.[36] Many government offices and courts are virtually paralyzed because they have no system for organizing, filing and accessing records and case files. In such cases the expedient of setting up a simple filing and retrieval system can be transformative.

Public justice transformation also requires the building of political will in communities and governmental agencies. When citizens and community leaders are educated to know their legal rights and what to do if those rights are violated, they begin to demand that the laws on the books be enforced. This public demand, in turn, ignites dormant calls for the rule of law among the middle class, which in turn spurs local officials to enforce the law and begins to marginalize obstructionists.[37] In many countries, pastors are an important resource in these efforts. Churches serve as centers of community life, and pastors are often community leaders who can be instrumental in teaching their congregations about the law and informing them of available legal resources.

While building functioning public justice systems in the developing world is a big goal, it is not impossible. As Haugen points out, "A century ago, police and the courts in the United States were nothing like the professional—albeit imperfect—U.S. law enforcement system that is now taken for granted."[38] Moreover, at the end of the day, it is God who calls his people to do the work of justice, and it is he who empowers the work, through prayer, wisdom, rigor, excellence and reliance on his power and authority.

We offer one final note before we leave the subject of procedural justice. Although adequate procedures are designed to produce accurate results, they sometimes fail to deliver substantive justice. For example, even a fair trial can result in the conviction of an innocent person. In a fallen world, it may be impossible (or too costly) to achieve absolute certainty, and procedural justice is sometimes the closest we can get to substantive justice. But

---

[36] Beginning in 2007 students and faculty from Pepperdine Law School's Global Justice Program have worked to build capacity in the court system in Uganda by doing legal research and serving as law clerks for high court judges, assisting Ugandan lawyers in representing juveniles who have been held for many years without trial, and helping the courts to develop a system for reducing the overwhelming backlog of criminal cases. See generally Jay Milbrandt, *Go + Do: Daring to Change the World One Story at a Time* (Carol Stream, IL: Tyndale House, 2012), pp. 179-98; see also http://law.pepperdine.edu/global-justice/.

[37] Haugen and Boutros, "And Justice for All," p. 61.

[38] Ibid., p. 58.

the prophets' reminder that God's justice is substantive (as well as procedural) should be a caution to the claim that, in every context, procedural justice is enough. In criminal cases, for example, no amount of formal process is enough if defendants have inadequate representation at trial. Even in relatively well-functioning legal systems such as in the United States, poor representation can lead to an alarming number of wrongful convictions, especially among poor and indigent defendants. While some US jurisdictions have excellent public defenders' offices, many do not, and contract attorneys are often poorly paid and unqualified to handle complicated criminal cases. Poor representation is one of the primary reasons behind wrongful convictions in the United States.[39]

Moreover, once a defendant has been convicted of a crime in an American court, an actual innocence claim is almost impossible to bring. While some permissible claims (for example, that a confession was coerced) could bear on the guilt of the convict, the one claim a convict can virtually never bring is that newly discovered evidence proves his innocence and he should be freed for that reason alone. While the right to be free from criminal punishment if one is innocent seems fundamental, the US Supreme Court has expressly declined to recognize a constitutional right to bring a claim of innocence.[40] The court has offered many weighty reasons for declining to recognize claims of actual innocence: it would undermine finality, invite frivolous or difficult-to-assess claims, raise difficult issues of proof and essentially require the federal court to relitigate the facts of the case in a nonadversarial setting.[41] While these issues are serious ones, it seems to us that a strong claim of actual innocence based on newly discovered evidence cannot—consistent with the claims of justice—be turned aside without some mechanism for assessing its merit.

Justice and vulnerable groups. We now turn to the substantive content of *mishpat.* God's call to do justice focuses on those in society who are most vulnerable to being oppressed by powerful individuals of higher status. The prophetic shorthand for this group is widows and orphans, prisoners (or the oppressed), the poor, and the alien (e.g., Is 1:16-17; Zech 7:8-10). The

---

[39]See generally Brandon L. Garrett, *Convicting the Innocent: Where Criminal Convictions Go Wrong* (Cambridge, MA: Harvard University Press, 2011) (discussing some of the reasons behind wrongful convictions).

[40]Herrera v. Collins, 506 U.S. 390 (1993). See generally Garrett, *Convicting the Innocent.*

[41]See generally Herrera v. Collins, 506 U.S. 390 (1993).

Hebrew word for "oppress" connotes the abuse of privilege or power. To oppress is to burden, trample or crush; to ill-treat or abuse; to deprive; or to treat with violence those of inferior social status who cannot protect themselves. Oppression of the defenseless is a grievous sin against God, "the Master of eternity," who has dealt graciously with sinful human beings (see Prov 14:31).[42] Conversely, to protect the weak and "crush" the oppressor is to imitate God, who works vindication and justice for all who are oppressed (Ps 72:4; 103:6).[43] It is not hard to translate the prophetic message into a modern application since these are some of the same groups that continue to be treated unjustly in various ways today.

Justice for the foreigner. As in ancient times, today's immigrants, especially illegal immigrants, continue to be vulnerable to unjust treatment. A relational feature of human sin is the tendency to resent or scapegoat those who are different. It is easy to find evidence around the world of discrimination, hatred and violence targeted toward disfavored ethnic, racial and religious groups, especially immigrants. Unfortunately, the attitude toward immigrants in the United States has a long and unhappy history, from antipathy toward Irish and German immigrants in the mid-nineteenth century to anti-Chinese legislation in the 1880s, to internment of Japanese-Americans during World War II, to the anti-Latino and anti-Middle Eastern sentiments of recent years.[44]

While the idea of citizenship in ancient Israel is not identical to modern notions of citizenship, it is clear that God's call to do justice is applicable to the treatment of aliens as well as citizens. In the Prophets, God forbids his people to "oppress" or to "do . . . wrong or violence" to the foreigner living among them, or to otherwise "deprive [him] of justice" (Jer 7:6; 22:3; Zech 7:10; Is 10:2 NASB). The word *foreigner* is translated from the Hebrew word *gēr*, which referred to someone who did not enjoy the rights usually possessed by the resident and was thus dependent on the hospitality of the native population. At many points in their history, often because of famine, the people of Israel, including Abraham, Israel and Isaac, lived as *gēr* or protected citizens outside the Promised Land. In Israel, the Old Tes-

---

[42]Harris, Archer and Waltke, *Theological Wordbook*, 2:705.
[43]Ibid.
[44]See generally Richard Vedder, Lowell Gallaway and Stephen Moore, "The Immigration Problem: Then and Now," *Independent Review* 4 (Winter 2000): 347-64.

tament law gave the foreigner many of the same rights as the native, and the Israelites were told not to mistreat or oppress the foreigner because they themselves had been oppressed as *gēr* in Egypt (Ex 22:21).[45]

While a detailed treatment of justice in immigration law is beyond the scope of this chapter, we offer some general observations. First, in today's legal and economic climate, noncitizen immigrants, particularly illegal immigrants, are vulnerable to precisely the kinds of injustices that the Prophets warn against. For example, in the United States many undocumented immigrants work as day laborers through unwritten, informal arrangements with employers and are therefore vulnerable to being hired but never paid.[46] Although illegal immigrants have the same legal rights as citizen workers to sue employees who refuse to pay them for completed work, many do not know their rights or are afraid to come forward for fear that they will be arrested and deported. In addition, many illegal immigrants are subjected to dangerous and illegal working conditions, denied basic safety precautions,[47] pressured to hide injuries, exposed to dangerous pesticides,[48] and exposed to violence and abuse by governmental officials.[49] The need to remain "invisible" also exposes illegal immigrants to an increased risk of unaddressed criminal violence because they are often afraid to come forward to report crimes. Laws in some states that empower local police as deputy immigration enforcers exacerbate immigrants' reluctance to report criminal activity committed against themselves or others. To their credit, many police departments have adopted explicit policies that they will not contact immigration authorities when illegal immigrants report crimes against themselves or others.

Second, while reasonable people may disagree on what kind of immigration reform or enforcement is appropriate to address the millions of il-

---

[45]Harris, Archer and Waltke, *Theological Wordbook,* 1:155.

[46]See Pamela Constable, "Advocates Speak Up for Illegal Day Laborers Cheated of Wages," *Washington Post,* July 8, 2008, http://www.washingtonpost.com/wp-dyn/content/article/2008/07/07/AR2008070702845.html.

[47]See, e.g., Harold Meyerson, "Protecting Undocumented Workers," *Los Angeles Times,* June 24, 2011, http://articles.latimes.com/2011/jun/24/opinion/la-oe-meyerson-undocumented-abuses-20110624.

[48]Mary Bauer and Mónica Ramírez, "Injustice on Our Plates: Immigrant Women in the U.S. Food Industry," Southern Poverty Law Center, November 2010, http://www.splcenter.org/get-informed/publications/injustice-on-our-plates.

[49]See, e.g., Staff reporter, "Report Alleges Physical, Sexual Abuse of Illegal Immigrants by Border Patrol," *International Business Times,* September 21, 2011, http://www.ibtimes.com/articles/217905/20110921/report-physical-sexual-abuse-illegal-immigrants-border-patrol.htm.

legal immigrants living in the United States, efforts to make it so oppressive that immigrants are forced to "self-deport" surely do not satisfy the dictates of *mishpat*. Examples of such legislation are laws prohibiting illegal aliens from contracting for utilities such as gas, water or sewer services, or renewing vehicle registrations or mobile home permits; statutes that would invalidate all contracts entered into by illegal immigrants (including mortgages, apartment leases and basic work agreements); and provisions that have driven immigrant children out of the public schools by requiring schools to determine the immigration status of students.

It is hard to imagine legal actions less in line with the biblical obligation to protect vulnerable groups from deprivations of basic societal goods and protections. While it would be just to deport those who are in the United States illegally pursuant to fair procedures and policies, it is not just to mistreat them while they live among us. We believe Christians should strongly oppose anti-immigrant legislation that is calculated to be oppressive. In our view, believers should seek the repeal of such laws and should prayerfully consider disobeying them as circumstances require.

Third, we believe it is consistent with the requirements of justice for churches and Christian social service organizations to provide assistance to illegal immigrants and for believers to support with monetary donations those that do. We reject the argument that illegal immigrants are criminals and that therefore it would be wrong to support their illegal presence by extending (or financing) basic services, such as food, shelter and education.[50]

Justice for widows and orphans. Prominent in the prophetic call to do justice is the obligation to protect widows and orphans. The Prophets call God's people to "defend the cause of the fatherless [and] plead the case of the widow" (Is 1:17; cf. 1:23), and they proclaim judgment on those who oppress or "withhold justice . . . making widows their prey and robbing the fatherless" (Is 10:2). The book of James renews the call to protect widows and orphans, mirroring the broader prophetic theme that worship without social justice is detestable to God: "Religion that God our Father accepts as pure and faultless is this: to look after orphans and widows in their distress and to keep oneself from being polluted by the world" (Jas 1:27).

---

[50]In fact, most undocumented immigrants in the United States are not subject to criminal prosecution because most immigration offenses—for example, overstaying a tourist or student visa—are civil violations, not criminal ones.

There is much one could say about justice for this vulnerable group. We will mention two contexts in which work is being done or needs to be done to protect widows and orphans. The first context involves protecting a widow's right to land. Throughout much of the world, access to and control over land is crucial to family well-being and food security. In many African countries, however, land is acquired through family inheritance of ancestral land, which is mostly passed down the male line. In these cultures, the death of a husband threatens serious harm to the widow and her children. She is often blamed for the family misfortunes and is punished by being chased away from her matrimonial home by her husband's extended family, often by violent means. Some African countries have laws against "land grabbing," but these laws are rarely enforced, in part because widows are afraid of violent reprisals from in-laws if they report the crime. A number of international human rights organizations and churches are working to protect widows and their families from land grabbing in Africa.[51]

A second area of vulnerability for women and children, especially in the developing world, is the threat of human trafficking for labor or sex. Human trafficking results in circumstances that amount to a modern form of slavery. In 2006, the United Nations Office on Drugs and Crime (UNODC) first attempted to identify human trafficking patterns.[52] According to the UNODC, sexual exploitation is the most common form of human trafficking, followed by trafficking for forced labor. Other forms of exploitation, which are likely underreported, are forced or bonded labor, domestic servitude and forced marriage, organ removal, and the exploitation of children in begging, sex trade and warfare. Adult women are the largest victim group, generally accounting for 65 to 75 percent of victims. Sadly, women are disproportionately involved in human trafficking, not only as victims but also as offenders. Children account for 15-25 percent of victims.[53]

In 2003, the United Nations adopted the Protocol to Prevent, Suppress,

---

[51]For example, Pepperdine's Global Justice Program has partnered with Saddleback Church's Justice Task Force to help address the problem of property grabbing in Rwanda. Together they published and distributed a legal handbook for Rwandan pastors detailing the biblical arguments against land grabbing and the rights of widows under Rwandan law. Subsequently, they sent teams of lawyers, law students and law professors to educate Rwandan pastors on how to protect widows and their families in their communities.
[52]See United Nations Office on Drugs and Crime, "Global Report on Trafficking in Persons," February 2009, at http://www.unodc.org/documents/Global_Report_on_TIP.pdf.
[53]Ibid., p. 57.

and Punish Trafficking in Persons, especially Women and Children, which has been signed by over one hundred countries. The protocol has inspired many countries around the world to pass laws against trafficking in persons, most prominently against sexual exploitation and forced labor. Many countries, however, have no laws against human trafficking, and of the ones that do, 40 percent have not registered a single conviction against perpetrators of trafficking. According to the United Nations, one of the most pressing needs is to develop a global understanding of human trafficking. This would require social scientists in academia and government to generate the logical categories and statistical information needed to formulate an evidence-based antislavery policy and facilitate international information sharing.[54]

Justice for the poor. The linchpin of the prophetic call to do justice is the requirement that God's people care for the poor and needy. "What do you mean by crushing my people and grinding the faces of the poor?" asks the prophet Isaiah (Is 3:15). "It is you who have ruined my vineyard," Isaiah accuses; "the plunder from the poor is in your houses" (Is 3:14). Conversely, that believers "loose the chains of injustice" and care for the poor is a sign of true religion. In the words of the prophet: "Is not this the kind of fasting I have chosen . . . ? Is it not to share your food with the hungry and to provide the poor wanderer with shelter—when you see the naked, to clothe him?" (Is 58:6-7). Jesus made the same point in the book of Matthew when he taught that on the Day of Judgment God will ask what each of us did to help the poor and needy, linking saving faith with acts of justice (Mt 25:31-46). The theological notion that God has special solicitude for the poor, defined broadly as all those who are marginalized in society, has been captured in Catholic social thought as the "preferential option for the poor."

In addition to the admonition to care for the poor by acts of generosity, the Prophets pronounce judgment on those who engage in extortion or deception toward the poor. While robbery and extortion are wrong regardless of the victim, the Prophets' special condemnation is reserved for those who use their power to defraud or extort those who are already weak and vulnerable. The prophet Amos condemns those who

---

[54]For a description of IJM's collaboration with local authorities in particular communities to rescue women and children trapped in brothels and prosecute the traffickers and pimps, see generally Haugen, *Good News About Injustice*, p. 186; Gary A. Haugen with Gregg Hunter, *Terrify No More* (Nashville: W Publishing Group, 2005) (describing IJM's work to end trafficking of children to work in brothels in Svay Pak, Cambodia).

trample the needy
    and do away with the poor of the land,
saying,
"When will the New Moon be over
    that we may sell grain,
and the Sabbath be ended
    that we may market wheat?"—
skimping the measure,
    boosting the price
and cheating with dishonest scales,
    buying the poor with silver
and the needy for a pair of sandals,
    selling even the sweepings with the wheat. (Amos 8:4-6)

All over the world, however, powerful individuals are "buying the poor with silver" through the extortionate practice of bonded labor.[55] Millions of men, women and children are in perpetual slavery to moneylenders. The bondage occurs when, in return for a money advance or credit—usually a very small amount—a person pledges his or her labor or that of a child for an indefinite amount of time. The bondage usually results from some unexpected expense, such as an illness or funeral expenses. Landless households or migrant workers are especially vulnerable to debt bondage as they have no financial reserve to meet unanticipated expenses.

Theoretically, bonded laborers can end their state of servitude by repaying the debt, but in fact this rarely happens. Since bonded debtors are often illiterate and uneducated, they are easy prey for deception by moneylenders. Moreover, the lenders pay low wages, charge usurious interest rates and require that the debt be paid back in a lump sum, which makes it virtually impossible for the debtor to repay the initial loan. In addition, the debt itself often increases because the employer will deduct payments for equipment or tools, food, lodging or mistakes. Sometimes the labor is used to repay only the interest on the loan and nothing ever goes toward the principal. Consequently, debt bondage is often generational. When the parent is no longer able to work, the debt is assumed by the child. In this way, entire families are

---

[55]See generally *The Use of Child Labor in U.S. Agricultural Imports & Forced and Bonded Child Labor*, vol. 2 of *By the Sweat and Toil of Children* (US Department of Labor, Bureau of International Labor Affairs, 1995), at http://www.dol.gov/ilab/media/reports/iclp/sweat2/sweat2.pdf.

trapped in perpetual servitude, and children are deprived of any opportunity to be educated. Child-bonded labor that results from the abduction or sale of children—often by parents seduced by the promise of a better life for their children—is particularly exploitative and abusive.

Forced and bonded child labor can be found in all sectors of the economy: in the carpet industries of India, Pakistan and Nepal; in the gold mines of Peru; in the fishing industries of Indonesia, Sri Lanka, the Philippines, India and Pakistan; in the sex industry in Thailand, India and Cambodia; in domestic service; and in the use of children as camel jockeys in Persian Gulf states. Regardless of the setting, bonded children are subject to sexual abuse, violence, dangerous and unhealthy work conditions, poor nutrition, and terrible living conditions. To cite one representative example of the life of a bonded child:

> Bonded children working in the carpet industries of India, Pakistan, and Nepal may work up to 20 hours per day, seven days a week. They often sleep, eat and work in the same small, damp room, and are sometimes locked in at night. Forced to work in cramped positions for long periods of time in poorly-ventilated sheds filled with wool fluff and dust particles, many of the children suffer from skin ailments, chronic colds, respiratory problems, spine deformities, and weakened eyesight.[56]

The misery is palpable.

There are an estimated twenty-seven million slaves in the world today—more than any other time in history! Tragically, children below the age of eighteen compose 40 to 50 percent of all forced-labor victims. Child slavery, including child bonded labor, is illegal in many of the countries where it is rampant. It exists because either those who practice it are able to evade the law or because governments are unable or unwilling to enforce the law against the perpetrators.[57]

For a less dramatic, but still troubling, example of short-term "slavery" to moneylenders, consider payday lending in the United States. Like bonded labor, payday lending often traps the poor in a cycle of indebtedness that exploits their precarious economic position. The thousands of payday-lending stores spread across America cater to the poor, the unbanked and those who

---

[56]*Use of Child Labor,* p. 5.

[57]For more information on child-bonded labor, see Haugen, *Good News About Injustice,* pp. 56-58; "Small Hands of Slavery: Bonded Child Labor in India," Human Rights Watch Children's Rights Project, September 1996, at http://www.hrw.org/legacy/reports/1996/India3.htm.

can't get a credit card or whose cards are maxed out. Many payday-lending stores are strategically located in distressed neighborhoods, in strip malls and near convenience stores. The stores extend small loans—typically between $100 and $500—which must be paid back in full within approximately two weeks (at the borrower's next paycheck). The vast majority (approximately 85 percent) of payday borrowers take out loans to cover emergency expenses.[58]

Payday lending has some troubling parallels with bonded labor. Each payday loan, which entitles the borrower to the use of the money for two weeks, comes with fees averaging around 16 percent of the total loan amount. This might not sound like much, but if calculated as an annual percentage rate (APR) the average payday loan commands well over 400 percent in interest! Moreover, very few borrowers pay only 16 percent, because most are unable to repay the full amount (plus fees and interest) in two weeks. Thus, the borrower has to take out a second payday loan—with a new fee of 16 percent—in order to pay off the first one. Studies indicate that over two-thirds or more of payday debtors extend their loans at least once, and the average number of "turn overs" annually is nine![59] With each flip, the borrower will find it more difficult to pay off the loan. According to the Center for Responsible Lending, on average, a customer borrowing $300 will repay $800, with $500 going toward fees.[60]

Payday lending is just one example of a larger phenomenon of financial practices that take advantage of the special vulnerabilities of the working poor. This should be of concern to anyone who is committed to pursuing justice. A number of states have passed legislation to ban or regulate payday lending. These efforts have had limited success, however, because payday lenders are masters at finding loopholes or new ways to structure their lending in order to avoid the legal restrictions.

In addition, closing the payday-loan stores will not solve the needs of the poor for occasional short-term loans. There is a crucial need for short-term credit that is available to the poor without entrapping them in extortionate contracts. In one creative solution called Grace Period, a Pittsburgh church

---

[58]"Congress Should Cap Interest Rates," CRL Research Brief (Center for Responsible Lending, March 2009), http://www.responsiblelending.org/payday-lending/policy-legislation/congress/ interest-rate-survey.pdf. All monetary references are in US dollars.

[59]See John P. Caskey, "Payday Lending: New Research and the Big Question," Working Paper No. 10-32 (Federal Reserve Bank of Philadelphia, October 2010) (summarizing research on payday lending).

[60]"Congress Should Cap Interest Rates."

entered into a partnership with a local credit union. The church encouraged its members to open accounts at the credit union, and the church also opened an account with a dedicated amount of its own money. Grace Period operates as a savings cooperative in which borrowers open accounts at the credit union and pay back small loans through payroll deductions. Fees for the loans are eventually reimbursed after the loan is paid off, and the payroll deductions include a savings component so that club members eventually accrue their own rainy-day fund to borrow against. Meanwhile, new club members are constantly being added into the loan pool, and as borrowers pay off their loans, many remain in the club so that their capital becomes available to new borrowers.[61] A smaller, more church-based model is underway in Richmond, Virginia. There the Jubilee Assistance Fund partners with two Methodist churches and a local credit union to make short-term loans available to active church members, with loans backed by collateral provided by church members.[62] In addition, a few credit unions around the country have begun to design loan products to compete with payday loans and create mechanisms for saving.

Another promising way to provide loan assistance for the poor around the world is through the use of microloans to support small-business entrepreneurs in developing countries. Nonprofit organizations such as Micro-Place invite individuals to invest their resources to capitalize small loans aimed at low-income populations. Loans are awarded for such purposes as developing communities, supporting women, promoting fair trade, providing affordable housing, preserving land and water, and promoting health.[63]

Justice and the advocate. We end by saying a bit about the prophetic role as a pattern for legal advocacy. One of the prophets' most important functions was to call attention to the requirements of justice and to condemn injustice where it persisted. Some of the prophets had access to the highest levels of power in Israel, using their influence with kings and religious

---

[61]In the first three years of its existence, Grace Period loaned (through its partnership with the Pittsburgh Central Federal Credit Union) over $1.5 million to over 1,800 individuals. For a more detailed description of this program, see Amy L. Sherman, "No Such Thing as a Free Loan," *Prism Magazine,* March/April 2011, pp. 2-3, reprinted at http://www.sagamoreinstitute.org/library-article/no-such-thing-as-a-free-loan/.

[62]Ibid., p. 3.

[63]Although Micro-Place is not itself a faith-based organization, it funds some faith-based projects in the developing world. Micro-Place reports since 2007 every investor has been repaid. For a description of Micro-Place and its work, see https://www.microplace.com/. Another similar organization is Calvert Foundation; http://www.calvertfoundation.org/.

leaders. Others raised a prophetic voice from outside the halls of power. In either case their role was to challenge the status quo in the service of justice. Lawyers in many parts of the world are in a unique position to act prophetically as advocates for justice.

Although modern lawyers are obviously not prophets in the same sense as the Old Testament prophets, by virtue of their training and role in society, lawyers are often well placed to be change agents for justice. In the United States and some other countries, many judicial, executive and legislative positions are held by lawyers. By education and training, lawyers are problem solvers, powerful advocates and skillful negotiators. For these and other reasons, attorneys in developed countries tend to be relatively powerful individuals and to have special cachet in the public square. Moreover, part of their intrinsic role is to step into contexts where legal rights are in dispute or where a challenge to the status quo is called for. All of this creates the potential for those with legal training to do a huge amount of good in the cause of justice. As legislators they can write and lobby for just laws; as advocates they can defend the cause of the poor and powerless; and as prosecutors and judges they can pursue and adjudicate cases fairly. In addition, lawyers change the law in incremental ways by making legal arguments that pave the way for particular policies or actions by others. More broadly, over time similar arguments in similar cases can move the law in significant ways, for good or for ill. A lawyer who cares about justice must consider whether the cases she accepts and the arguments she chooses to offer in these cases— over the course of her legal career—make the world a more or less just place.

Finally, that lawyers are the natural change agents in a country's legal culture underlines the crucial role lawyer training must play in the cause of justice. In many developing countries lawyers are scarce, poorly trained and inadequately paid. In countries with histories of genocide or exodus by the educated classes, a whole generation of legally trained individuals may have been lost. In such circumstances, it is crucial to support the training of a new generation of attorneys to do the work of justice in their nations.

6

THE KINGDOM OF GOD,
LAW, AND THE HEART

JESUS AND THE CIVIL LAW

Robert F. Cochran Jr. and Dallas Willard

A̶s THE PREVIOUS CHAPTER NOTED, the Hebrew prophets spoke both about future things and about justice. These roles merged in the prophecies of a coming Messiah who would inaugurate a reign of justice. Isaiah said:

> Here is my servant, whom I uphold,
>   my chosen one in whom I delight;
> I will put my Spirit on him
>   and he will bring justice to the nations. . . .
> In faithfulness he will bring forth justice;
>   he will not falter or be discouraged
> till he establishes justice on earth.
>   In his law [Israel will put its[1]] hope. (Is 42:1, 3-4)[2]

The Gospel writer Matthew identified Jesus as the Messiah of this prophecy (Mt 12:18-21).[3]

---

[1]Literally, "in which the islands will put their hope." In the view of many scholars, "islands" here would have been understood to include the coastal regions, including Israel.

[2]Scripture quotations in this chapter are from NIV unless otherwise noted.

[3]Our discussion of Jesus and the law draws most heavily from the Gospel of Matthew. Of the Gospel writers, Matthew, apparently writing primarily to a Jewish audience, gives the most at-

Though Matthew identified Jesus as Isaiah's champion of justice, the Gospel of John contrasted law with Jesus' gifts to humankind: "the law indeed was given through Moses; grace and truth came through Jesus Christ" (Jn 1:17 NRSV). In this chapter, we will explore the ambiguous nature of Jesus' relationship to law suggested in these and other passages.

JESUS' LIFE AND ENCOUNTERS WITH LAW AND LEGAL AUTHORITIES

During Jesus' life, Rome ruled Palestine, but it gave some authority to local Jewish leaders. Jesus encountered both Roman and Jewish legal officials. Most of these encounters were not pleasant.

The location of Jesus' birth was determined by Roman law.[4] Shortly before his birth, Jesus' earthly father, Joseph, and his mother, Mary, traveled from their home in Palestine to Bethlehem because "Caesar Augustus issued a decree that a census should be taken of the entire Roman world. . . . And everyone went to their own town to register" (Lk 2:1, 3). There was no housing available in Bethlehem, so Jesus was born in a stable. Shortly after Jesus' birth, the local king, Herod, heard a rumor that "the king of the Jews" had been born in Bethlehem, and Herod ordered the murder of all the young male children, in hopes that he would kill the would-be usurper. But an angel warned Jesus' parents and they escaped (Mt 2:1-3, 13, 16). We know little about Jesus' childhood, other than that by age twelve he was already conversing at a sophisticated level with Jewish rabbis (Lk 2:42, 46-47).

At age thirty, Jesus became an itinerant preacher, teacher and rabbi, traveling about Palestine, healing people and gathering disciples. He issued a starkly simple, but audacious, call: "Follow me" (Jn 1:43). People were struck by a couple of things about Jesus. He "taught as one who had authority, and not as their teachers of the law" (Mt 7:29; Mk 1:22) and yet he ate and drank with sinners (Mt 9:11; Lk 15:2). Jesus was often condemned by the Jewish law teachers and the Pharisees (a strict, law-abiding Jewish group) for his violations of the then-current interpretations of Jewish law.

Much of Jesus' teaching addressed the Jewish law. John P. Meier notes

---

tention to the Old Testament in general, and to the Mosaic law in particular.
[4]Augustine said, "An unjust law is no law at all" (*Free Will*, 1.1.5). Though we have sympathies with this notion, we will generally use the term *law* as it is commonly used today in the West, to refer merely to the officially implemented commands or decisions of those in authority.

that Jesus "[thought] long and hard about the Mosaic Law and [came] up with some startling and at times unprecedented pronouncements about it."[5] But Jesus was more than a thoughtful rabbi who commented on the law.[6] On occasion, he contrasted his teaching with that of the Mosaic law and its then-current interpretation with the bold phrase, "But I tell you . . ." (see, e.g., Mt 5:22, 28, 32, 34, 39, 44, addressing murder, divorce, oaths, retributive justice and treatment of enemies). Jesus did not merely comment on and draw insight from the law; he announced its true meaning.

Many Jews in Jesus' day hoped for a military and political Messiah who would free them from the rule of the Romans. Jesus rejected that role. Nevertheless, at the instigation of the leading Jewish legal authorities (who did not have the authority to impose the death penalty), the Roman authorities crucified Jesus. To the Jews, Jesus' crime was that he claimed to be God. They reported to the Romans that he was guilty of sedition, that he claimed to be "king of the Jews" (Mt 27:11).

Following Jesus' crucifixion, his followers dispersed in fear. But they soon returned to Jerusalem and preached that Jesus had risen from the dead. They worshiped him as Immanuel ("God with us," Mt 1:23), Messiah

---

[5]John P. Meier, *Law and Love,* vol. 4 of *A Marginal Jew: Rethinking the Historical Jesus* (New York: Doubleday, 2009), p. 527. For example, in Mark 12:29-31, Jesus quotes Deuteronomy 6:4-5 and Leviticus 19:18 and argues that their commands to love God and neighbor are the first and second greatest commandments. Here, he employs an unusual, if not unique at the time, hermeneutical technique, later adopted by Jewish rabbis and called *gĕzērâ šāwâ* (ibid.). This technique allowed a rabbi to use commandments from different books of the Mosaic law for mutual interpretation if both contained the same phrase. The phrase "and you shall love" appears in these passages (two of only four times that it is used in the Jewish Scriptures). In doing so "Jesus shows a remarkable knowledge of the Hebrew text of the Mosaic Torah" (ibid., p. 493). "Anyone can declare himself a charismatic prophet. Getting the *gĕzērâ šāwâ* right requires study" (ibid., p. 575).

Meier and other critical scholars reject the reliability of many of the reports of the Gospel writers. He says, for example, "we find in the Gospels not simply Jesus' interpretation of the Law but, first of all, the four evangelists' reinterpretation of Jesus' interpretation of the Law" (ibid., p. 41). Meier and other critical scholars are likely to see much of our essay as a comment on the early church's views of law, rather than on Jesus' views. In our view, Meier unjustifiably limits what one can know about the historical Jesus. There are many reasons to trust the reports of the Gospel writers. Most of the Gospels were written within forty years of Jesus' death by people who were either his disciples or who carefully interviewed eyewitnesses (see Lk 1:2). In addition, as Meier himself notes, Jesus taught that "one should restrict oneself to simple, direct, and always honest speech" (ibid., p. 198). For Jesus' followers, all statements rose to the level of oaths. It is difficult to imagine that, with this as one of Jesus' central moral teachings, his followers, for their own purposes, would intentionally put words into Jesus' mouth. They would be likely to revere and take special care with the words of their Lord and Savior.

[6]William R. G. Loader, *Jesus' Attitude Towards the Law: A Study of the Gospels* (Grand Rapids: Eerdmans, 2002), p. 267.

(the savior who came to free humans from our sins and give us a meaningful life, Mt 16:16), and Lord (1 Cor 12:3).

JUSTICE AND THE MESSIAH

As noted above, Matthew identified Jesus as the Messiah who Isaiah had
said would "bring forth justice." In his first reported sermon, Jesus, also
quoting Isaiah, identified himself as the one anointed "to preach good
news to the poor," "to proclaim release to the captives," "to let the oppressed go free" and "to proclaim the year of the Lord's favor" (Lk 4:17-21
NRSV, quoting Is 61:1-2). On another occasion, Jesus exclaimed, "Will
not God bring about justice for his chosen ones, who cry out to him day
and night? Will he keep putting them off? I tell you, he will see that they
get justice, and quickly" (Lk 18:7-8).

As Nicholas Wolterstorff notes, justice may have been an even more
important theme of Jesus' teaching than is generally realized.[7] A Greek
word in Jesus' teaching, *dikaiosynē*, rendered "righteousness" in many
English translations, could also be translated "justice" (as translators do
in English versions of Plato's *Republic*).[8] Consider the difference in
meaning of two of Jesus' well-known beatitudes if *dikaiosynē* is translated
"justice" rather than "righteousness":

---

[7]Nicholas Wolterstorff, *Justice: Rights and Wrongs* (Princeton, NJ: Princeton University Press, 2008), pp. 111-12.

[8]The Septuagint, a second- and third-century B.C. Greek translation of the Old Testament, shows that "in the linguistic circles of the New Testament writers, *dikaiosynē* did not clearly refer to ei-ther [justice or righteousness], but was ambiguous as between the two" (ibid., p. 112). If so, the proper translation should be determined based on the context. Wolterstorff suggests that it is especially likely that "justice" is the better translation in the second beatitude quoted in the text:

> Apparently, the translators [of the most common English translations] were not struck by the oddity of someone being persecuted because he is righteous. My own reading of human affairs is that righteous people are either admired or ignored, not persecuted; people who pursue justice are the ones who get in trouble. (ibid., p. 111)

It may be that *dikaiosynē* is a richer word than any English equivalent, referring to both an inner goodness and a just society. Plato in his *Republic* taught that *dikaiosynē* is not only a public qual-ity of a city that treats its citizens appropriately but also an inner quality of a really good person.

The unstated, traditional assumption in Wolterstorff's discussion of the beatitudes is that they identify qualities that are worthy of reward. One of us has argued, however, that the beati-tudes identify qualities that would have been seen as negative within that culture and that the primary message of the beatitudes is that the kingdom of God is open to all. The poor and those who mourn are blessed—a big surprise to everyone in that culture. See Dallas Willard, *The Di-vine Conspiracy: Rediscovering Our Hidden Life in God* (San Francisco: HarperSanFrancisco, 1998), pp. 114-19.

> Blessed are those who hunger and thirst for [justice],
>> for they will be filled. (Mt 5:6)

> Blessed are those who are persecuted because of [justice],
>> for theirs is the kingdom of heaven. (Mt 5:10)

Whatever the proper translation of *dikaiosynē* in the New Testament, "Jesus is identified as inaugurating the reign of justice."[9] When his followers pursue justice, they follow his call.

THE KINGDOM OF GOD, LAW AND THE HEART

Though law was important in Jesus' teaching, it was not his most important concern. The primary focus of his teaching was the condition of the heart. First, we will address Jesus' terminology.

***Jesus' use of the term* law.** Jesus used the term *law* to refer to different types of law. In many situations, we must look to the context to determine to which type he refers. At times Jesus referred to God's eternal moral law—God's intention for human life and action. This is the law that God promised through the prophet Jeremiah to place in the believer's mind and heart:

> I will put my law in their minds
>> and write it on their hearts. (Jer 31:33)

At other times, Jesus referred to the civil law—the positive law—the rules and practices of those in human authority. God's moral law may or may not be reflected in the civil law. In Jesus' discussion of divorce, he contrasted the civil law with God's moral law. "Moses permitted you to divorce your wives because your hearts were hard [the civil law]. But it was not this way from the beginning" (Mt 19:8). God intended that husband and wife be "no longer two, but one flesh. Therefore what God has joined together, let no one separate [God's moral law]" (Mt 19:6 NRSV). We return to the distinction between civil law and God's moral law in the following section "Law, Love and Character."

Jesus encountered three types of civil law: Roman law, the Mosaic law as originally given by Moses, and the Mosaic law as expanded and interpreted by the Jewish tradition of Jesus' day. At various times, Jesus defied, obeyed, criticized, praised, reinterpreted and affirmed the civil law; he invariably

---

[9]Wolterstorff, *Justice*, p. 107.

obeyed and praised God's law. The major concern of this essay is the implications of Jesus' teaching for the civil law.

Law and the heart in God's kingdom. The focus of Jesus' preaching was "the good news of the kingdom" (Mt 4:23; Mk 1:15; Lk 4:43). This kingdom's availability was inaugurated with Jesus' ministry.[10] "The kingdom of God is in your midst" (Lk 17:20-21; see also Mt 11:12). It was what C. H. Dodd describes as "realized eschatology."[11] But Jesus also spoke of a future manifestation of the kingdom. "Truly I tell you, I will not drink again from the fruit of the vine until that day when I drink it anew in the kingdom of God" (Mk 14:25).[12] Jesus' kingdom was both the present and future kingdom.

Jesus' most thorough teaching about the nature of the kingdom of God came in his Sermon on the Mount. He taught that the kingdom is primarily about a change in the heart and will, rather than outward conformity to law. He contrasted the Jewish legal code with his heart-based kingdom. The Jewish law prohibited murder, but Jesus called the citizens of this new kingdom not to even be angry (Mt 5:21-22). The Jewish law prohibited adultery, but Jesus called the citizens of this new kingdom not to even indulge in cultivated lusting (Mt 5:27-28). The Jewish law required oaths in some contexts, but Jesus prohibited oaths and taught that his followers' word should be binding in all contexts (Mt 5:33-37). The Jewish law imposed reciprocal penalties, "eye for eye, and tooth for tooth" (Ex 21:24; Lev 24:20; Deut 19:21), but Jesus called the citizens of his new kingdom not to respond to violence in kind and to love their enemies (Mt 5:43-48). Compliance with these startling, seemingly impossible commands required (and requires) a change in heart.

The citizens of the new kingdom would go beyond the requirements of Roman law as well. The Roman law required Jews to carry the packs of Roman soldiers a mile. The citizens of this new kingdom would carry them two miles (Mt 5:40). If someone sued them for their coat, they would give them their cloak as well (Mt 5:41).

Jesus' kingdom was designed to generate a far more radical change than human law could bring. The commitment to follow him would yield a trans-

---

[10]Willard, *Divine Conspiracy.*
[11]C. H. Dodd, *The Parables of the Kingdom,* rev. ed. (New York: Charles Scribner's Sons, 1961).
[12]See Rudolf Bultmann, *Jesus and the Word,* trans. Louise Pettibone Smith and Erminie Huntress Lantero (New York: Charles Scribner's Sons, 1958); and Richard A. Horsley, *Jesus and the Spiral of Violence: Popular Jewish Resistance in Roman Palestine* (Minneapolis: Fortress, 1993).

formed heart. This change of heart would cause someone to want to do the good, in most cases automatically to do the good. "A good [person] brings good things out of the good stored up in his heart" (Lk 6:45). On the other hand, evil comes from the evil heart. "It is from within, out of a person's heart, that evil thoughts come—sexual immorality, theft, murder, adultery, greed, malice, deceit, lewdness, envy, slander, arrogance and folly" (Mk 7:20-22).

Though Jesus' emphasis on the heart stood in marked contrast to the common Jewish teaching of the day, in fact it recaptured a theme that was prominent in the Jewish Scriptures. Israel was to love God "with all your heart" (Deut 6:5). When David committed adultery and murder, he prayed "create in me a pure heart" (Ps 51:10). Through Isaiah, God said, "[The people's] hearts are far from me. Their worship of me is based on merely human rules they have been taught" (Is 29:13). At one point Jesus quoted this last verse to some Jewish law teachers and said, "You have let go of the commands of God and are holding on to human traditions" (Mk 7:8).

The transformed heart can do much for law. Those with transformed hearts will be far more likely to comply with most aspects of law than those who do not have such a heart. They will go beyond the requirements of law. Following the change in heart called for by Jesus, disciples of Jesus can be left free to do what they want to do. Moreover, a changed heart will lead one to be greatly concerned with justice, and thus with law. Justice alone will never do justice to justice, but a heart of love will promote and require justice (and much more).

Jesus' teaching about the heart is a check on his modern followers who might want a political or military kingdom. Christians must keep their priorities in order. God's kingdom may have implications for law, law may further kingdom values, but the kingdom does not come through law. Indeed, in his kingdom, there is likely to be far less need for law. Moreover, law can have little influence on the heart. The transformation of the heart, like other components of following Christ, cannot be coerced.

Is Jesus pro- or antilaw? The Gospels give substantial attention to Jesus' violations of the Jewish law and his arguments with Jewish legal authorities. Was Jesus antilaw? A careful look at Jesus' references to law reveals that he unswervingly affirmed God's moral law and took a mixed approach to the civil law.

Jesus was often critical of the Jewish law of his day. In some respects it did too little—law, by its very nature, can have only a limited effect on the heart. In other respects it did (or tried to do) too much—it had grown so large and complex that it was very difficult for anyone to comply with it. To the law teachers, he said: "You load people down with burdens they can hardly carry" (Lk 11:46). Law had evolved in ways that overlooked the original purpose of law—to serve people.

Jesus, like the prophets before him, often contrasted the Jewish legal practices of his day with God's deeper and more important moral law.

> Woe to you, teachers of the law and Pharisees, you hypocrites! You give a tenth of your spices—mint, dill and cumin. But you have neglected the more important matters of the law—justice, mercy and faithfulness. You should have practiced the latter, without neglecting the former. You blind guides! You strain out a gnat but swallow a camel. (Mt 23:23-24)

Concern with the minutiae of law can lead one to overlook the heart of law—justice, mercy and faithfulness. (We often find this misplacement of priorities today in government administrative offices.)

Given some of Jesus' teaching and actions, some in his day appeared to think he had come to abolish the law. Jesus answered that concern in the Sermon on the Mount.

> Do not think that I have come to abolish the Law or the Prophets; I have not come to abolish them but to fulfill them. For truly I tell you, until heaven and earth disappear, not the smallest letter, not the least stroke of a pen, will by any means disappear from the Law until everything is accomplished. Therefore anyone who sets aside one of the least of these commands and teaches others accordingly will be called least in the kingdom of heaven, but whoever practices and teaches these commands will be called great in the kingdom of heaven. For I tell you that unless your righteousness surpasses that of the Pharisees and the teachers of the law, you will certainly not enter the kingdom of heaven. (Mt 5:17-20)[13]

This section raises three questions (at least). First, what does it mean that Jesus "fulfilled" the law? In our view, Augustine was correct to identify two meanings. Jesus fulfilled God's moral law by obeying all of its require-ments.[14] As we have noted, Jesus disobeyed the law as interpreted by the

---

[13]For additional discussion of Matthew 5:17-20 in this volume, see "Jesus fulfilled the Law and Prophets" in chapter five.

[14]Augustine, *Sermon on the Mount*, 1.8.

Jewish law teachers of his day. For Jesus to say that he obeyed all the law's requirements, then, implied that their interpretation was wrong. He obeyed God's law, not their defective human law.

Jesus also fulfilled the law by adding to the Mosaic law what it lacked. As Oliver O'Donovan has put it, Jesus presented "an advance upon both the oral interpretations and the bare text."[15] Jesus gave us a fuller understanding of God's moral law. We have seen that Jesus adds to the law by explaining its relationship with the heart. In the section "Trials in Acts," we will explore other ways that his teaching may have added to the Mosaic law what it lacked. Finally, Jesus fulfilled the law by enabling people to obey it.

A second question arising from this section is: what does it mean that "not the smallest letter, not the least stroke of a pen, will . . . disappear from the Law"? Initially, Jesus' teaching here seems to be inconsistent with other parts of his teaching, which emphasize the importance of the heart, rather than obedience to the letter of the law. In our view, Jesus' affirmation here is best understood as affirming the details of God's moral law. "Not the smallest letter, not the least stroke of a pen, will by any means disappear from [God's moral] Law."

Alternatively, Jesus may have been using irony, possibly making a play on phrases that were used by the strictest of the Jews. Jesus may have been saying, with calculated sarcasm, "I am more legalistic than the legalists, for I teach the deeper meaning of the law—the transformation of the heart."

Finally, what does it mean that his followers' righteousness must "surpass[] that of the Pharisees and the teachers of the law"? This brings us back to the central message of the Sermon on the Mount: true righteousness requires a changed heart living interactively with God, not obedience to rules. Jesus recognized the continuing validity of God's moral law, while being critical of what the Jewish teachers had done with the Mosaic law.

Though Jesus was critical of many aspects of the Jewish law, in general, he obeyed it, even its technical requirements. He instructed those he had healed to comply with the law. "Go, show yourself to the priest and offer the sacrifices that Moses commanded" (Mk 1:44). Indeed, William Loader notes that the "most striking feature of Luke's presentation, both in the gospel and in Acts, is that there is an underlying assumption that both Jesus and those

---

[15]Oliver O'Donovan, *The Desire of the Nations: Rediscovering the Roots of Political Theology* (New York: Cambridge University Press, 1996), p. 109.

who surround him or later follow him are faithful to [the details of] Torah."[16]

In addition, Jesus suggested that people needed to be instructed both about the law *and* the kingdom of God. "Every teacher of the law who has become a disciple in the kingdom of heaven is like the owner of a house who brings out of his storeroom new treasures as well as old" (Mt 13:52). Law is valuable, but it needs to be understood in light of the teaching of the kingdom of God that the condition of the heart is primary. Jesus changed the Mosaic law in some respects (e.g., Mt 5:33-37 [oaths] and Mk 7:19 [dietary laws]), but generally, his teaching about the law concerned the interpretation of the law, rather than whether one should obey it. Jesus presumed that the law, rightly understood, should be obeyed.

As we note in the introduction to this chapter, John contrasts the Mosaic law with Jesus' message and purpose. "The law was given through Moses; grace and truth came through Jesus Christ" (Jn 1:17). But as Loader notes:

> John's account of Jesus' attitude towards the Law assumes the Law as God's gift
> to Israel through Moses. It is appropriate to a level of reality which is both inferior and preliminary to the realm of the Spirit opened by Jesus. It nevertheless
> pointed towards it and through its institutions to some degree prefigured it.[17]

Nevertheless, Jesus' most striking response to law in his culture was to challenge it as a distorted expression of God's moral law and of life in God's kingdom. His was a legalistic culture, where law had forgotten its purpose, where law served itself and its experts, rather than people.

Jesus' response to modern culture might be more mixed.[18] Indeed, in our view, Jesus presented a balance regarding the importance of law that is sorely lacking in American legal culture. Today, he would probably condemn the overly regulated areas of the modern legal system. A striking example is the New York City housing regulation that rejected a homeless shelter operated by Mother Teresa's Missionaries of Charity because it did not have an elevator.[19] Some areas of Western life are so heavily regulated that people are prohibited from taking actions that would assist human flourishing. Law

---

[16]William R. G. Loader, *Jesus' Attitude Towards the Law: A Study of the Gospels* (Grand Rapids: Eerdmans, 2002), p. 379.

[17]Loader, *Jesus' Attitude Towards the Law*, p. 490.

[18]He might be more like Paul, who challenged Christians who participated in the permissive practices of Greece and Rome. See 1 Corinthians 5-7.

[19]Phillip K. Howard, *The Death of Common Sense: How Law Is Suffocating America* (New York: Warner Books, 1994), pp. 3-5.

still, at times, "strain[s] out a gnat," while "swallow[ing] a camel" (Mt 23:24).

But as to some areas of modern life, we believe Jesus would present a very different message. In some areas the lack of law yields great injustice. As O'Donovan notes:

> It is a Western conceit to imagine that all political problems arise from the abuse or over-concentration of power; and that is why we are so bad at understanding political difficulties which have arisen from a lack of power, or from its excessive diffusion.[20]

A visit to countries that have no operative legal system (Somalia is an example at the time we write) is likely to convince anyone of the importance of law.

The most common subject of controversy between Jesus and the law teachers of his day concerned the sabbath. Whereas Jesus encountered those who had a legalistically rigid view of the sabbath, that is not the problem in our largely antinomian era. Today, the sabbath and its underlying principles are completely ignored by personally driven workaholics (to their and their families' great detriment), as well as owners of Asian sweatshops, worldwide cruise lines, and elite American law and accounting firms. Modern workweek-limitation statutes share some of the humane objectives of God's original sabbath. As we note below, the sabbath was rooted in creation and it "was made for man" (Mk 2:27).[21] Law should serve human good. It can miss that objective when it is either so consumed with details that it loses sight of people or so weak that it fails to protect them.

A place for civil law in the kingdom? Some Christians believe that there is no place for Christian support of civil law because of the coercion that is an inherent part of it. The foremost proponents of this view have been Anabaptists.

> The sword is ordained by God outside the perfection of Christ. It punishes and kills evil people and protects and defends the good. In the law the sword is established to punish and to kill the wicked, and secular authorities are established to use it. But in the perfection of Christ the ban [excommunication] alone will be used to admonish.[22]

---

[20]O'Donovan, *Desire of the Nations,* p. 94.

[21]See the section "Lawmaking as an act of love." For additional discussion of the sabbath in this volume, see also chapter three.

[22]Michael Sattler, "*The Schleitheim Articles:* The Brotherly Agreement of Some Children of God Concerning Seven Articles," in *The Radical Reformation,* ed. Michael G. Baylor (Cambridge: Cambridge University Press, 1991), pp. 176-77.

The belief that Christians may not use force, a necessary element of government, leads Anabaptists to separate themselves from coercive political and legal culture. Nevertheless, there is a place for Anabaptist influence in the world. They are to influence the world by modeling the teachings of Christ. Modern proponents of this view, Stanley Hauerwas and William Willimon, argue that "the political task of Christians is to be the church rather than to transform the world."[23]

Anabaptists find support for their position in Jesus' rejection of political power. Following Jesus' arrest, when asked by Pilate whether he was the king of the Jews, Jesus said, "My kingdom is not of this world. If it were, my servants would fight to prevent my arrest by the Jewish leaders. But now my kingdom is from another place" (Jn 18:36). Anabaptists argue that Christians should reject governmental authority as Christ did.[24]

We agree that Jesus should be our model in everything we do, but in our view, the question should be, What would Jesus do if he were me? Jesus rejected political power, but he also rejected a lot of other options. During his time as a rabbi, he was not a farmer, businessman or lawyer. We cannot all follow his vocation. The fact that Jesus did not exercise political or legal power should not keep Christians from doing so, so long as they can do so consistent with his moral teaching. That, of course, is the key question. We will return to it.

Other Christians, including Martin Luther, have agreed with Anabaptists that the rules of Jesus' kingdom are inconsistent with the rules of this world's kingdoms. They believe that the kingdoms of this world cannot operate on Jesus' rules, but they argue that government service can be an appropriate manifestation of love. Political and military service are "necessary to the common life, and [are] therefore spheres in which the neighbor could be served and God be obeyed."[25] However, in his "Sermon on 'The Sermon on the Mount,'" Luther says, "Do you want to know what your duty is as a prince or judge or a lord or a lady, with people under you? You do not have

---

[23]Stanley Hauerwas and William H. Willimon, *Resident Aliens: Life in the Christian Colony* (Nashville: Abingdon, 1989), p. 38.

[24]See Sattler, *"Schleitheim Articles,"* p. 177, citing John 6:15, in which a crowd sought to make Jesus king by force, but he withdrew.

[25]H. Richard Niebuhr, *Christ and Culture* (San Francisco: HarperSanFrancisco, 2001), pp. 156-57, summarizing Luther's view.

to ask Christ about your duty. Ask the imperial or the territorial law."[26]

Some find support for the separation of Jesus' teaching from the governmental realm in one of Jesus' exchanges:

> Some . . . Pharisees and Herodians [sought] to catch [Jesus] in his words. . . . [They asked:] "Is it right to pay the imperial tax to Caesar or not? Should we pay or shouldn't we?"
>
> But Jesus knew their hypocrisy. "Why are you trying to trap me?" he asked. "Bring me a denarius and let me look at it." They brought the coin, and he asked them, "Whose portrait is this? And whose inscription?"
>
> "Caesar's," they replied.
>
> Then Jesus said to them, "Give to Caesar what is Caesar's and to God what is God's."
>
> And they were amazed at him. (Mk 12:13-17)

In our view, this is a story of Jesus' cleverness, rather than a story from which an important theological truth about Jesus and the state can be drawn. Matthew set the story up that way. Jesus' inquisitors asked a question that was designed to trap Jesus. If he answered that the Jews should pay taxes, he would get into trouble with the rebellious elements of Judaism. If he answered that the Jews should not pay taxes, he would get into trouble with the Romans. "But Jesus knew their hypocrisy." His answer merely begged the question of what is due to Caesar. As O'Donovan notes, "'Render to Caesar . . .' was not a means of Jesus acknowledging a twofold authority. The crowds admired his clever answer—he did not deny [his inquisitors'] claim, but brushed it aside."[27]

Though we disagree with Luther's view that Jesus' teachings have no implications for government, we share his view that some portions of Jesus' teachings were meant to address Christians in their individual capacity, not in a governing capacity. Turning the other cheek (Mt 5:39) is difficult for an individual Christian; it would be impossible for a government. But as we noted earlier, justice was an important theme in Jesus' teaching. Short of a universal change of heart, law and its required coercion are necessary means to obtain justice. The development and enforcement of just laws are

---

[26]Martin Luther, "Sermon on 'The Sermon on the Mount,'" in *From Irenaeus to Grotius: A Sourcebook in Christian Political Thought, 100–1625*, ed. Oliver O'Donovan and Joan Lockwood O'Donovan (Grand Rapids: Eerdmans, 1999), p. 599.

[27]O'Donovan, *Desire of the Nations*, p. 93.

significant means whereby Christians can show love to their neighbors. As Paul teaches, God appoints governing officials as servants for human good, agents of God to bring punishment on wrongdoers (Rom 13:1-5).[28] In our view, Jesus' followers properly seek to bring about justice through law.

Jesus taught Christians to pray "Your kingdom come, your will be done, on earth as it is in heaven" (Mt 6:10). He encouraged us to: "Seek first his kingdom and his righteousness [or justice!]" (Mt 6:33).[29] Though Jesus taught that the primary method of bringing in his kingdom is through changes in the heart, we believe that just laws are a part of that kingdom. The change of a person's heart is not merely a private event, as is so often thought, but has a vast range of insuppressible implications for life, including life as a citizen. God's kingdom has come to the extent that his will is done on earth. God is a God of justice, and—though not as important as changes to the human heart—adoption and enforcement of fair laws are means whereby his will is accomplished.

The character of those who administer law is profoundly important for how law is practiced and received, and its effects. A cruel or irrational judge, prosecutor or policeman can have a devastating effect upon public and private well-being and righteousness. Who better than a person living with Christ in Christ's kingdom to administer law in a just manner? As Augustine argues: "[The rule of Christians] is beneficial, not so much for themselves as for their subjects."[30] As we argue in the following section, unlike Luther we believe that Jesus' teachings have much to teach governing officials about how government power should be exercised.

LAW AS A MEANS OF LOVING ONE'S NEIGHBOR

Jesus enjoined his followers to love broadly. They were to love neighbors, Samaritans and enemies. Jesus placed love at the center of the law. Love of God and neighbor are the first and second greatest commandments (Mk 12:28-34). Indeed, they are the framework on which all of the law hangs (Mt 22:35-40). "In everything, do to others what you would have them do to you, for this sums up the Law and the Prophets" (Mt 7:12). As Calvin put it, the

---

[28]For additional discussion of Romans 13 in this volume, see "Christians and the Civil State in the New Testament" in chaper seven and "The State, Law and Empire" in chapter eight.

[29]See also Luke 12:31.

[30]Augustine, *The City of God,* trans. Gerard G. Walsh et. al. (New York: Doubleday, 1958), 4.3, p. 88.

purpose of the Mosaic civil law was "to preserve that very love which is enjoined by God's eternal law."[31] "Every nation is left free to make such laws as it foresees to be profitable to itself. Yet these must be in conformity to that perpetual rule of love."[32] Love can be reflected in laws as dramatic as those prohibiting murder and those ensuring that criminal defendants have fair trials to laws as seemingly mundane as those prohibiting drivers from double parking.

Lawmaking as an act of love: law was made for humans, not humans for law. Lawmaking itself can be an act of love toward the neighbor. Jack Sammons suggests this possibility in his discussion of the story of the Good Samaritan.[33] Jesus, in conversation with an expert in the law, established that the greatest commandments are that we are to love God and to love our neighbor. The expert in the law, "want[ing] to justify himself," asked Jesus: "Who is my neighbor?" (Lk 10:29). Jesus responded with the story of the Good Samaritan, in which the hated Samaritan served as the role model, caring for the needs of a man, presumably a Jew, who had been beaten and robbed.

Without diminishing the importance of the Samaritan's individual acts of care, we should recognize that those who develop laws can also serve humankind through legislation. Legislation might deal "with the underlying problems of the dangerousness of passage to Jericho, or the need for medical care to travelers in distress, or, for that matter, the hardhearted financial shrewdness of innkeepers."[34] The development and enforcement of wise laws can be among the most loving acts in which a person can engage.

On another occasion, Jesus made it clear that the purpose of law is to serve people. Some Jewish legal officials criticized Jesus' disciples for picking grain on the sabbath. Jesus said: "The Sabbath was made for man, not man for the Sabbath" (Mk 2:27). Note that Jesus grounded the sabbath in creation, rather than the Mosaic law. God *created* it for man. In addition, as Loader says, Jesus "sees the sabbath as more gift than command."[35] Moreover, in contrast to the dominant rabbinic teaching that the sabbath

---

[31]John Calvin, *Institutes of the Christian Religion,* in *John Calvin: Selections from His Writings,* ed. John Dillenberger (New York: HarperCollins, 2001), 4.20.15, p. 490.
[32]Ibid.
[33]Jack L. Sammons, "Parables and Pedagogy," in *Gladly Learn, Gladly Teach: Living Out One's Calling in the 21st-Century Academy,* ed. John Marson Dunaway (Macon, GA: Mercer University Press, 2005), p. 46.
[34]Ibid., p. 53.
[35]Loader, *Jesus' Attitude Towards the Law,* p. 130.

was made for the Jews, Jesus taught that the sabbath was made *for all of humanity.*[36] Implicit in this teaching is the notion that all law was made for humankind. Human law has instrumental value; it is not an ultimate value. Law should be evaluated based on its impact on human lives.

Jesus was particularly harsh with those who criticized him and his disciples for failure to abide by ceremonial laws but failed to care for their elderly parents (Mk 7:1-13). He criticized the teachers of the law who meticulously tithed their mint, dill and cumin but "neglected the more important matters of the law—justice, mercy and faithfulness" (Mt 23:23). Note that these "more important matters of the law" all have to do with humans flourishing. Justice, mercy and faithfulness should be the focus of law.

Law and poor people. As we have seen throughout this volume, the Old Testament identified the most vulnerable of society—the poor, the widow, the orphan and the alien—as special objects of God's love.[37] Jesus shared this compassion. In his inaugural sermon, quoting Isaiah, Jesus identified himself as having come "to proclaim good news to the poor, . . . to proclaim freedom for the prisoners and . . . to set the oppressed free" (Lk 4:18-19, quoting Is 61:1-2; see also Mt 12:15-21). Jesus' "radical concern for people in need" is reflected in his teaching on law.[38]

Jesus' call to care for those in need is challenging to the individual. It is also challenging to those who are concerned with law. At times, we have been in classes or other gatherings in which we have discussed the nineteenth-century fight against slavery and the slave trade, led in England largely by William Wilberforce, the Clapham Circle and other Christians. This was followed by the fight against slavery in the United States and the American Civil War. People ask how previous generations could have allowed something so obviously wrong as slavery. The answer is probably a combination of both lack of moral insight and lack of economic insight. The discipline of economics was in its early development. The abolition of slavery required the development of new economic structures.[39] But many in slave-holding generations did not even recognize that there was a problem.

---

[36]See Meier, *Law and Love*, pp. 281-83.
[37]For additional discussion in this volume, see "The message of the Prophets" in chapter five.
[38]Loader, *Jesus' Attitude Towards the Law*, p. 130, commenting on Mark's Gospel. Loader also notes that "Much of Jesus' distinctive Torah interpretation in Matthew reflects the value of compassion for the needy" (ibid., p. 265).
[39]O'Donovan, *Desire of the Nations*.

In such discussions, after a bit of self-righteous criticism of slave-holding generations, the question arises whether there are aspects of modern society on which generations two hundred years from now will look back, shake their heads and wonder how we could have been so blind. We suspect that the persistence of world poverty may be such an issue. Many innocent people in the world, including many children, live on the edge of starvation. We suspect that Jesus would lament the persistence of poverty and applaud attempts to develop laws that alleviate it.

Poverty is, of course, a complex problem. We witnessed the heady days of the Great Society in America in the 1960s, when many expected that doing away with poverty was just around the corner. In that same era, many Christians applauded the work of Tanzania's idealistic Christian philosopher/president Julius Nyerere, who sought to implement Christian socialism.[40] The results of both efforts were deeply disappointing. Many attempts to alleviate poverty have been counterproductive, generating dependence, undercutting the generation of wealth and damaging the family (one of the institutions that does the best job of combating poverty).

As we have noted, Jesus' primary concern was with the heart. One of the firstfruits of hearts changed by Jesus will be a deep concern for the poor. Here, as in many areas, Jesus did not provide easy answers. We suspect that he would affirm the Catholic teaching that laws (and all actions) should be evaluated first based on their impact on the poor. This change of heart will manifest itself in the work of economists, entrepreneurs, social workers and, yes, those who write and enforce laws, crafting means both to care for the poor and to enable them to develop skills and disciplines that will equip them to flourish and contribute to the common good.

Legal administration as an act of love: legal officials are made for man, not man for legal officials. As Gary Haugen and Victor Boutros have noted, many of the greatest injustices to which poor people in developing countries are subjected are not a result of the content of their countries' laws.[41] Their laws prohibit slavery, extortion, land grabbing, human trafficking, child labor and prostitution, but no one enforces these laws. The law on the

[40]Martin Meredith, *The State of Africa: A History of Fifty Years of Independence* (New York: Free Press, 2005), pp. 249-74.
[41]Gary Haugen and Victor Boutros, "And Justice for All: Enforcing Human Rights for the World's Poor," *Foreign Affairs* 89 (May/June 2010): 51-62.

books is different from the law on the street. Government corruption is at the root of much of this problem; only those who can pay get justice. Police, prosecutors, court personnel and judges—those who are supposed to protect poor people—take advantage of them.

Jesus suggested that law administration, as well as lawmaking, can be an exercise of love. On one occasion, Jesus' disciples and the mother of two of his disciples were verbally jockeying for position in Jesus' future kingdom. Jesus gave them a challenging picture of leadership.

> You know that the rulers of the Gentiles lord it over them, and their high officials exercise authority over them. Not so with you. Instead, whoever wants to become great among you must be your servant, and whoever wants to be first must be your slave—just as the Son of Man did not come to be served, but to serve, and to give his life as a ransom for many. (Mt 20:25-28; see also Lk 22:24-30)

Jesus criticized a familiar characteristic of political leaders—they "lord it over" the people who are subject to their control—they push them around. Law is, of course, a common means that leaders use to push people around. Jesus' criticism of Gentile leaders suggested that leaders, as well as laws, should serve people. He set a high standard for leaders, holding up his own sacrifice as a model.

On another occasion, Jesus provided a similar challenge to legal experts. "And you experts in the law, woe to you, because you load people down with burdens they can hardly carry, and you yourselves will not lift one finger to help them" (Lk 11:46). Good leaders will help people comply with law, not merely wait around to catch them when they fail. Good leaders will teach, interpret and give direction.

Legal administration, as well as lawmaking, can be a means of loving people. Those who enforce and administer the law, from a country's president to the clerk at the Division of Motor Vehicles, have an enormous impact on people's lives. Jesus' model is that of servant/leader.

Law, love and character. Jeffrie Murphy advocates organizing law around the value of Christian love.[42] But he notes that Christian love is not

[42]Jeffrie G. Murphy, "Christian Love and Criminal Punishment," in *Christianity and Law: An Introduction,* ed. John Witte Jr. and Frank S. Alexander (New York: Cambridge University Press, 2008), p. 219.

cuddly. It seeks the best for people and is not simply concerned with making their lives more pleasant. If Christian love is our aim, we will "design legal practices and institutions with a view to the moral and spiritual improvement in virtue of affected citizens."[43] Law, from regulations governing pornography to the treatment of those in prison, will be concerned with citizens' character.

Character is largely what one does without thinking. Most often our character determines what we do. Law creates habits, good and bad, and these habits can become virtues and vices—good and bad moral habits. Young people can be formed by law, especially when they see law as good, sensibly exemplified in elders. The ancients and the entire biblical tradition sought the goodness of the lawgivers, a concept that is foreign today. Law can and must reinforce the practices of the good.

Law can even be a means of teaching citizens to love one another. The Mosaic law *required* Jews to show love toward their neighbors. It required farmers to allow poor people to take the crops at the edges of the farmers' fields (Lev 23:22), thereby, hopefully, teaching them to love poor people and to be generous. Just as parents teach their children to love each other by requiring them to go through the motions of forgiving and sharing, it may be that laws requiring citizens to behave well toward one another, appropriately implemented, will teach them to love their neighbors.

But there is a significant limit to what law can do to influence character. Further development of character requires the exercise of free choice. Too much law gives little room for character to operate and develop. Morality is primarily an internal matter—choosing the right thing for the right reason. Nevertheless, law can slow people down, limit their passions' control and enable them to appreciate the good.[44] Enhancing freedom that is consistent with justice should be a primary goal of law. Wise laws will work themselves out of a job, building character and creating the possibility for citizens to exercise greater freedom.

The good and evil in us all. Jesus taught another lesson, by both his actions and his words. As we noted earlier, one of the primary things people noticed about Jesus was that he ate and drank with sinners. He crit-

---

[43]Ibid., p. 224.
[44]Robert P. George, *Making Men Moral: Civil Liberties and Public Morality* (New York: Oxford University Press, 1995), p. 25, commenting on Aristotle's thought.

icized the "good people"—the Pharisees and law teachers—and welcomed as friends the outsiders—sinners, prostitutes and tax collectors. Jesus did not recognize a comfortable distinction between the bad people and the rest of us. The rewards to the self-righteous were merely the ego trips they enjoyed—"they have received their reward" (Mt 6:5, 16); Jesus befriended and forgave repentant tax collectors and prostitutes.

Jesus not only loved and forgave "the bad people," he taught that his followers are to do the same; they are to love their enemies and forgive those who wrong them (Mt 5:38-48; 18:21-22). Miroslav Volf, who experienced the ethnic violence of late-twentieth-century Bosnia, sees a tie between forgiveness and the recognition of the evil and the good in us all:

> Forgiveness flounders because I exclude the enemy from the community of humans even as I exclude myself from the community of sinners. But no one can be in the presence of the God of the crucified Messiah for long without overcoming this double exclusion—without transposing the enemy from the sphere of monstrous inhumanity into the sphere of shared humanity and herself from the sphere of proud innocence into the sphere of common sinfulness. When one knows that the torturer will not eternally triumph over the victim, one is free to rediscover that person's humanity and imitate God's love for him. And when one knows that God's love is greater than all sin, one is free to see oneself in the light of God's justice and so rediscover one's own sinfulness.[45]

This recognition should affect our treatment of people who are charged with and convicted of crime. As Jeffrie Murphy notes, Christian love "does not forbid punishment. What it forbids is *punishment out of hatred or other vindictive passions.*"[46] Jesus' love can be contrasted with the indifference, hatred and cruelty that often underlie criminal punishment. Jesus would, no doubt, be distressed at countries that lock up so many of their citizens, hide them away and expose them to inhumane conditions.

Injustice, love and forgiveness: personal and social implications. Jesus calls for both justice and love. Both concepts have implications for law, but many commentators find tension between them. By some definitions, justice yields what people deserve; love yields what is best for them whether they deserve it or not. Jesus seems to generally teach that in our personal relations

---

[45]Miroslav Volf, *Exclusion and Embrace: A Theological Exploration of Identity, Otherness, and Reconciliation* (Nashville: Abingdon, 1996), p. 124.
[46]Murphy, "Christian Love and Criminal Punishment," p. 231 (emphasis in original).

(at least), love trumps justice. Victims should not seek an eye for an eye. Irrespective of our rights, when attacked we should turn the other cheek (Mt 5:38-39), when sued for our tunic we should give our cloak as well (Mt 5:40), when wronged we should forgive (Mt 18:21-22) and when asked we should give (Lk 6:30). Jesus speaks to wrongdoers, as well as victims. If someone has something against me, my top priority—higher than worship!—is to go and be reconciled (Mt 5:23-24). These teachings present challenges to private individuals, lawyers, social groups and governing officials.

When individuals are the victims of injustice, should they seek their legal rights? In the Sermon on the Mount, Jesus addresses those who face litigation and (as throughout the Sermon) focuses on the heart (Mt 5:25-26). We are to be well disposed or kindly minded (*eunoōn*) toward our adversaries in the interactions that lead up to a trial. We are to try, with genuine love for the adversaries, to resolve the matter. If we fail to resolve our dispute, we limit ourselves and our adversaries to the resolution that law and the human system might yield. Jesus does not say that we should simply give in to the demands of adversaries. Rather, we are to be genuinely committed to what is good for them, seeking their well-being. This may require that we *not* give into their demands.

Calvin argues, citing Romans 13:4, that Christian use of the courts is appropriate, for "the magistrate is minister of God for our good." Those who are "undeservedly oppressed" may put themselves "in the care of the magistrate" and seek "what is fair and good," so long as they are "far from all passion to harm or take revenge, far from harshness and hatred, far from burning desire for contention." Calvin acknowledges, however, that "as the customs of these times go, an example of an upright litigant is rare."[47] Unfortunately, in this respect, customs have not changed over the last five centuries.

In God's kingdom, apology, forgiveness and reconciliation are the preferred means of resolving a wrong. Sadly, attorneys often undercut these possibilities. Attorneys often, as a matter of course, instruct clients not to speak to the opposing party. This practice is encouraged by the rules in many jurisdictions, which treat an apology as an admission of guilt. In client-counseling sessions, many attorneys inflame the client's most selfish instincts, rather than serve as wise, objective counselors. Attorneys almost reflexively excuse

---

[47]Calvin, *Institutes*, 4.20.15, in *John Calvin*, ed. Dillenberger, p. 493.

the client and blame the opposing party for any loss. Too often they serve to exacerbate rather than resolve conflict. This is not to suggest that lawyers do not exercise an important role within a legal system, speaking for clients and presenting the client's side of a case. The justice system depends on such advocacy. But lawyers should raise for discussion with clients the possibility of apology, forgiveness and reconciliation. A lawyer thereby can be an instrument of peace and serve the deepest interests of clients.

Jesus' call for justice and love of enemies presents challenges at the social, as well as the individual, level. Whereas some social activists, including theologian Cornel West, argue that despair and rage are essential elements in the struggle for justice,[48] Jesus calls for us to resist the fire of anger (Mt 5:22). Anger imposes a high price on the parties on both sides of a conflict and on the public as well. Those who encourage anger are sowing the wind, and they will reap the whirlwind and the tornado. Indeed, we are reaping it now among people increasingly sick with rage and resentment. But there is nothing that can be done with anger that cannot be done better without it. Jesus' call is to right wrongs with persistent love.[49]

Injustice, love and forgiveness: implications for the state. And what are love's demands on governing officials who have the responsibility to protect citizens and ensure justice? If government officials followed Jesus' command to forgive those who do wrong and to give to all who ask, it would destroy the government's ability to comply with Jesus' call for justice and probably destroy the government's ability to govern.[50] To forgive those guilty of crime would often be unjust to past and future victims. To give to all who ask might be unjust to others. A legislator cannot give to all who ask (when everyone is asking).

The nature of Christian love resolves some of the apparent tension between love and justice. As noted previously, Christian love can be tough love: it will give a person what he needs, not necessarily what he wants. But even tough love may be inconsistent with justice: giving someone what he needs may be inconsistent with fairness to everyone else.

---

[48]*NBC News*, June 2, 1996.

[49]See Willard, *Divine Conspiracy*, pp. 147-51.

[50]Paul appears to call for an exercise of different roles in different capacities. Compare Romans 12:19 NIV 1984 ("Do not take revenge, my friends, but leave room for God's wrath") with Romans 13:4 NIV 1984 (the magistrate is "God's servant, an agent of wrath to bring punishment on the wrongdoer"). For additional discussion of Romans 13 in this volume, see "Christians and the Civil State in the New Testament" and "The State, Law and Empire" in chapter eight.

Some, including this book's coeditor David VanDrunen, have argued that Jesus' demanding kingdom ethics apply institutionally only within the church.[51] By this view, the *lex talionis,* "an eye for an eye," remains the standard of justice for the state: though Christians rightfully manifest forgiving and reconciling love within the church and with their neighbors, they should support the state's imposition of proportionate retributive justice. This institutional division of Christian standards into love within the church and retributive justice administered by the state is analogous to Luther's division of authority, discussed previously. But, where Luther argued that government operates on its own rules, VanDrunen finds the state's standards in the Old Testament's *lex talionis* and in Paul's teaching in Romans 13.

In our view, this too neatly avoids the difficult work of determining the implications for the state of Jesus' teaching on love. There is no basis for such a division of authority in Jesus' teaching. Indeed, he taught that love is the framework on which law hangs. Love is the standard by which law, including the *lex talionis,* should be judged. Moreover, Jesus' kingdom is primarily about a change in the heart, not about the application of rules. That change of heart, and its accompanying Christian virtues, should affect all of life. Are Christians involved in government leadership to have one heart for the home and the church and another heart for the office and the courtroom? This is not to say that it will be easy to determine the implications of Jesus' teachings for law. We see that as the challenge that Jesus presents to his followers who are concerned with law.

From one view, justice is not merely consistent with love; it is the way that love is manifested by one with responsibilities to a group. As William Temple said, justice is "the primary form of love in social organization."[52] One in authority should not show special love to privileged individuals, but to all who might be affected by an action. We are communal beings and must attend in love to everyone involved. In the family setting, not everyone can determine where to go on a family vacation. If agreement cannot be reached, fair decision-making measures (e.g., taking turns) must be identified. In a country, government leaders must develop and implement

---

[51]David VanDrunen, "Bearing Sword in the State, Turning Cheek in the Church: A Reformed Two-Kingdoms Interpretation of Matthew 5:38–42," *Themelios* 34, no. 3 (2009): 322-34.
[52]Jeffrie G. Murphy, "Christian Love and Criminal Punishment," p. 219.

fair procedures. Justice is generally the most loving thing that one can do for all the people in a family or a state.

In our view, the best resolution of conflicts between love and justice at the institutional level may be the traditional Christian formulation: "justice tempered with mercy."[53] The primary goal of one in authority—whether legislator, administrator or judge—should be justice. In cases where circumstances warrant, a concern for mercy might vary an outcome. A judge might reduce a sentence based on the illness of a defendant or the needs of his family; a legislature might give welfare caseworkers discretion to give greater benefits to those encountering unexpected needs. The advice of Augustine still captures the sort of judgment that a heart transformed by Christ might dispense:

> We call those Christian emperors happy who govern with justice. . . . We call
> them happy . . . when they are slow to punish, not out of private revenge, but
> only when forced by the order and security of the republic, and when they
> pardon not to encourage impunity, but with the hope of reform; when they
> temper with mercy and generosity the inevitable harshness of their decrees.[54]

GOD'S MORAL LAW, THE MOSAIC LAW AND LEGISLATION

In some of Jesus' most helpful teaching regarding the relationship between God's moral law and civil law, he addressed the only section of the Mosaic law that discusses divorce.[55] The Mosaic law prohibited a man from remarrying his ex-wife following her remarriage and her divorce from or the death of her second husband. Nevertheless, the law appeared to accept the husband's divorce if the wife "becomes displeasing to him because he finds something indecent about her, and he writes her a certificate of divorce" (Deut 24:1-4). The meaning of this section was hotly disputed in Jesus' time among Jewish legal scholars. Shammai took the stricter view: "A man should not divorce his wife unless he has found her guilty of some unseemly conduct"; whereas Hillel said that he may divorce her "even if she has merely spoilt his food."[56] Here is the account of Jesus' discussion of the matter:

---

[53]Oliver O'Donovan traces this formulation to Ambrose. O'Donovan, *Desire of the Nations*, p. 200.
[54]Augustine, *City of God,* trans. Walsh et. al., 5.24, p. 118.
[55]For additional discussion in this volume of the Mosaic law's and Jesus' teaching on divorce, see "Marriage, Divorce and Sexuality" in chapter three.
[56]"Tractate Gittin: Folio 90a," in *Soncino Babylonian Talmud,* ed. Isidore Epstein (London: Soncino Press, 1952), reporting the views of each.

> Some Pharisees came to [Jesus] to test him. They asked, "Is it lawful for a man to divorce his wife for any and every reason?"
>
> "Haven't you read," he replied, "that at the beginning the Creator 'made them male and female,' and said, 'For this reason a man will leave his father and mother and be united to his wife, and the two will become one flesh'? So they are no longer two, but one flesh. Therefore what God has joined together, let no one separate."
>
> "Why then," they asked, "did Moses command that a man give his wife a certificate of divorce and send her away?"
>
> Jesus replied, "Moses permitted you to divorce your wives because your hearts were hard. But it was not this way from the beginning. I tell you that anyone who divorces his wife, except for marital immorality, and marries another woman commits adultery." (Mt 19:3-9, quoting Gen 1:27; 2:24)

Jesus pushed the Pharisees beyond the controversy back to God's moral law, back to God's original design that marriage be a permanent union of two lives. As in Jesus' teaching on the sabbath—"the Sabbath *was made* for man"—Jesus looks back to creation (Mk 2:27). God's moral law takes us back to the Garden. Jesus bases his position on Genesis 1:27 and Genesis 2:24, two verses that do not appear to have been have been paired before in addressing divorce. Jonathan Burnside notes that Jesus thereby employed a "remarkable" exegetical technique: "Jesus combines two distinct and unrelated texts that have nothing to do with divorce, and this leads to something that does address the issue."[57]

For our purposes, the important part of the exchange is Jesus' reference to the Mosaic law: "Moses permitted you to divorce your wives because your hearts were hard. But it was not this way from the beginning." Moses allowed, but did not approve of, divorce. Jesus does not criticize Moses for allowing divorce. He notes that Moses allowed divorce "because your hearts were hard." The Israelites suffered from, in John Meier's words, "a stubborn refusal at the core of [their] being to hear and obey God's word."[58] Knowing all too well our fallen human nature and consequent inability to conform to God's moral law, Jesus approved of civil law that explicitly permitted and even identified the procedures for deviations from God's moral law. "Jesus

---

[57]Jonathan Burnside, *God, Justice, and Society: Aspects of Law and Legality in the Bible* (Oxford: Oxford University Press, 2011), p. 407 (emphasis in original).

[58]Meier, *Law and Love*, p. 122.

[here] makes the radical claim that *it is halakhically permissible to divorce in circumstances when it is not morally right to do so.*"[59]

It is likely that Moses (and Jesus) envisioned the harmful consequences that would have arisen if divorce were not allowed: some husbands would abandon wives and take other women without benefit of divorce, or, worse, husbands might kill their wives in order to get rid of them; husbands would father illegitimate children; it would be unclear whether abandoned women were free to remarry; prospective husbands would risk being accused of adultery if they married abandoned wives; abandoned wives and children would be destitute; inheritance rights would be unclear and inheritance disputes would generate conflict; and children of new relationships would not be provided for at death. Law that yielded these consequences would be the opposite of love. In light of these consequences, Moses allowed divorce. Civil law has instrumental value; it is not the ultimate value.

Many commentators speak of the Mosaic divorce legislation as a grudging acceptance of divorce, as if it is an unusual deviation from God's moral law:

> Hebrew law . . . does not institute divorce, but tolerates it, in view of the imperfections of human nature.[60]

> Divorce is a bad custom which has grown up amongst a degenerate people, and the Mosaic law tolerated it as an accommodation to a low level of moral custom.[61]

> [Moses] did not give a law about divorce and approve of it by his consent, but when men's wickedness could be restrained by no other means, he applied the most tolerable remedy, so that a man might at least bear witness to his wife's chastity.[62]

Though we do not disagree with these statements, we think that divorce may not be the only place where, in light of the hardness of human hearts, the Mosaic law permitted and regulated activity that deviated from God's moral law.

---

[59]Burnside, *God, Justice, and Society*, p. 406 (emphasis in original).

[60]S. R. Driver, *A Critical and Exegetical Commentary on Deuteronomy* (Edinburgh: T & T Clark, 1902), p. 272.

[61]Willoughby C. Allen, *A Critical and Exegetical Commentary on the Gospel According to St. Matthew* (New York: Charles Scribner's Sons, 1907), p. 204.

[62]Ibid., p. 245.

Both Justin Martyr and Irenaeus argued very early in the Christian tradition that a good portion of the Mosaic law did not belong to unchanging moral standards—some of it was simply God's wise and prudent way of providing an appropriate framework for the communal life of his people at that unique time in history.[63] In addition, the view that Jesus affirmed Moses' creation of best-practical-alternative human laws may provide a basis for understanding some of the troubling aspects of the Mosaic law. For example, the Mosaic law need not be taken to have approved of slavery, any more than to have approved of divorce. Jesus' reaction to slavery provisions in the Mosaic code might well have been similar to his reaction to divorce: "Moses permitted slavery because your hearts were hard. But it was not this way from the beginning." Augustine argued that it was not God's intention in the beginning that there be slavery. According to Augustine, man was appointed to rule over the rest of God's creation (citing Gen 1:26) but not one another. "God wanted rational man, made to His image, to have no dominion except over irrational nature. He meant no man, therefore, to have dominion over man, but only man over beast."[64] Augustine appears to have accepted the necessity of man ruling over man as a result of the fall, but Jesus' comments on divorce suggest that it is appropriate for legislation to seek to get back to God's original standard. Under this view, if the social circumstances are such that people will follow a rule that is closer to God's moral law (on divorce or slavery), the wise legislator will pursue it. Jesus' comments on divorce suggest that it is appropriate for legislation to seek to get back to God's moral law.

Jesus might also have said similar things about some of the harsh punishments of the Mosaic code, possibly including capital punishment in many cases. As noted elsewhere in this volume,[65] the Mosaic law imposed the death penalty for many offenses, including being disrespectful to one's parents, engaging in homosexual activity and engaging in adultery. It may be that Moses ordered capital punishment for many of these offenses because "your hearts were hard." Such punishment was a prudential response

---

[63]See, e.g., Justin Martyr, *Dialogue with Trypho*, trans. Thomas B. Falls, rev. Thomas P. Halton, ed. Michael Slusser (Washington, DC: Catholic University of America Press, 2003); Irenaeus, *Against Heresies*, in *The Ante-Nicene Fathers*, vol. 1, ed. Alexander Roberts, James Donaldson and A. Cleveland Coxe (1885; repr., Grand Rapids: Eerdmans, 2001), esp. Book IV.
[64]Augustine, *City of God*, trans. Walsh et. al., 19.15, p. 461.
[65]See "Criminal law" in chapter three.

to the situation of the time—a nomadic people who did not have the option
of life imprisonment—but in a different situation, law might more closely
approach God's ideal; the death penalty might be abolished or reserved
only for the worst of crimes.[66] This is consistent with the current Catholic
position on the death penalty:

> Assuming that the guilty party's identity and responsibility have been fully
> determined, the traditional teaching of the church does not exclude recourse
> to the death penalty, if this is the only possible way of effectively defending
> human lives against the unjust aggressor.
>
> If, however, non-lethal means are sufficient to defend and protect people's
> safety from the aggressor, authority will limit itself to such means, as these
> are more in keeping with the concrete conditions of the common good and
> more in conformity with the dignity of the human person.[67]

The use of oaths in the Mosaic law (see Ex 22:9-10; Num 5:11-31) may
also have been a concession to the hardness of human hearts. It is necessary to discern the truth in a legal setting, whereas God's moral law
requires truthfulness in all settings—"Simply let your 'Yes' be 'Yes,' and
your 'No,' 'No'" (Mt 5:37 NIV 1984).

Civil law deviates from God's moral law for very practical reasons. As
Thomas Aquinas argued, human law establishes minimum standards rather
than the moral ideal because not everyone is capable of abiding by the ideal.

> The purpose of human law is to lead men to virtue, not suddenly, but grad-
> ually. Wherefore it does not lay upon the multitude of imperfect men the
> burdens of those who are virtuous, viz., that they should abstain from all evil.
> Otherwise these imperfect ones, being unable to bear such precepts, would
> break out into yet greater evils.[68]

If law imposes too heavy a burden on the population, people will give up on
compliance. Such open resistance to law would create a risk of law falling into
disrespect. It is best that we have what William Stuntz and David Skeel have
labeled a "modest" positive law,[69] one that prohibits only the greatest of evils.

---

[66]For discussion in this volume of capital punishment in the case of murder, see "The Covenant
with Noah" in chapter one.

[67]*Catechism of the Catholic Church: Second Edition* (Doubleday: New York, 1995), pp. 604-5.

[68]Aquinas, *Summa Theologica* 1a2ae q. 96 a. 2.

[69]David A. Skeel Jr. and William J. Stuntz, "Christianity and the (Modest) Rule of Law," *University
of Pennsylvania Journal of Constitutional Law* 8 (2006): 809.

Jesus' comments on the Mosaic divorce law suggest an enormous opportunity (and responsibility) for judges and legislators. They must prudently and creatively craft laws with eyes fixed both on God's moral law and on practical reality. The lawmaker should exercise pragmatic judgment in light of the hardness of human hearts. The task of the Christian legislator or judge is to identify God's moral law and to determine how to advance it in light of the current social situation.

Some have criticized modern lawmakers for failing to enact God's moral law or even the less stringent Mosaic standards into contemporary law. On the issue of divorce, one American commentator has said: "I believe that our lawmakers are to blame for allowing [no-fault divorce] laws to exist as they do, and not bringing the law of divorce in these United States to the scriptural standard."[70] But if our understanding of Jesus' teaching on the law of divorce is correct, the civil law should not necessarily adopt God's moral law. Human law should reach for the ideal, but should do so in light of its practical impact.

Modern divorce law is an area where Jesus' model could be applied. The ideal—permanent union—has not changed, nor has the hardness of human hearts or the danger that a rule prohibiting divorce would yield worse results than a rule allowing it. In the 1960s and 1970s in the United States, legislatures in almost all jurisdictions moved from a fault-based divorce system to a no-fault system. Divorce today can be obtained easily by either party for any or no reason. The law provides little or no deterrence to divorce.

The hardness of human hearts may warrant laws that discourage divorce without demanding God's ideal of permanent marriage. Thoughtful lawyers, legislators and legal academics wrestle with alternatives to easy no-fault divorce, proposing longer waiting periods (especially for parents of young children), counseling requirements and covenant-marriage legislation (which allows couples to agree at marriage to certain impediments to divorce).

Jesus' comments regarding the Mosaic divorce law suggest that all who have responsibility for law—including citizens—have a high calling. They do God's work as they prudently seek to create laws that will move us toward God's ideals in light of the practical problems of the hardness of hearts in the current situation.

---

[70]A. Cressey, as cited in Joseph S. Exell, "Matthew," in *The Biblical Illustrator* (Grand Rapids: Baker Books, 1992), 11:418.

CONCLUSION: A WOMAN CAUGHT IN ADULTERY

We conclude our look at Jesus' view of law with the well-known story of Jesus and a woman caught in adultery. It suggests many of the themes we have identified in this chapter. Like many stories about Jesus, its meaning is not entirely clear.[71]

> At dawn [Jesus] appeared again in the temple courts, where all the people gathered around him, and he sat down to teach them. The teachers of the law and the Pharisees brought in a woman caught in adultery. They made her stand before the group and said to Jesus, "Teacher, this woman was caught in the act of adultery. In the Law Moses commanded us to stone such women. Now what do you say?" They were using this question as a trap, in order to have a basis for accusing him.
>
> But Jesus bent down and started to write on the ground with his finger. When they kept on questioning him, he straightened up and said to them, "Let any one of you who is without sin be the first to throw a stone at her." Again he stooped down and wrote on the ground.
>
> At this, those who heard began to go away one at a time, the older ones first, until only Jesus was left, with the woman still standing there. Jesus straightened up and asked her, "Woman, where are they? Has no one condemned you?"
>
> "No one, sir," she said.
>
> "Then neither do I condemn you," Jesus declared. "Go now and leave your life of sin." (Jn 8:2-11)

Jesus' final comment makes clear his rejection of adultery as a moral matter, but what other conclusions might we draw from this story? Does this story teach us anything about law? The explanation for Jesus' actions may be one or some combination of the following.

- *The priority of the heart.* This may have been a teaching moment for the woman's accusers. Jesus may have been using this occasion to challenge their hearts. A comment addressed to those who are "without sin" is likely to generate self-reflection in almost anyone. "Let any one of you who is without sin" stop reading. (Let the rest of us read on.) In the Sermon on the Mount, Jesus tells would-be judges that they should first take the

---

[71]The earliest and most reliable manuscripts of the Gospel of John do not include this story. Nevertheless, "throughout the history of the church, it has been held that, whoever wrote it, this little story is authentic" (Leon Morris, *The Gospel According to John*, rev. ed., New International Commentary on the New Testament [Grand Rapids: Eerdmans, 1995], p. 779).

plank out of their own eyes so that they will see clearly to take the speck from a brother's eye (Mt 7:1-5; Lk 6:37-42). Which of these accusers' sins came to mind? He forced them to examine their own hearts, and they found themselves wanting. Jesus accepted the outcast who turned to him; he cut to the heart the attitude of those who considered themselves good.

- *Unjust enforcement of law.* This may have been a story about the unjust enforcement of law. Jesus is one who brings justice. The Mosaic code said that if two people were caught engaging in adultery, both were to be stoned. Here, the men only brought the woman to Jesus. They may illustrate what we see in many cultures—a tendency to hold women to strict sexual mores while "boys will be boys." To stone the woman, without the man, would have been unjust to her. Her accusers very well knew they were not really keeping the law. In context, Jesus' statement may have meant: "Any of you who is without sin [in this prosecution] must cast the first stone." Here as well, the accusers found themselves wanting.

- *Justice tempered with mercy.* In this case, justice may have demanded the woman's punishment. It appears, at least, that the Mosaic law did. Adultery is one of the most damaging acts in which people can engage. Adultery can easily break up two families and damage two sets of spouses and two sets of children. If adultery becomes common, it can lead to the destruction of the institution of the family and, ultimately, a country. But Jesus concluded that in this case, at least, mercy should trump law.

- *"Any one of you who is without sin."* If we take Jesus literally (which is the habit of our Anabaptist brethren), this story may prohibit followers of Jesus from participating in the coercion that is a necessary part of human law. No one is "without sin." If Jesus' example here is normative, his followers might challenge sin through verbal admonition, but not law.

- *Jesus filling up the law.* It may be that this story teaches us something about the substance of law. Jesus filled up the law; he added what it lacked. O'Donovan argues that though the Mosaic law permitted an eye for an eye, Jesus' "fulfilling of the law will mean the end of our thirst for public vindication."[72] In this story, Jesus may have rejected particularly punitive legal systems.

---

[72]O'Donovan, *Desire of the Nations*, p. 112.

- *Abolition of the death penalty.* Finally, Jesus may have concluded that Moses commanded the death penalty for adultery because of the hardness of human hearts but that the death penalty was no longer necessary. At the time Moses gave the law—to a nomadic group of recently freed slaves—it might have been that nothing less would have protected the family. But Jesus may have concluded that in his day the family was on a sufficiently secure footing that the death penalty, at least for adultery, was not needed.

We wish we could tell you which, if any, of the above lessons Jesus intended to teach us in his encounter with the woman caught in adultery. Jesus does not always explain everything. We hesitate to make things clear where Jesus seems to have intentionally left them unclear. We leave the interpretation of this story to you, as Jesus did.

7

CIVIL LAW AND CIVIL DISOBEDIENCE

The Early Church and the Law

Joel A. Nichols and James W. McCarty III

INTRODUCTION

The book of Acts (or Acts of the Apostles) is the only book of the Bible that tells the history of the early church.[1] In a volume such as the present one, which seeks to explore the relationship between the Bible and the civil law, Acts thus plays an important descriptive *and* normative role, for the actions of the earliest followers of Christ carry special import for modern application. Acts is structured as a historical narrative, with scholars alternately contending that a set of central speeches frame the text, that a set of trials provide the movement within the text, or that the book has the literary qualities of a memoir.[2] Scholars agree, however, that the purpose of this historical narrative is *theological*: the book of Acts provides an authoritative interpretation of the gospel (especially as conveyed in the Gospel of Luke)

---

[1]See Bruce M. Metzger, *The New Testament: Its Background, Growth, and Content*, 3rd ed. (Nashville: Abingdon, 2003), p. 196.

[2]See, e.g., Bart D. Ehrman, *The New Testament: A Historical Introduction to the Early Christian Writings*, 4th ed. (New York: Oxford University Press, 2008) (speeches), pp. 142-44; Matthew L. Skinner, *The Trial Narratives: Conflict, Power, and Identity in the New Testament* (Louisville, KY: Westminster John Knox, 2010) (trials); Martin Dibelius, *The Book of Acts: Form, Style, and Theology*, ed. K. C. Hanson (Minneapolis: Fortress, 2004), pp. 10-12 (memoir).

and seeks to persuade readers both of the truth of the evangelistic message of Jesus as savior and of the respective roles of the community (the church) and the Holy Spirit in that message.[3]

Acts tells the story of the early church, its tenuous relation to various religious, local and international governing authorities and its functioning as an increasingly autonomous body that cared for its own members. Acts recounts how God calls not just individuals but a community to be the church; God creates "a people for himself" (Acts 15:14)[4] and, accordingly, these believers are "witnesses" (Acts 1:8) to God's name.[5] Importantly, Acts highlights the priority of early Christians' loyalty to the church rather than to national, ethnic or familial groups: followers of God are asked to put God's commands and God's leading above all else. If other authorities give contrary commands, believers respond, "We must obey God rather than men!" (Acts 5:29).

In this chapter, then, we will see two main themes. First, there is not a single answer for how Christians should relate to civil authority; that relationship must be discerned in the context of the Christian community and through the Holy Spirit. Second, on those occasions when it *is* clear that there is a conflict between God's command and that of the civil authority, God is to be obeyed.

This chapter first provides an overview and introduction to the book of Acts. Next, it addresses three major areas of interaction between Christians and the law. First, as Acts shows, the resolution of conflict within the church contains the seeds of internal church law. Second, Acts relies on the motif of legal trials as a vehicle to carry its narrative. This has interesting implications both theologically and practically. Third, Acts speaks emphatically of the primacy of God's command over contradictory earthly authorities. Because this last section arguably contradicts Romans 13 (which calls for submission to earthly rulers)—and because we believe the present application of biblical themes is best understood contextually—we provide a modern example of the principles of Acts. We describe how many South African Christians responded to the evil of apartheid by claiming allegiance to God first, rather

---

[3]See, e.g., Carl R. Holladay, *A Critical Introduction to the New Testament: Interpreting the Message and Meaning of Jesus Christ* (Nashville: Abingdon, 2005), pp. 225-60.
[4]Unless otherwise indicated, Scripture quotations in this chapter are taken from the NIV 1984.
[5]C. Kavin Rowe, *World Upside Down: Reading Acts in the Graeco-Roman Age* (New York: Oxford University Press, 2009), p. 18.

than to the civil state, and self-consciously followed the example of the early church. Finally, we offer concluding reflections on what modern Christians can learn from the book of Acts and the South African experience.

ACTS: AUTHORSHIP, AUDIENCE AND THEMES

The book of Acts is addressed to Theophilus and begins by explicitly mentioning the author's "former book" (Luke), in which the author "wrote about all that Jesus began to do and to teach until the day he was taken up to heaven, after giving instructions through the Holy Spirit to the apostles he had chosen" (Acts 1:1-2). Acts is uniformly considered the sequel to the Gospel of Luke, and biblical commentators frequently refer to these books simply as Luke-Acts.[6] Ancient sources, from as early as the second century, have designated the author as Luke—a Gentile physician and Paul's co-worker (mentioned in Col 4:14 and elsewhere). We follow this authorial designation, even though it cannot be firmly established.

The unity of Luke-Acts provides a critical basis for interpretation, including within this chapter. The use of geography in Luke-Acts is especially important, for Luke uses geography "as a literary and theological instrument."[7] The center of the Luke-Acts narrative is Jerusalem—with the Gospel of Luke moving *toward* Jerusalem and the book of Acts moving *away from* Jerusalem. The key section in the Gospel begins in Luke 9:51, where Jesus "resolutely set out for Jerusalem." It is in Jerusalem where Jesus is put on trial, adjudged guilty and sentenced, and then executed. And it is in Jerusalem where Jesus appears to his disciples after his resurrection, telling them that they will be "witnesses" for him "to all nations, beginning at Jerusalem" (Lk 24:47-49).

Acts begins exactly where Luke leaves off—in Jerusalem, with Jesus proclaiming that the disciples "will be my witnesses in Jerusalem, and in all Judea and Samaria, and to the ends of the earth" (Acts 1:8). And just as Jesus (in

---

[6]See Luke Timothy Johnson, *The Writings of the New Testament: An Interpretation,* 3rd ed. (Minneapolis: Fortress, 2010), p. 188. Many interpreters put the inseparability even stronger still: "Luke-Acts must be read together. The Gospel helps to interpret Acts, and Acts helps to interpret Luke" (William H. Willimon, *Acts,* Interpretation: A Bible Commentary for Teaching and Preaching [Atlanta: John Knox, 1988], pp. 7-8). But see contentions otherwise in *Rethinking the Unity and Reception of Luke and Acts,* ed. Andrew F. Gregory and C. Kavin Rowe (Columbia: University of South Carolina Press, 2010).

[7]Johnson, *Writings of the New Testament,* p. 194. See also Fred B. Craddock, *Luke,* Interpretation: A Bible Commentary for Teaching and Preaching (Louisville, KY: John Knox, 1990), pp. 139-42.

Luke) has to set his face (Lk 9:51) to fulfill his mission *toward* Jerusalem, so
Paul (in Acts) has to set his face to fulfill his mission *away from* Jerusalem to
Rome—to the ends of the earth, which is what Rome symbolizes. While the
movement of Luke is toward Jerusalem, where Jesus will be put on trial before
Jewish and Roman authorities for his bold proclamations of his messianic
nature, the movement of Acts is toward Rome, where Paul will be put on trial
for his proclamations that Jesus is the Messiah and King. This geographic
movement and the use of trials as literary devices is significant. Luke uses
trials less to convey ideas about justice or about the nature of law than he uses
them as vehicles to further the evangelistic work of God's kingdom.

Many other themes of Luke are carried forward in Acts as well.[8] For example, a key Lucan theme is the idea of "reversals" as expressed in Mary's
Magnificat (Lk 1:46-55), where God elevates the poor and humbles the rich.
And a related paradigmatic theme is that God's kingdom has broken in on
earth through the person of Jesus, who sets prisoners free, gives sight to the
blind and proclaims the year of the Lord's favor: "Today this scripture [from
Isaiah] is fulfilled in your hearing," Jesus says (Lk 4:18-21). So, too, the book
of Acts gives the poor, hungry and humble a special place through shared
possessions (Acts 4:32-37) and pulls down the mighty in power, as when
Herod is struck down by God while the disciples go about their work (Acts
12:1-23). Further, Jesus' followers in Acts are empowered by the Holy Spirit
to continue his mission of healing, even to the point of raising the dead
(Acts 9:32-43). The disciples and church are empowered to continue Jesus'
ministry in these ways so that all who hear and see may "repent and be
baptized . . . for the forgiveness of your sins. And you will receive the gift of
the Holy Spirit" (Acts 2:38). Luke and Acts together proclaim that God's
salvation has come in the person of Jesus Christ, that all are welcome to
receive this salvation (including Gentiles) and that Jesus' followers are
empowered by the Holy Spirit to continue his evangelistic message as his
"witnesses" even "to the ends of the earth" (Acts 1:8). Acts thus portrays the
early Christians as possessing a foundational commitment to God, be-
lieving that the kingdom of God has broken in through the person of Jesus
and that Christians and the church are tasked with bearing witness to God's
message of salvation and continuing his ministry.

---

[8]For parallels in Luke and Acts, see Ehrman, *New Testament*, p. 147.

CHRISTIANS AND THE LAW IN ACTS

Internal church functioning. Luke describes the newly formed Christian community in terms that are both descriptive and prescriptive. The members of the community are said to care for each other in ways that model the kingdom of God, and God blesses them as they live together in community; their community's functioning (and not just the spoken word) is itself evangelistic. This sacrificial fellowship of believers is described immediately after the coming of the Holy Spirit at Pentecost and Peter's subsequent address to the crowd, which persuaded about three thousand people to join the Christians. Thereafter, Luke reports that they devoted themselves increasingly to prayer, fellowship, communal sharing of goods, Eucharistic celebration and the teaching of the apostles (Acts 2:44-47). Luke repeats the theme of community sharing of possessions in Acts 4. Again, the passage follows a speech by Peter (and John) and follows a declaration that the Holy Spirit filled them all (Acts 4:32-35). To emphasize the point further, Luke's next story is that of Ananias and Sapphira, who sold a piece of property (as was expected of them) and secretly kept part of the proceeds for themselves but gave the rest to the apostles. Peter rebuked them for their deception, and they were both struck dead (Acts 5:1-11).

Such passages that focus on the early church's sharing of possessions should be highlighted for two reasons. First, they have, at times, been used as a prescriptive formula for the state, tending toward socialism. They have been used by others as a prescriptive formula for the church. We think there is little textual support for extrapolating such wide-scale sharing into an agenda supporting central state control, and Luke was surely not writing a paean to or brief for socialism. This is not at all to say that Luke prescribes unfettered capitalism (and in fact we think he does not), but rather to say that one needs to be cautious in pushing this text beyond its original intent. We *do*, however, believe that Luke intends to be both descriptive *and* prescriptive regarding sharing possessions, and we think the church has too often underplayed the importance of some kinds of internal communal sharing. Such sharing is an indication that the Holy Spirit is active within the church, is an evangelistic sign that draws in nonbelievers, and is a portent of the kingdom of God that Jesus sought to usher in.[9]

---

[9]Luke Timothy Johnson, *Sharing Possessions: What Faith Demands,* 2nd ed. (Grand Rapids: Eerdmans, 2011), p. 122.

A second reason to highlight these passages is that they show the beginnings of internal community norms, or law. There are acknowledged leaders (apostles) whose authority is reinforced by the laying of money at their feet (Acts 4:35). All were invited into God's community, whether rich or poor. There were some who had needs, but the community coalesced around them to provide for them in an orderly fashion. When the orderliness of meeting the believers' needs waned, the early church established additional procedures and structures. Acts 6 details this need for more law, which arose because some of the needy widows "were being overlooked in the daily distribution of food" (Acts 6:1). To meet this need and resolve the dispute, the twelve apostles delegated authority to seven deacons or ministers. These seven, including Stephen, successfully took on the task. The apostles thus resolved the first reported internal dispute, and the good news spread rapidly as soon as these tangible needs were met.[10]

The greatest internal dispute in Acts, however, pertained to the inclusion of Gentiles as full members of the Christian community. Some contended that they needed to be circumcised, and others—including Paul and Barnabas—argued forcefully against this proposition. The argument was so divisive that the first recorded church council was convened at Jerusalem. The Jerusalem Council was convened to discuss these issues (Acts 15), and Luke reports an impassioned speech by Peter as particularly persuasive. Peter contended that God "accepted [the Gentiles] by giving the Holy Spirit to them, just as he did to us. He made no distinction between us and them, for he purified their hearts by faith" (Acts 15:8-9). Barnabas and Paul then told of the signs and conversions among the Gentiles, and James proposed a response that did not require circumcision but did require abstaining from certain foods and from sexual immorality. Luke recounts that "the apostles and elders, with the whole church," then agreed by choosing a number of men to travel and convey this decision in person and by letter (Acts 15:22-35).

This event is important for three reasons. First, the Jerusalem Council is essential in Acts because the gospel would not be able to reach "the ends of the earth" (Acts 1:8) if there were a major obstacle to Gentiles joining the

---

[10]Further delegation of apostolic authority to local churches, which is a precursor to the development of church laws and norms, may be seen in the appointment of elders for local churches. See, e.g., Acts 14:23.

community. Second, the Jerusalem Council is foundational organizationally as the first church council, serving as a model for future dispute resolution. Many modern scholars look directly to the Jerusalem Council as the beginning of internal church law and regulation. It led to the eventual establishment (over time) of an entire body of canon law to govern internal church affairs.[11] Third, these two instances of dispute resolution within Acts (feeding widows and resolving the issue of acceptance of Gentiles) suggest that the early church resolved internal disputes internally. There was no contemplation of recourse to the civil courts. The strongest statement of that principle is not in Acts but in a Pauline epistle: in 1 Corinthians 6:1-11, Paul exhorts believers not to take another believer to civil court in a lawsuit. Instead, he seemingly commands the resolution of the dispute within an internal forum, judged by a disinterested but wise fellow Christian.[12] Although there is no record of church courts at this early stage of church history, the 1 Corinthians passage provides strong precedent for their later development, or at least for the development of some internal church method to resolve disputes between believers.

We believe that a distinction might be drawn between resolution of church doctrinal disputes (such as in the Jerusalem Council) and the determination of internal procedures for effective ministry (such as for feeding the widows), on the one hand, and "legal disputes" between Christians, on the other. The former situations are the kind of thing that should be resolved outside the civil legal system precisely because they involve matters of doctrine, belief and distribution of church resources. This accords with a strong line of case precedent in the United States, in which the US Supreme Court has stated that internal church matters must be decided by internal church norms and forums.[13] This is one offshoot of the "separation of church and state," which protects the church from an intrusive state decision maker that lacks knowledge about how to make internal decisions,

---

[11]See, e.g., Amleto Giovanni Cicognani, *Canon Law,* trans. Joseph M. O'Hara and Francis Brennan (Philadelphia: Dolphin Press, 1934), pp. 68, 98; Hamilton Hess, *The Early Development of Canon Law and the Council of Serdica,* Oxford Early Christian Studies (New York: Oxford University Press, 2002), p. 5.

[12]Jesus also seemingly counseled believers to resolve disputes among themselves in Matthew 18:15-17. For additional discussion of 1 Corinthians 6:1-11 in this volume, see "Civil Litigation in 1 Corinthians 6:1-11" in chapter eight.

[13]E.g., Hosanna-Tabor Evangelical Lutheran Church and School v. Equal Employment Opportunity Commission, 565 U.S. __, 132 S.Ct. 694 (2012); Kedroff v. Saint Nicholas Cathedral, 344 U.S. 94 (1952); Watson v. Jones, 80 U.S. 679 (1872).

and also protects the state from having to adjudicate matters of faith and thereby take sides in, essentially, doctrinal disputes.[14]

Whether to take legal disputes between Christians to civil courts is a much harder issue, in our view. There are some Christians who contend that *every* dispute between Christians must be resolved outside the civil court system. Practically, this raises several unanswered questions. These include what disputes are encompassed: Do they include disputes between married couples seeking to divorce? Child custody disputes? Business or contractual disputes? Disputes about an injury that occurred on a neighbor's property? Claims of improper discrimination? Questions also include whether churches have functioning dispute-resolution mechanisms (courts or arbitral panels or the like), and whether there is sufficient procedural protection for applicants. They also include whether a modern liberal state will or even should permit exclusive resolution of claims by its citizens if the state is not sure that the procedural and substantive rights of vulnerable persons will be respected (for example, women in divorce actions or children in custody actions).[15]

Trials in Acts. Trials are an important part of the narrative of Luke-Acts. In the Gospel of Luke, the arrest, trial and imposition of a death sentence on Jesus form the central part of the book. This trial fulfills God's predicted purpose of bringing salvation to all people through the death, burial and resurrection of Jesus.

In the same way, Jesus' tripartite commission of Acts 1:8 (that the disciples will be witnesses in Jerusalem, Judea and Samaria, and the ends of the earth) is fulfilled, in each instance, by a trial scene. The gospel spreads in Jerusalem alongside the trials of Peter and John and the other apostles in Acts 4–5. The gospel first spreads to Samaria in Acts 8, immediately after the trial and stoning of Stephen. And the gospel spreads to the ends of the earth when Paul is on trial in Philippi and Thessalonica (Acts 16–17) and, much more, when Paul is arrested in Jerusalem, appeals to Rome and participates in several trials en route to Rome (Acts 21–28).

---

[14]See John Witte Jr. and Joel A. Nichols, *Religion and the American Constitutional Experiment,* 3rd ed. (Boulder, CO: Westview, 2011), pp. 241-62.

[15]See, e.g., Michael A. Helfand, "Religious Arbitration and the New Multiculturalism: Negotiating Conflicting Legal Orders," *New York University Law Review* 86 (2011): 1231 (commercial disputes); Joel A. Nichols, ed., *Marriage and Divorce in a Multicultural Context: Multi-Tiered Marriage and the Boundaries of Civil Law and Religion* (New York: Cambridge University Press, 2012) (marriage and divorce).

In Jerusalem, there are two similar trial episodes in Acts 4 and 5, with Peter as the main speaker/defendant in each. Both trial episodes are sparked by the apostles' teaching of the people and their popularity among them (Acts 4:2; 5:12-17). Both center on a charge against the apostles concerning "what power" or "what name" authorizes their teaching and the accompanying physical healings and miracles (Acts 4:7; 5:28). And both trial episodes conclude with the disciples' prayer for the success of the gospel message, and then the actual success of that message (Acts 4:29, 31; 5:42). The trials of Peter and the apostles conclude not with an acquittal from the religious tribunal but with an ambivalent and ambiguous speech by one of the members of the court, which leads to the release of the apostles—but not before they are flogged and ordered not to speak in Jesus' name again. The speech by Gamaliel, a Pharisee and teacher of the law, in one of these instances suggests a wait-and-see approach: if the apostles' message "is from God, you will not be able to stop these men; you will only find yourselves fighting against God" (Acts 5:39). The officials reluctantly follow this advice, and Luke shows the reader that the gospel continues to spread as many others hear and believe even more after the trials.

Before the gospel spreads to Samaria, Stephen is put on trial before the Sanhedrin (or religious court). Stephen was not an apostle but is described as "a man full of God's grace and power, [who] did great wonders and miraculous signs" (Acts 6:8); he was also one of the seven deacons selected to minister to the widows within the church. Stephen is falsely accused of blasphemy and is hauled before the Sanhedrin and accused by false witnesses. He responds with an impassioned speech, which infuriates his accusers and the court itself, and he is taken outside and stoned to death. This scene, by the end, comes across to modern readers more as a mob scene than a fair trial with due process. But the end result in the text is that the gospel continues to be preached and believed all the more, including Philip's spreading of the gospel in Samaria (Acts 8:4-5).

Trials also accompany the gospel's spread to the "ends of the earth." Paul began by preaching the gospel in Gentile areas away from Jerusalem. As a result, he was beaten and put in jail in Philippi (Acts 16). That night an earthquake opened the doors of the jail, and the jailer himself was converted when Paul declined to escape. Paul and Silas, his companion, were put on trial before the magistrate the next morning. The magistrate ordered them released, but when Paul claimed that he was a Roman citizen (implying that he had due process rights that were not followed) he was escorted out of the city rather than just released. Paul next entered Thessalonica, where a mob rioted after Paul and Silas preached and converted a large number of people. While there is not a formal record of a trial, the city officials forced Paul's host to post bond before they allowed Paul and Silas to leave the city (Acts 17:1-10).

After some further travels, Paul followed the Spirit's leading and returned to Jerusalem in Acts 21. This is the starting point for the gospel's final journey toward Rome, which was seen as the center of the known world at the time and the avenue to the "ends of the earth." Paul was warmly received by the Christians in Jerusalem, but not by some other Jews there. They stirred up a mob that began to beat Paul, who was rescued, ironically, by Roman soldiers. As the Roman commander questioned him, the trial scene culminated in Paul proclaiming that he was a Roman citizen just as he was about to be flogged (Acts 22:25-29). The trial then moved to the religious authorities, the Sanhedrin, who were so opposed to Paul's message that he again had to be rescued from injury by the Roman commander. That night, Paul had a dream in which God told him that just as he had "testified about me in Jerusalem, so you must also testify in Rome" (Acts 23:11). This is a central piece of the story, for now the reader clearly sees that Paul's journey to Rome is part of God's plan to spread the gospel. After Paul appeared before other civil authorities he eventually "appeal[ed] to Caesar" (Acts 25:11). In this milieu of Paul's trials before the Jewish court system and the Roman system, then, Paul appears to avail himself of the advantages of his Roman citizenship—and the advantages of the Roman civil court system itself—when it suits his needs and God's purposes, since it was long Paul's desire to get to Rome and take the gospel there. Acts concludes with Paul in Rome, not on trial and not even with any stated resolution to the earlier trials, but preaching the gospel (though under guard).

Three themes may be gleaned from these trial scenes, and we flag a fourth issue as well. *First,* the trial narratives provide historical context for the spread of the gospel. If Luke-Acts is determined to provide an "orderly account" (Lk 1:3) of "the things that have been fulfilled among us" (Lk 1:1), then conveying the trial scenes of Stephen, Peter and Paul is an important part of that historical endeavor. And if Jesus proclaimed that the disciples would be his "witnesses . . . to the ends of the earth" (Acts 1:8), then communicating the path that the gospel took to get to Rome was also important. Because the gospel was spread in large part by Paul's imprisonment, which posed a stigmatizing and practical problem, Luke simultaneously had to "defend or justify the prisoner missionary Paul to the reader" in his depiction of the custody and trial while presenting the orderly account.[16] *Second,* the trials serve a key literary purpose for Luke: they place the tenets of the Christian faith "on trial" for the reader at the same time that those tenets are literally on trial in the story. Luke intends for his readers to hear the arguments at trial—whether from Stephen, Peter or Paul—and to be persuaded by the truth of the gospel.[17] *Third,* the trial scenes not only provide an opportunity for powerful civil authority figures to hear the gospel and judge it; they provide a window into Christianity's "ambiguous and potentially precarious relationship to the sociopolitical structures" of the civil authorities.[18] The trial scenes depict the gospel itself "making claims upon or sometimes against the religious and political structure of the first-century world."[19] That is, *the trials are ways for Luke to show the reader that the gospel is more authoritative than the power exerted by earthly authority.* Even if a trial ends badly for the defendant, as in the stoning of Stephen, the gospel message is still conveyed and the reader is left to see that God is in control of the situation and takes care of his faithful followers. Thus, Stephen dies at the hands of the earthly authorities but forgives his executioners in the midst of it and is comforted by looking up and seeing "the Son of Man standing at the right hand of God" (Acts 7:56). There is irony here, as the trial ends with Stephen's vindication by the ultimate authority (God) even though he is adjudicated guilty by the earthly authority (the Sanhedrin and other religious authorities).

Finally, what are we, as twenty-first-century readers, to do with these stories? Are we meant merely to understand the truth of the gospel message better because of them, and to appreciate the difficult road undertaken by the

---

[16]Brian Rapske, *The Book of Acts and Paul in Roman Custody,* The Book of Acts in Its First Century Setting 3 (Grand Rapids: Eerdmans, 1994), p. 2. See also H. W. Tajra, *The Trial of St. Paul: A Juridical Exegesis of the Second Half of the Acts of the Apostles* (Tübingen: Mohr Siebeck, 1989).

[17]Alexandru Neagoe, *The Trial of the Gospel: An Apologetic Reading of Luke's Trial Narratives* (New York: Cambridge University Press, 2002), p. 22.

[18]Skinner, *Trial Narratives,* p. 3.

[19]Ibid.

early disciples to ensure the spreading of the gospel? Or should we take away some larger normative premise about our own ability to interact with the civil judicial system and the larger sociopolitical system? As mentioned above, although some modern Christians eschew resort to the civil judicial system (at least for disputes between believers), we do not believe that Acts counsels a full bifurcation of Christians' lives as citizens of a civil state and citizens of God's community (for instance, Paul willingly exercised his rights as a Roman citizen to continue his missionary work). We also do not believe such a bifurcation is practical in today's age, if it ever was, as the civil state now touches so many aspects of every citizen's life: roads and transit, schools and education, food supply and delivery, health care, family law, and so much more. We do believe, however, that the trial narratives carry forward the message of Acts that Christians' first allegiance is to God. When there is a conflict between the civil state and God's will, the latter trumps and Christians must actively follow God even if it means disobeying the civil state. Other passages in Acts make this point emphatically, and it is to those that we now turn.

Christians and the civil state in the New Testament. Scholars have long argued about the message of Acts regarding the relationship of Christians to the civil state. Whereas Hans Conzelmann and others have contended that Luke intended to show the political harmlessness of Christianity to the Roman state,[20] others contend forcefully that this is incorrect. For example, C. Kavin Rowe calls Acts a "political document that aims at nothing less than the construction of an alternative total way of life—a comprehensive pattern of being—one that runs counter to the life-patterns of the Graeco-Roman world."[21] This is not to suggest that Christians in Acts were presenting and planning a counterstate, and in fact "such a construal of Christian politics is resolutely and repeatedly rejected."[22] Instead, the early Christians were fundamentally wedded to a different culture entirely as their primary normative allegiance. Their confessions of faith and baptisms placed them within the new order of the kingdom of God, with the advancement of God's purposes first.[23] At times

---

[20]See, e.g., Hans Conzelmann, *The Theology of St. Luke* (London: Faber & Faber, 1960); Neagoe, *Trial of the Gospel*, pp. 4-21.

[21]Rowe, *World Upside Down*, p. 4.

[22]Ibid., p. 87.

[23]See, e.g., David W. Pao, *Acts and the Isaianic New Exodus* (Tübingen: Mohr Siebeck, 2000; repr., Grand Rapids: Baker Academic, 2002), p. 5.

Christians' a priori commitments will not contravene allegiance to the state, and at other times they will.

The quintessential text of disobedience and resistance to ruling authorities in the New Testament is Acts 5:27-30:

> Having brought the apostles, [the captain and his officers] made them appear before the Sanhedrin to be questioned by the high priest. "We gave you strict orders not to teach in this name," he said. "Yet you have filled Jerusalem with your teaching and are determined to make us guilty of this man's blood."
>
> Peter and the other apostles replied: "We must obey God rather than men! The God of our fathers raised Jesus from the dead—whom you had killed by hanging him on a tree."

As mentioned above, the Sanhedrin (the governing Jewish religious body) had commanded Peter and the other apostles to cease preaching about Jesus. Following such a command would cut against the heart of the most important aspect of the Christian faith, in Peter and the apostles' view, for it would undercut the good news itself and the clear command of Jesus in Acts 1:8. A command by a ruling authority cannot stand in the way of this movement of God and should not stand in the way of the actions of God's followers in carrying out God's message of salvation. Peter and the apostles rejected the admonition of the religious leaders to keep quiet; they chose to follow God's commands instead.

A similar conflict occurred just one chapter earlier in Acts, when Peter and John were called before the Sanhedrin and commanded not to speak. In that instance, they replied, "Judge for yourselves whether it is right in God's sight to obey you rather than God. For we cannot help speaking about what we have seen and heard" (Acts 4:19-20). When the authorities command silence but God commands the sharing of the good news of Jesus, Christians must follow God's command.

It is a short step to look to the whole of Jesus' ministry in Luke-Acts and conclude that his life also teaches that Christians must follow God as preeminent. In Luke-Acts, we are taught that Jesus came to inaugurate the good news of God on earth—not just in proclaiming the good news, but in enabling sight for the blind, freedom for the prisoners, release of the oppressed and a return to jubilee principles (Lk 4:18-19, referring to Is 61:1-2). He inaugurated a kingdom in which the rich and the poor (Lk 16:19-31), first and last (Lk 13:30),

greatest and least (Lk 22:26-27), and powerful and weak (Lk 14:15-24) experience reversals. He taught the priority of mercy over sacrifice, service over
"lord[ing] it over" others (Lk 22:25), and a special concern for society's outcasts
and most vulnerable. So, when a government actively works against the equality
of people, the lifting up of the poor and freedom for the oppressed, then the
government is working against the core theological principles of God's coming
kingdom and—by extrapolation of the Acts passages—the government is to be
disobeyed when it enforces and imposes such laws upon Christians.[24]

The book in the New Testament following Acts is Paul's letter to the
Romans, which includes the longest passage in the New Testament about
the civil state. It counsels, and from a surface reading seems to require
without qualification, submission to ruling authorities.

> Everyone must submit himself to the governing authorities, for there is no
> authority except that which God has established. The authorities that exist
> have been established by God. Consequently, he who rebels against the au-
> thority is rebelling against what God has instituted, and those who do so will
> bring judgment on themselves. For rulers hold no terror for those who do
> right, but for those who do wrong. Do you want to be free from fear of the one
> in authority? Then do what is right and he will commend you. For he is God's
> servant to do you good. But if you do wrong, be afraid, for he does not bear
> the sword for nothing. He is God's servant, an agent of wrath to bring pun-
> ishment on the wrongdoer. Therefore, it is necessary to submit to the author-
> ities, not only because of possible punishment but also because of conscience.
>
> This is also why you pay taxes, for the authorities are God's servants, who
> give their full time to governing. Give everyone what you owe him: If you
> owe taxes, pay taxes; if revenue, then revenue; if respect, then respect; if
> honor, then honor. (Rom 13:1-7)

This is a difficult passage to square with what we have seen in Acts, for it
does not seem to contain caveats for Christians facing persecution or injustice but, on its face, appears to be a clear statement of obedience and
submission (even if the authorities prohibit preaching). The text further
establishes the notion that God is sovereign, and this seemingly includes
the placement of particular governing authorities over their subjects.

---

[24]Although the passage says nothing explicit about the method of resistance, whether violent or
nonviolent, the example of Jesus, Peter and the apostles was clearly that of nonviolent civil
disobedience.

Despite the seemingly clear text in Romans 13, however, some scholars resist reading the text as a once-for-all statement about how Christians should relate to the civil government.[25] We know that some of the earliest Christians were struggling with antinomianism,[26] for they were living with the idea that Jesus' return was imminent and that they did not need to engage in civil life. Paul wrote against that tendency elsewhere[27] and offered that, until the second coming of Christ (and the time and date are truly unknown, insisted Paul[28]), there will be and should be some state or civil authority. Whether Paul intended more than this, even in Romans 13, is unclear in light of the overall Christian Scripture and Paul's writings elsewhere.[29]

These differing themes have come into tension and even conflict at various times throughout history—with ruling Christians in power often relying upon the theme of submission to the state from Romans 13 and disenfranchised, out-of-power Christians at times looking to a theme of biblical resistance to authority via Acts 5. One of the starkest instances of this tension in recent history is the case of Christians in apartheid South Africa.

A CASE STUDY: APARTHEID SOUTH AFRICA

South Africa was, for the majority of the twentieth century, a land governed by racialized political policy and legal mandates. The peak of this racist and unjust history was nearly fifty years of an apartheid government that denied citizenship to all nonwhite Africans living within its borders. In this context, education, wealth, housing, occupations and even leisure were racialized in such a way that imposed a deplorable life on nonwhites, especially black Africans. One of the most heinous aspects of this oppressive rule by the Afrikaners, descendants of Dutch immigrant traders who settled in South Africa, was that it was given a Christian theological

---

[25]Thomas L. Hoyt Jr., "Romans," in *True to Our Native Land: An African American New Testament Commentary,* ed. Brian K. Blount et al. (Minneapolis: Fortress, 2007), pp. 249, 269.

[26]Antinomianism is the theological belief that one is no longer obliged to abide by legal or moral rules or laws after receiving God's grace. It is against such a stance that Paul writes in Romans 6, for example.

[27]For instance, Christians in Thessalonica had apparently stopped working in anticipation of the second coming. Paul writes against this and encourages those Christians to continue working in their daily occupations. See 2 Thessalonians 3:10-12.

[28]1 Thessalonians 5:2, stating that the day of the Lord will come "like a thief in the night."

[29]For further discussion of Romans 13:1-7 in this volume, see "The State, Law and Empire" in chapter eight.

warrant and blessing by many of its political and religious leaders.[30] This Afrikaner theology had three key features: a narrative reading of Scripture that emphasized racial difference and divinely ordained separation;[31] a "performance" of key biblical stories[32] that was manifested in an appropriation of a divinely ordained ethnic identity by the Afrikaner people; and a strong emphasis on Romans 13, read through a peculiar kind of Calvinistic lens.[33] Afrikaner theologians, pastors and politicians all emphasized Paul's admonition in Romans 13 that everyone must submit to the governing authorities as the central Scripture concerning Christian relations to the state. Read through an Afrikaner Calvinist lens that emphasized "sphere sovereignty,"[34] theologians claimed that the apartheid state was ordained by God and must be obeyed by all living in South Africa. In this account, the state is under God's rule and implements God's will in the political sphere. The different spheres of life are inviolable and function within their own divinely appointed goals and norms. So, the "sphere of the state," or the "political sphere," is autonomous and is "so important that even sin" committed by those exercising political authority cannot alter its authority.[35] Read this way, the injunction in Romans 13 to be subject to the governing authorities is an inviolable command that even the church cannot transgress. It is binding in all times and in all places, especially in apartheid South Africa. In fact, soldiers were given Bibles with an inscription on the first page that linked their harsh treatment of dissident political groups with their religious convictions and obligations.[36]

---

[30]See additional sources and discussion in Joel A. Nichols and James W. McCarty III, "When the State Is Evil: Biblical Civil (Dis)Obedience in South Africa," *St. John's Law Review* 85 (2011): 593.

[31]See Samuel A. Paul, *The Ubuntu God: Deconstructing a South African Narrative of Oppression* (Eugene, OR: Pickwick, 2009), pp. 13-57.

[32]Throughout history some people have "performed" key stories that are found in Scripture by attempting to relive or reenact scriptural stories in their contemporary situation. When doing so, they often interpret their lived realities as carrying the same theological import as the stories they are reenacting. For example, American Puritan settlers often understood themselves to be reliving the story of Israel entering Canaan. See Richard T. Hughes, *Myths America Lives By* (Urbana, IL: University of Illinois Press, 2003), pp. 19-44.

[33]Hans Engdahl has described this brand of Calvinism as "Afrikaner Calvinism." Hans S. A. Engdahl, *Theology in Conflict: Readings in Afrikaner Theology* (New York: Peter Lang, 2006), p. 46.

[34]See J. A. Loubser, *A Critical Review of Racial Theology in South Africa: The Apartheid Bible*, Texts and Studies in Religion 53 (Cape Town: Maskew Miller Longman, 1987; reprint, Lewiston, NY: Mellen, 1990), pp. 38-39 (citing Kuyperian sphere sovereignty); Engdahl, *Theology in Conflict*, p. 138.

[35]Loubser, *Critical Review*, p. 39.

[36]Pumla Gobodo-Madikizela, *A Human Being Died That Night: A South African Story of Forgiveness* (Boston: Houghton Mifflin, 2003), p. 53.

In this politically and theologically charged context, there were many religious leaders and political activists, primarily but not exclusively black Africans, who drew upon the example of the apostles in Acts to resist through civil disobedience what they considered unjust, evil and even blasphemous laws. Many Christians, both black and white, even argued that obedience to God *required* disobedience to the apartheid government. Three of the loudest of these voices were the Kairos theologians, Beyers Naudé and the Christian Institute of Southern Africa, and Anglican Archbishop Desmond Tutu.

The Kairos theologians. *The Kairos Document,*[37] composed by an anonymous group of South African theologians, was a theological statement that was circulated throughout South Africa and the world.[38] The document provided a theological denunciation of the apartheid regime and laid the theological foundation for resistance to, and eventual overthrow of, the regime. Included in this statement was a biblical defense of civil disobedience as a means to achieving this end and a condemnation of the use and abuse of Romans 13 and "state theology" by defenders of apartheid.[39]

The Kairos theologians began their rebuttal of state theology's use of Romans 13 by claiming that the passage has often been misused throughout history by unjust, totalitarian and sinful governments and authorities to legitimize their rule and justify their oppression. Paul was not, as state theology assumes, claiming to write a once-for-all, final-word-on-the-subject declaration about the relationship of Christians to governing authorities and the state.[40] To treat the text in such a way is inappropriate because it reads it out of its immediate context in Romans, its context within the entire biblical witness and the context of first-century Christians living in Rome. Instead, in the book of Romans "Paul was writing to a particular

---

[37]Charles Villa-Vicencio, ed., "The Kairos Document," in *Between Christ and Caesar: Classic and Contemporary Texts on Church and State* (Grand Rapids: Eerdmans, 1986), p. 252 (hereinafter *Kairos Document*).

[38]See Peter Walshe, "The Evolution of Liberation Theology in South Africa," *Journal of Law and Religion* 5 (1987): 299, 309.

[39]"State theology" is the name given by *The Kairos Document* to the theology that emphasized Romans 13 and the sovereignty of God over the nations because of its usage to justify the existence of the apartheid state. See *Kairos Document*, p. 252.

[40]The modern concept of the nation-state did not exist at the time Paul was writing, but we will sometimes use this language for ease of discussion. Further, Paul was addressing many political subjects who were not citizens (Jews, women and slaves, for instance). The modern idea of a democratic citizen who participates in an election of government officials who form and shape civil law did not exist and poses additional difficult questions.

Christian community in Rome, a community that had its own particular problems in relation to the State at that time and in those circumstances."[41] Those original readers, according to the Kairos theologians, were most likely Christian antinomians who believed that they were not required to obey the laws of any governing authority other than their one Lord, Jesus Christ. Their allegiance to Christ and his kingdom meant that they were no longer subject to any earthly authority. Paul's emphasis, therefore, was simply that Christians do have a duty to be good citizens. One way in which Christians should fulfill this duty is to be subject to governing authorities. However, in this reading the emphasis is not on the extent to which that duty applies,[42] but simply that it is a duty that Christians cannot easily dismiss as irrelevant to the spiritual life. In particular, the passage does not teach that obedience is a duty that can never be transgressed (in contrast to the prohibitions against murder or adultery, for example).

This is especially important in light of the entire biblical witness. The Kairos theologians claimed straightforwardly that "in the rest of the Bible God does not demand obedience to oppressive rulers."[43] The Israelites, while slaves in Egypt, were led by God in a social revolt. God raised up prophets consistently to denounce the prevailing ethos and social standards of their day. Some of those prophets, like Isaiah walking around naked for three years (Is 20), used civil disobedience as a creative, nonviolent protest against rulers of the day. The book of Daniel includes three key stories of faithful civil disobedience.[44] Even Jesus, on multiple occasions, broke either custom or law for the causes of justice, love, mercy and compassion. In the context of the entire biblical witness, Paul could not have meant his brief statement in Romans 13 about being subject to governing authorities to be the only rule for how Christians should relate to government.

Finally, the Kairos theologians insisted that one could not read Romans 13 apart from Revelation 13. In Revelation 13 a governing authority, probably the Roman Empire, is described as a beast who receives its authority and

---

[41]*Kairos Document*, p. 253.
[42]Ibid.
[43]Ibid.
[44]These stories are Daniel and his friends refusing to eat the ceremonially unclean food of the Babylonian king (Dan 1); Shadrach, Meshach and Abednego refusing to bow to the statue of King Nebuchadnezzar (Dan 3); and Daniel refusing to obey the Babylonian law that forbade prayer to any god other than King Darius (Dan 6).

blessing from a dragon, Satan.[45] In Romans 13 we see that, in some way, God granted the Roman Empire its authority; but in Revelation 13 we see that, in some way, Satan granted the Roman Empire its authority. Inasmuch as a government is in line with God's will and is fulfilling its purpose of rewarding what is right and punishing what is wrong, it can be viewed as blessed and ordained by God and worthy of one's obedience. Inasmuch as a government does not fulfill its mission, and even does the exact opposite by punishing what is right and rewarding what is wrong, it cannot be viewed as blessed and ordained by God.

Beyers Naudé and the Christian Institute of Southern Africa. Beyers Naudé was a white Afrikans pastor.[46] He was moving through the ranks of the Dutch Reformed Church, a member of the Broederbond (South Africa's elite fraternal order) and destined for leadership in the country, possibly even as prime minister.[47] He was, as a younger man, a strong defender of apartheid.[48] But slowly from 1955 to 1960 he began to have a change of heart as a result of an intense period of biblical study. And then the violence of the Sharpeville Massacre in 1960 provided the impetus for a Damascus Road experience for him; he thereafter became one of apartheid's staunchest opponents, for he believed "separateness" could be neither biblically nor theologically justified.[49] By 1963, Naudé was forced to choose to renounce his anti-apartheid views or face ouster from his pastorate.[50] In a September 22, 1963, sermon announcing his decision to step down rather than temper his anti-apartheid activity, Naudé pleaded with his congregants to follow God rather than humans. His sermon was

---

[45]Whether one interprets Revelation 13 as describing primarily the Roman Empire that governed at the time of its writing (as most scholars do) or as predicting a future government, the passage still teaches that some governments are "ordained" by Satan. On varying ways of interpreting Revelation see Carl R. Holladay, *A Critical Introduction to the New Testament: Expanded CD-ROM Version* (Nashville: Abingdon, 2005), pp. 812-15.

[46]See Colleen Ryan, *Beyers Naudé: Pilgrimage of Faith* (Grand Rapids: Eerdmans, 1990), pp. 2-11; Charles Villa-Vicencio, "A Life of Resistance and Hope," in *Resistance and Hope: South African Essays in Honour of Beyers Naudé*, ed. Charles Villa-Vicencio and John W. De Gruchy (Grand Rapids: Eerdmans, 1985), p. 3.

[47]Ryan, *Beyers Naudé*, pp. 32-39; G. McLeod Bryan, "Introduction," in *Beyers Naudé, The Struggle for Liberation in South Africa*, Baptist Peacemaker International Spirituality Pamphlet 5 ([S.I.]: Baptist Peacemaker International Spirituality, 1986).

[48]See Villa-Vicencio, "Life of Resistance and Hope," pp. 5-7.

[49]See Ryan, *Beyers Naudé*, pp. 40-72.

[50]See J. C. Pauw, "The Life and Legacy of Beyers Naudé," in *The Legacy of Beyers Naudé*, ed. L. D. Hansen (Stellenbosch, South Africa: Sun Press, 2005), pp. 16-17.

titled "Obedience to God," and it expressly rested upon Acts 5:29. After recounting the story of Peter and John before the Sanhedrin, Naudé asked: "And what does it mean to follow God if it does not mean proclaiming the kingship of Jesus Christ over all peoples, . . . and this applies also to our ecumenical and race relations." He urged the parishioners to action: "Oh my Church, I call today with all the earnestness that is within me: awake before it is too late, stand up and stretch the hand of Christian brotherhood to all who reach out to you in sincerity. There is still time, but time is becoming short, very short."[51]

It was Naudé's founding of the Christian Institute of Southern Africa (CISA) in 1963, and his attendant publication of the journal *Pro Veritate* in an effort to advance ecumenical dialogue and work against apartheid, that led to his forced departure from his parish. Undaunted, Naudé and the other, mostly white, South African Christians in CISA continued to combat apartheid. CISA (and Naudé himself) were ultimately "banned" by the government in the 1970s for their work toward equality for blacks. During a state trial concerning CISA, Naudé and others defended the right and duty of Christians to disobey an unjust government.[52]

In the 1973 statement "Divine or Civil Obedience" (some twelve years prior to *The Kairos Document*), Naudé emphasized Paul's statement in Romans 13 that governing authorities exist to be "God's servant" for the people's good.[53] He argued that as long as a government or state is acting as God's servant by pursuing policy and law that reflect God's will, Christians should be subject to such a state. If a government is not acting as God's servant, however, but rather in service of itself, it becomes the Christian's duty to resist such a state. Historically, the emphasis of interpretation in Romans 13 had been on the words "be subject" when it should have been on the fact that the state or governing authorities exist to be "God's servant," he said. This interpretive move en-

---

[51]Rev. C. F. B. Naudé, *My Decision* (Christian Institute of Southern Africa, 1963), a sermon preached on Sunday, September 22, 1963. Naudé also famously preached on a passage from Jeremiah in his farewell sermon to his congregation in 1963, wherein he insisted that God used the Bible as a "sledgehammer" of judgment upon all human systems, social customs and traditions—including apartheid. See Rev. C. F. B. Naudé, *Flame of Fire and Sledgehammer* (Christian Institute of Southern Africa, 1963), a sermon preached on Sunday, November 3, 1963.
[52]See, e.g., Ryan, *Beyers Naudé*, pp. 73-186.
[53]See Charles Villa-Vicencio, ed., "Divine or Civil Obedience," in *Between Christ and Caesar: Classic and Contemporary Texts on Church and State* (Grand Rapids: Eerdmans, 1986), pp. 217, 219.

abled Naudé to turn the conversation away from the individual and onto the government.

According to Naudé, when a government ceases to function as God's servant, it becomes idolatrous because it then begins serving itself and its own interests rather than God's will. This is the story of Revelation 13 (the apocalyptic biblical story of "the beast") recurring in the modern day.[54] Naudé argued that in such a situation, it is the duty of Christians to disobey their idolatrous government:

> When the Government deviates from the Gospel, the Christian is bound by his conscience to resist it. Even if this results in breaking the law, it has to be done because God's will must be maintained above the law of man (Acts 4). The Government is God's servant and this means that it cannot arbitrarily place itself above the rule of law without impinging on the highest authority. If it does it, it becomes the evil-doer, (Romans 13) which must be resisted in obedience to God.[55]

Therefore, it is not government and authorities as such that are appointed by God. It is only those authorities that act as God's servants on earth that are approved by God.

Desmond Tutu. The most well-known theological critic of the apartheid state was Anglican Archbishop Emeritus of Cape Town Desmond Mpilo Tutu.[56] Archbishop Tutu was president of the South African Council of Churches during an important period of the anti-apartheid struggle and was awarded the Nobel Peace Prize in 1984 for his work in resisting nonviolently the apartheid government in multiple marches and acts of civil disobedience. After the establishment of a democratic government, President Nelson Mandela appointed him as chair of the South African Truth and Reconciliation Commission (TRC). Tutu became one of the world's leading moral voices and became synonymous with the struggle for freedom and forgiveness on the African continent.

In his public sermons, speeches and writings Tutu raised similar points concerning civil disobedience to those raised by the Kairos theologians and Naudé.

[54]Ibid., p. 218.
[55]Ibid., p. 220.
[56]See John Allen, *Rabble-Rouser for Peace: The Authorized Biography of Desmond Tutu* (New York: Free Press, 2006).

He criticized politicians who quoted Romans 13 while ignoring Revelation 13.[57] He pointed out that according to Romans 13 governments are to act as God's servants and are no longer worthy of Christian obedience if they fail to do so.[58] Tutu often pointed out that there are multiple stories in Scripture of civil disobedience, especially from Jesus, that are used as examples of faithfulness.[59]

Tutu was especially adamant, citing the Christian Scriptures, that a Christian's allegiance to God trumped any responsibility to an unbiblical and sinful government, such as the apartheid government. He drew on the example of Peter, John and the apostles, who boldly proclaimed in a courtroom, "We must obey God rather than any human authority."[60] Whenever a human authority demands that Christians act in an unchristian way, their allegiance to God trumps their duty to obey such a government.[61] Tutu drew great inspiration from this example of the apostles' fearlessness in the face of imprisonment, violence and death.[62] Their example provided a precedent for Christian civil disobedience. Whenever someone accused Tutu of acting in an unchristian way because he broke the law or accused him of not respecting law and order, he reminded them of Peter's bold words before a council of religious, social and political leaders in the first century.

Tutu said very bluntly, "Our marching orders come from Christ himself and not from any human being. . . . When laws are unjust then Christian tradition teaches that they do not oblige obedience."[63] On another occasion he said, "[The Bible] says when a ruler gives you unjust laws, disobey. You are not disobeying the ruler, you are obeying God. . . . The church says, an unjust law does not oblige obedience."[64] At such times civil disobedience is a religious obligation because "not to oppose injustice is to disobey God."[65]

---

[57]See Desmond Tutu, "Your Policies Are Unbiblical, Unchristian, Immoral and Evil (1988)," in *The Rainbow People of God: The Making of a Peaceful Revolution*, ed. John Allen (New York: Doubleday, 1994), pp. 145, 152.

[58]Ibid.

[59]See, e.g., Desmond Tutu, "They Have Power but No Authority (1989)," in *The Rainbow People of God: The Making of a Peaceful Revolution*, pp. 169, 171.

[60]Tutu, "Your Policies Are Unbiblical," pp. 151-52 (quoting Acts 5:29 NRSV).

[61]Tutu, "They Have Power but No Authority," p. 171.

[62]Tutu, "Your Policies Are Unbiblical," pp. 151-55.

[63]Ibid., pp. 150-51.

[64]Tutu, "They Have Power but No Authority," p. 171.

[65]Desmond Tutu, *God Has a Dream: A Vision of Hope for Our Time* (New York: Doubleday, 2004), p. 63.

Conclusion

The book of Acts is important for understanding the way Christians should relate to civil authorities. Therein, we see Peter declaring that he would obey God before men, and Paul using the Roman court system as a means of advancing his missionary efforts. We also see the early Christians laying the foundations of later internal church law so that Christian communities could function with appropriate autonomy from civil authorities. This helped to create structures that allow Christianity to adapt to the political system in which it finds itself.

The primary lesson in all of this, it seems to us, is that the relationship of Christians to the state or governing authority is a contextual matter. There are times when Christians should submit to the governing authorities; in fact, this is usually the case. Even in instances where there is blatant injustice, even religious oppression, Christians still should submit to the majority of the laws of the governing polity (and in democratic governments they should also participate, with an eye toward creating a more just civil society). Following the example of the first Christians, however, we see that there are times when civil disobedience is justified, and even required. This is clearest in instances where the Christian faith itself is made illegal, but we believe it is not limited to these most extreme cases.

There have been Christians throughout history who have, through prayer and communal discernment, deemed it necessary to disobey certain laws out of obedience to God's calls for love, mercy and justice. For instance, Christians in the French village of Le Chambon,[66] and throughout Europe, disobeyed the laws declaring that no one should aid Jews during World War II. Christian abolitionists in the United States frequently broke immigration laws when operating the underground railroad. A century later, Christians broke a litany of Jim Crow laws in nonviolent civil disobedience as they sought social change toward racial justice. And, as explored above, Christians in South Africa participated in nonviolent civil disobedience against apartheid. They understood their actions as not simply a political tactic but a requirement of the Christian faith. We believe that those Christians who discerned that their faith required such drastic action were faithful to the tradition of Peter and John when they faced the Sanhedrin in Acts 4–5. If

---

[66]Philip P. Hallie, *Lest Innocent Blood Be Shed: The Story of the Village of Le Chambon, and How Goodness Happened There* (New York: Harper & Row, 1979).

one understands that Christian faith demands the pursuit of justice and acts of mercy as much as it does the task of preaching, the congruence between a contemporary figure like Desmond Tutu or Beyers Naudé and the early Christians is not hard to recognize.

Is there room for such actions in a contemporary American context (for example)? All citizens, except convicted felons, now have the right to vote, and discrimination based on race, religion or gender is illegal. There are still many situations, however, in which Christians have deemed it necessary to break the law to be faithful to God. For instance, several churches in the American Southwest provide water and transportation to illegal immigrants who are crossing through the deserts. In some places such aid is illegal, but these Christians believe that their faith (for example, the parable of the good Samaritan) requires that they meet the immigrants' needs because hundreds of people die every year making the journey.[67] Other Christians, frequently Catholic priests and nuns, have been imprisoned over the past several decades for their ongoing symbolic protests of America's proliferation of nuclear weapons.[68] And other Christians attempt to save the lives of unborn children by protesting outside clinics, sometimes even blocking the entrances, in their effort to prevent women from exercising their legal right to abortions. While the reasons Christians give for claiming that these laws are so unjust that they demand disobedience are varied (theologically and politically), and the forms of disobedience also vary, the common thread is a strong belief that a commitment to the Christian faith sometimes requires the willful violation of human laws.

Our conclusion is that in this context it is appropriate at times for Christians to participate in civil disobedience. In most situations, most of the time, submission—combined with prayer, acts of piety and participation in the established democratic processes—is the appropriate Christian response.

---

[67]See, e.g., Darryl Fears, "Desert Samaritans Stand by Duty: Move to Outlaw Aid for Immigrants Called Contrary to Bible," *Washington Post,* December 18, 2005, p. A10 (describing Christian assistance to migrants); United States Government Accountability Office, *Illegal Immigration: Border-Crossing Deaths Have Doubled Since 1995; Border Patrol's Efforts to Prevent Deaths Have Not Been Fully Evaluated,* report to the Honorable Bill Frist, Majority Leader, US Senate, prepared by the United States Government Accountability Office (Washington, DC, August 2006), http://www.gao.gov/assets/260/251173.pdf (reporting thousands of deaths from 1990 to 2005 from desert crossings).
[68]See, e.g., Joshua J. McElwee, "A Prophetic, Transforming Priest: Jack McCaslin," *National Catholic Reporter,* April 1, 2011, p. 1.

But there are times when Christians must declare unashamedly that we obey God rather than humans. It is not for us to declare beforehand when those times will be. Instead, we believe the leading of the Holy Spirit in real Christian communities is the best guide for such decisions—just as in the book of Acts. Our reading of both Scripture and history make it clear that there are times when faithfulness to the way of Christ requires disobedience to the way of the world and its governing institutions. May God grant his Spirit to all Christians in discerning when those times arise.

8

LIVING AS CHRISTIANS
UNDER CIVIL LAW

The New Testament Letters,
Law, and Politics

David M. Smolin and Kar Yong Lim

THE DISTANCE IN TIME, place, language and culture between that of the biblical authors and contemporary readers presents a primary interpretive dilemma. There is the constant question of what the text means to persons today—persons themselves living within complex, varied and dynamic contexts. This dilemma is made both more urgent and more difficult by our belief that the Scriptures are inspired, reliable and authoritative. Hearing both the voice of God and the voice of the human authors across the space of almost two thousand years requires a trained ear: "Whoever has ears to hear, let them hear" (Lk 8:8).[1]

The words *law* and *politics* in our title accentuate these interpretive dilemmas. Monotheists and others who believe in some kind of ultimate and binding authority (God, morality, etc.) tend to connect that ultimate authority to some kind of authoritative, binding and universal law. Even those who discount such absolutes and think in terms of merely situational ethics may have a layperson's view of positive law—law enacted by governments—

---

[1]Unless otherwise indicated, all Scripture quotations in this chapter are from the NIV.

as clear and definitive. Thus, many would assume that any law discussed in the Christian Scriptures must be authoritative, binding, universal and clear.

Further, the word *law* has been made problematic by centuries of intra-Christian disputes about theological subjects such as justification by faith and the role (if any) of obedience in salvation. These controversies about the role of law have been intensified by debates over whether the apostle Paul's discussions of law primarily address the issue of salvation by faith or primarily address the relationship between Jew and Gentile (or both). In these contexts, questions related to the nature of Mosaic, Old Testament, Jewish and rabbinic laws, in both biblical and historical contexts, can become critical.

By contrast, for some the word *politics* is almost the opposite of *law*, evoking a domain of the state and raw (lawless) power. Even idealistic or Aristotelian definitions of politics may perceive politics as a form of practical reason in which it is necessary to vary actions according to the needs of the situation. From this perspective, politics is perceived as situational and contextual rather than universal and fixed.

We acknowledge these difficulties primarily to prevent them from becoming distractions from the primary purpose of this essay, which is to focus on the civil law, meaning that law which is enforced by the state, in the context of the New Testament letters. This is not an essay about the question of salvation or the related doctrine of justification, nor is it an exploration of the role of Jewish law in Christian theology or ethics. At the time and in the Scriptures under discussion, the governing authority or state was the Roman Empire and those acting locally on its behalf. The civil law enforced by this empire was neither Mosaic law nor its rabbinic elaborations, and to the degree there were directly religious elements to that law, they related either to the imperial religious cult or to other pagan religious practices or beliefs.

To encounter this law—the law of the pagan Roman Empire—as a Christian is necessarily to explore the question of the relationship of the state and empire to the church. The primary question in view is therefore whether a Christian theology of politics and civil law emerges from the New Testament letters. A related question is how such a theology is to be heard and expropriated today, in our own varied contexts.

Our interpretive position is obviously different from that of the original recipients of the New Testament letters, as a matter of language, culture and political situation. We have the record of the long advance of the church, over some three hundred years, amidst the difficulties of life in the pagan Roman Empire, culminating in a "Christian" Roman Empire that then declines and "falls." Indeed, we are divided from the authors and original generations of readers by multiple histories of Christendom, or Christian empire, in both the Eastern and Western branches of the church. Many of the possible interpretations of a Christian politics are before us as lived experiments that have, for us, occurred in the past. Some of the embodiments of those experiments are decidedly unattractive.

Keeping these interpretive difficulties in view, this essay will try to discern the political and legal contexts and meanings of the New Testament letters, focusing primarily on the Pauline corpus. We will also explore specific applications within diverse, contemporary contexts. Topically, the primary issues addressed will be: (1) state, law and empire, through Romans 13 and other relevant texts; (2) the concept of natural law, through Romans 1 and 2, and as relevant to Romans 13; (3) the Pauline adoption texts in the context of the anti-imperial reading of Paul; and (4) lawsuits between Christians, in 1 Corinthians 6, once again in the context of the anti-imperial reading of Paul.

THE STATE, LAW, AND EMPIRE THROUGH ROMANS 13
AND OTHER RELEVANT TEXTS

Paul and the Roman imperial order. Twenty-first-century developments in the study of Paul have witnessed a shift from merely seeing Paul as the apostle of Jesus Christ who proclaims the gospel to the Gentiles to also perceiving Paul the citizen within the Roman Empire who navigates, confronts and critiques the political and social structures of his day. This additional perspective reveals an anti-imperial Paul, an apostle who is deeply concerned with the injustice and corruption that were prevalent in the world of his day. These additional understandings of Paul can be seen, for example, in the work of Neil Elliott on the gospel as a direct challenge to the power of Caesar in the epistle to the Romans; N. T. Wright's recognition of the imperial cult as a fitting background for a number of Paul's letters, especially Romans; and Richard Horsley's examination of Paul's theological and practical response to political issues of his day.[2]

---

[2]See Neil Elliott, *The Arrogance of Nations: Reading Romans in the Shadow of Empire* (Minneapolis: Fortress, 2008), pp. 59-85; N. T. Wright, *Paul: Fresh Perspectives* (London: SPCK, 2005), pp. 59-

Some, like New Testament scholar Seyoon Kim, are critical of these anti-imperial readings of Paul. Kim dismisses the anti-imperial interpretation in large part by portraying Paul as expecting an imminent *parousia* of such a cosmic nature as to deny any ordinary political aspirations that could be realized in this world.[3] However, it is important to note the common ground. Kim acknowledges that Paul "would certainly have included the Roman imperial system in his criticism of the idolatrous and immoral pagan world (Rom. 1:18-32), of unjust pagan courts (1 Cor. 6:1), of the 'rulers of this age' often acting as agents of Satan (1 Cor. 2:6-8; 1 Thess. 2:18; cf. 2 Cor. 4:4), of slavery (1 Cor. 7:21; Phlm), and so forth."[4] Kim further understands that the anti-imperial reading of Paul is a natural reading of the text, despite his rejection of that reading:

> The various assumptions about the pervasive imperial cult in the Roman East, Paul's apocalyptic thinking, and his gospel of the crucified Jesus as the Lord and Savior, as well as the parallelism of important terms (e.g., *kyrios, soter/ soteria, evangelion, dikaiosyne, pistis, eirene, eleutheria, elpis, parousia, apantesis*) between the Roman imperial ideology and Paul's preaching of the gospel of Jesus Christ, all seem to invite an anti-imperial reading of the Pauline Epistles. It appears natural to suppose that in the Roman world Paul's proclamation of Jesus as the messianic king, Lord (*kyrios*), and Son of God, and as the Savior (*soter*) who would come (*parousia*) to destroy the rulers of this age/ world and establish the Kingdom of God, could have been understood as proclaiming a rival king to Caesar and subverting the Roman imperial order.[5]

Given the substantial common ground, and the concession of how "natural" the anti-imperial reading of Paul is to the text, it seems important to identify the concerns that animate Kim and other critics of this anti-imperial reading. First, some concerns may arise from a desire to retain traditional readings of Paul regarding justification.[6] As noted above,

---

79; Richard A. Horsley and Neil Asher Silberman, *The Message and the Kingdom: How Jesus and Paul Ignited a Revolution and Transformed the Ancient World* (Minneapolis: Fortress, 2002), pp. 184-223. See also Richard A. Horsley, ed., *Paul and the Roman Imperial Order* (Harrisburg, PA: Trinity Press International, 2004).

[3]See Seyoon Kim, *Christ and Caesar: The Gospel and the Roman Empire in the Writings of Paul and Luke* (Grand Rapids: Eerdmans, 2008), pp. 66-71.

[4]Ibid., p. 42.

[5]Ibid., p. 65.

[6]It may be worth noting that Seyoon Kim is also the author of *Paul and the New Perspective* (Grand Rapids: Eerdmans, 2001), and of course N. T. Wright is a central proponent of the

however, these controversies over justification are not the subject of this
chapter. More importantly, there is nothing inherently incompatible with
Paul being read traditionally regarding justification while acknowledging
that Paul is deliberately contrasting the imperial cult and political order
with the reign of Christ and God's kingdom. More than one thing can be
going on within the obviously complex and dense writings of Paul. Further,
it is necessary theologically to disentangle what Paul is saying about empire
and civil law from what he is saying about justification and salvation.

Second, there may be concern that some of these readings of Paul as
anti-imperial go too far in remaking Paul into a political author concerned
primarily with social and political revolution and reformation. Here, the
concerns may have some validity. While Paul properly places the political
within the context of the cosmic vision of Christ and the kingdom, it could
be a confusion of categories to see Paul as primarily concerned with improving the political order through reforming or replacing the Roman
Empire. This difficulty is sharpened by those in the new movement who
may want to situate the anti-imperial readings of Paul in the context of anti-
American, anti-Western, postcolonial literature.[7] Whatever the flaws and
grievous sins of the various Western empires, there are dangers of reducing
either Paul or the Christian faith to merely an echo of secular critical political perspectives on the various empires of this world.

Eschatology and the political theology of the Reformers. Eschatology[8]
necessarily looms large over this discussion, as indicated by Seyoon Kim's
use of Paul's purported eschatological expectations to dismiss the anti-
imperial reading of Paul.[9] What would Paul make of a Christian empire?
Would he see such as a sign of the progress of Christ's kingdom, or as a
contradiction in terms? Can the kingdom "come" politically ahead of the
parousia—the return of Christ—in any meaningful sense? Short of the full
establishment of Christ's kingdom by Christ personally, is a severe contrast
and tension between earthly political rulers and the kingdom inevitable
and permanent? These questions are implicitly at the center of any attempt

---

so-called new perspectives and also writes favorably of the anti-imperial reading of Paul.
[7]See Neil Elliott, "Paul and the Politics of Empire," in *Paul and Politics: Ekklesia, Israel, Imperium,
Interpretation, Essays in Honor Krister Stendahl,* ed. Richard A. Horsley (Pittsburgh: Trinity Press
International, 2000), p. 17.
[8]For additional discussion in this volume of eschatology ("last things"), see chapter nine.
[9]See Kim, *Christ and Caesar,* pp. 66-70.

to read Paul politically, for they concern the question of what Paul would think of the replacement of the Roman pagan empire with some other empire, be it a Roman Christian empire or any other. If all empires are equally and necessarily in tension with Christ's kingdom, then Paul's political goals, if any, would have been quite modest. If improving the political order in a religious or moral sense is somehow connected to the progress of the kingdom, then a more political reading of Paul becomes more plausible.

Different eschatological views are implicit in the diverse approaches to politics that arose within Western Christendom after the Protestant Reformation. The Anabaptist emphasis on a separationist church and rejection of Christian involvement in politics implies an eschatology that expects tribulation rather than progress in the political history of the world. From this perspective a Christian empire or state is a contradiction in terms, and the kingdom will not be established until the literal second coming of Christ. Thus, the foundational Anabaptist Schleitheim Confession of 1527 begins with a reference to "perseverance in all tribulation until the end" and ends with a reference to the "blessed hope, and the glorious appearance of the Great God and our savior Jesus Christ."[10] Like the Anabaptists, Luther perceived the political order as something other than Christ's coming kingdom but still viewed Christian participation in political office as a positive service to both God and humankind. For Luther, recognition of the positive function of the state in a fallen world had more to do with the order of creation and the common needs of humanity to restrain evil and provide social order, issues to be sharply distinguished from the proclamation of the gospel and the growth of the kingdom.[11]

By contrast, the multi-jurisdictional, one-kingdom vision underlying neo-Calvinist political theology is compatible with a more optimistic eschatology and the positing of a link between the advancement of the

---

[10]See "The Schleitheim Confession (1527)," in *Creeds of the Churches: A Reader in Christian Doctrine, from the Bible to the Present*, ed. John H. Leith, 3rd ed. (Atlanta: John Knox, 1982), pp. 282-91.

[11]See David M. Smolin, "A House Divided? Anabaptist and Lutheran Perspectives on the Sword," in *Christian Perspectives on Legal Thought*, ed. Michael W. McConnell, Robert F. Cochran Jr. and Angela C. Carmella (New Haven, CT: Yale University Press, 2001), pp. 370-85; Marie A. Failinger and Patrick R. Keifert, "Making Our Home in the Works of God: Lutherans on the Civil Use of the Law," in *Christian Perspectives on Legal Thought*, ed. Michael W. McConnell, Robert F. Cochran Jr. and Angela C. Carmella (New Haven, CT: Yale University Press, 2001), pp. 386-405; Martin Luther, "On Governmental Authority (1523)," in *The Protestant Reformation*, ed. Hans J. Hillerbrand (New York: Harper & Row, 1968), p. 43.

kingdom and politics. Here, the belief in the positive possibilities for a Christian social and political order, even a Christian kingdom or nation, becomes determinative of Christian political viewpoints.[12] Calvin himself argued for Christian disobedience to political rulers, and even political revolution, under certain circumstances. He stated that there is no higher calling than being a magistrate and approved of the use of the sword by the Christian without any sense of moral or spiritual ambivalence.[13] Regardless of the formal eschatological label we apply to contemporary neo-Calvinists, their viewpoint is optimistic in looking for signs of progress of the kingdom in political and historical events.

History of and problems in the interpretation of Romans 13:1-7. Seyoon Kim calls Romans 13 "the Achilles heel for all anti-imperial readings of Paul."[14] Certainly, a careful analysis and application of Romans 13 is necessary to assess whether this central text on civil government can be made compatible with other Pauline texts that appear to use the Roman Empire and imperial cult and household as a foil to illustrate the glories of Christ and the kingdom.

> Let everyone be subject to the governing authorities, for there is no authority except that which God has established. The authorities that exist have been established by God. Consequently, whoever rebels against the authority is rebelling against what God has instituted, and those who do so will bring judgment on themselves. For rulers hold no terror for those who do right, but for those who do wrong. Do you want to be free from fear of the one in authority? Then do what is right and you will be commended. For the one in authority is God's servant for your good. But if you do wrong, be afraid, for rulers do not bear the sword for no reason. They are God's servants, agents of wrath to bring punishment on the wrongdoer. Therefore, it is necessary to submit to the authorities, not only because of possible punishment but also as a matter of conscience.
>
> This is also why you pay taxes, for the authorities are God's servants, who give their full time to governing. Give to everyone what you owe them: If you owe taxes, pay taxes; if revenue, then revenue; if respect, then respect; if honor, then honor. (Rom 13:1-7)

---

[12]See, e.g., Abraham Kuyper, *Lectures on Calvinism* (1931; repr., Grand Rapids: Eerdmans, 1987); Smolin, "House Divided?"

[13]See John Calvin, "Civil Government," in *Institutes of the Christian Religion,* ed. John T. McNeill, vol. 2 (Philadelphia: Westminster, 1960), 4.20.

[14]Kim, *Christ and Caesar,* p. 36.

The opening verses of Romans 13:1-7[15] appear to suggest, at first sight, that Paul is propagating an uncompromising endorsement of political authority. In Romans 13:1-2, Paul seems to declare that all political authority is ordained by God and should not be resisted. Romans 13:3-4 states that those who do good will have no fear for the authorities and will be commended for their good deeds. However, the sword will be wielded against those who practice evil. And in order to stay out of trouble, one has no choice but to be subject to the authorities, as stated in Romans 13:5. Finally, in Romans 13:6-7, it is instructed that one should give all that is due—whether it is taxes, revenue, respect or honor—to the governing authorities. Taking these exhortations at face value, Paul's words can appear to be an unqualified endorsement of political authority that would stifle any opposition to political systems: perhaps even political systems of domination and oppression. Further justification for submission to governing authorities is often made by referring to later parallel texts found in 1 Peter 2:13-17, 1 Timothy 2:1-4 and Titus 3:1-3.[16] It has often been argued that the parallels among these texts suggest that Paul's and Peter's view of the relationship between the believers and the governing authorities was widely held among early Christians.[17]

How does one make sense of Romans 13:1-7 in a way that would reconcile it with Paul's critique of rulers and authorities elsewhere, as seen, for example, in 1 Corinthians 2:8, where he held the rulers responsible for crucifying Christ? The difficulty in interpreting Romans 13:1-7 is demonstrated by positions taken by Christians throughout the centuries, ranging from complete surrender to critical submission to the ruling authorities.[18]

Whatever position one takes, the offensiveness of this passage has been noted by numerous authors. J. C. O'Neill has exclaimed that these verses "have caused more unhappiness and misery in the Christian East and West than any other seven verses in the New Testament by the license they have given to tyrants," as they "have been used to justify a host of horrendous

---

[15]For additional discussion in this volume of Romans 13:1-7, see "Christians and the civil state in the New Testament" in chapter seven. In the view of the editors, this section of Scripture is sufficiently important to deserve two extensive discussions.

[16]See also *1 Clement* 60:2–61:2.

[17]See Thomas H. Tobin, *Paul's Rhetoric in Its Contexts: The Argument of Romans* (Peabody, MA: Hendrickson, 2004), p. 397.

[18]Mark Reasoner, *Romans in Full Circle: A History of Interpretation* (Louisville, KY: Westminster John Knox, 2005), pp. 129-42.

abuses of individual human rights."[19] But perhaps equally shocking is his speaking so positively of the Roman authorities, and ascribing such an exalted status to Rome in his own time, as if he is oblivious to the brutality surrounding him. It is as if Paul is hypocritical and untrue to his whole theological position when he advocates submission and subordination to the ruling authorities.[20] This difficulty is accentuated by Neil Elliott's argument that the vivid condemnation of human depravity in Romans 1:18-32 includes God's judgment on the imperial household.[21]

Reading Paul in context. In our view, what Paul advocated in Romans 13:1-7 was not an elaborate set of principles or a theory of political power or his theology of the state. Rather it was Paul's guidance to a minority group who lived under the reality of a Roman hegemony and power that was unjust and oppressive. It was this vulnerable group of Christians that Paul addressed.

The focal point of Romans 13:1-7 has been largely on the clause "let everyone be subject to the governing authorities" (Rom 13:1), and it has often been assumed that the duty of all Christians is to submit themselves to the ruling government. However, this reading fails to take into account Paul's wider discourse within the verses that follow. While there is no denying that Paul affirms that all ruling authorities are established by God, he is also quick to describe how godly ruling authorities should act. Paul is thus calling the authorities themselves to account, challenging whether they, as divinely appointed governors and rulers, have been carrying out their responsibilities in a just manner. Ruling authorities are to rule justly and to exercise their divinely appointed powers rightly. They are to punish those who do wrong and commend those who do right. They are to rule for the good of the people (see Rom 13:2-4). For Paul, if all authority comes from God, who rules justly, any authority that wishes to rule as a divinely appointed instrument must also rule consistently with the justice of God. In other words, what Paul seems to be advocating here is willing submission with the clearly implied assumption that this submission is only appropriate to a power that deserves such obedience, a power that rules justly.

The recipients living in the heart of the Roman Empire would have im-

[19]J. C. O'Neill, *Paul's Letter to the Romans* (London: Penguin, 1975), p. 209.
[20]James Kallas, "Romans 13:1-7: An Interpolation," *New Testament Studies* 11 (1965): 365-74. "Paul could not have ascribed such an exalted status to Rome without being not only hypocritical and servile, but untrue to his whole theological position" (ibid., p. 369).
[21]Elliott, *Arrogance of Nations*, pp. 59-85.

mediately recognized that what Paul identified as the proper characteristics of governing authorities are the direct opposite of the caesars and their representatives. The early Christians would have recognized that the Roman emperors did not primarily rule for the good of the people, giving rise to the question, What will be the response of the Roman Christians now that they know Caesar has failed the test to be God's appointed ruler? This is the context for Paul's admonition in Romans 13:7: "Give to everyone what you owe them: If you owe taxes, pay taxes; if revenue, then revenue; if respect; then respect; if honor, then honor." Paul here elaborates four specific items that the believers are to pay if these are due: taxes, revenue, respect and honor. Paul begins with the two forms of taxes that are to be paid to the authorities: the direct and indirect taxes.[22] This is what they owe the state, and Paul argues that believers should not refrain from paying what is due. The two forms of taxes that Paul addresses were historically documented in the middle of the first century by the Roman writer Tacitus:

> In the same year, as a result of repeated entreaties from the people, which complained of the excesses of the tax farmers, Nero hesitated whether he ought not to decree the abolition of all indirect taxes [*vectigalia*] and present this as the noblest of gifts to the human race. His impulse, however, after much preliminary praise of his magnanimity, was checked by the senators who pointed out that the dissolution of the empire was certain if the income on which the state subsisted were to be curtailed: "For, the moment the duties on imports were removed, the logical sequel would be a demand for the abolition of the direct taxes [*tributorum*]."[23]

Tacitus's account gives us a glimpse into the situation in Rome at about the time Paul wrote the letter to the Christians in Rome. There were complaints from the population about the taxes imposed by the tax collectors. If Nero were to abolish the indirect taxes, demands might also be made to abolish the direct taxes. This suggests that the population deemed both forms of tax excessive and unjust.[24] It is therefore interesting that we see Paul exhorting the Roman Christians to exercise restraint by paying what is due to the authorities, be it direct (*phoros*) or indirect (*telos*) taxes.

---

[22]In Romans 13:7, Paul specifically refers to two forms of taxes: *phoros* and *telos*, direct and indirect taxes, typically translated as "taxes" or "tribute" and "revenue" or "custom," respectively.
[23]Tacitus, *Annales* 13.50.
[24]See Tobin, *Paul's Rhetoric in Its Contexts*, p. 400.

However, readers often overlook Paul's assertion that respect and honor should be paid to those to whom it is due, implying that they should not be paid to those to whom it is not due! If one lives under ruling authorities who have defied instead of honored their divinely appointed role, and seem to have promoted injustice instead of justice, as argued by Elliot,[25] how should one respond to the authorities? Paul is less explicit in this respect, and this is where most interpretation has unfortunately missed the significance and power of Paul's rhetoric. What Paul may be advocating here is a subversive call for the Christians living under Roman hegemony, power and injustice to examine whether respect and honor should be rendered to those who have failed to discharge their divinely appointed duties (Rom 13:1). Even if some degree of respect and honor is due to the office no matter how unjust and oppressive the rule, and even though unjust rulers often punish ordinary criminal acts and thereby preserve order, Paul's language nonetheless should be seen as a tacit mandate for Christians to examine critically the acts and status of ruling authorities, and to act accordingly. The rulers, after all, are not (as they may claim) gods but instead are appointed by and accountable to God himself. Thus, if one is to apply the Word of God correctly, one must examine what is due to the ruling authorities. Moreover, Paul is making clear what is *not* due to political rulers: worship, or the complete and absolute obedience one owes to the divine. Christians might give Caesar some degree of respect and honor, but they would not render him worship.

Of course, it has long been recognized that the Bible teaches disobedience to the ruling authorities when there is a direct conflict between God's commands and the law or commands of human rulers. The classic examples include the Hebrew midwives who "feared God" and disobeyed Pharaoh's command to kill the Hebrew male infants, and were rewarded by God (Ex 1:15-21), and Peter's statement in Acts 5:29, when told not to preach the gospel, that "we must obey God rather than human beings." Interpreted correctly, Romans 13:1-7 reinforces rather than conflicts with these texts on disobedience, for it places rulers in a position subordinate to, and accountable to, God and subject to God's standards of justice. Even while being subject to the ruling authorities, one can and must look beyond those

---

[25]Elliott, *Arrogance of Nations,* pp. 59-85.

authorities and seek direct guidance from God himself. And the measure of respect and honor one owes to the ruling authorities is bounded by the absolute respect and honor—and worship—owed to God, the ruler of all.

Reading Romans 13:1-7 under a present-day regime hostile to the church. In the next two sections, we think it will be useful to acknowledge the different voices, backgrounds and concerns of the authors. As a part of acknowledging the critical roles of perspective on biblical interpretation, these sections will include some material in a first-person voice, as opposed to the more objective or joint voicing found elsewhere in this chapter.

Paul, of course, wrote to Christians in the capital of the Roman Empire. Such a community would have been more conscious than others of the imperial authority. Although the persecution of Christians had yet to intensify at the time Paul wrote Romans, there were other forms of oppression, such as the edict of Claudius, which expelled the Jews from Rome (cf. Acts 18:2). In the capital of the Roman Empire, where the worship of the imperial cult was popular, one could only imagine that there would have been hostility toward Gentile Christians who refused to participate in such cultic activities. How should this passage be understood today within a context where there is political and religious oppression by a dominant group against a Christian minority?

I (Kar Yong Lim) can offer some reflections from the perspective of a member of the Christian minority living in the multireligious, multiethnic and multicultural context of Malaysia, where Islam is not only the dominant religion but also the official religion.

In Malaysian society, religious beliefs, identity and ethnic boundaries are intricately interconnected. The Malays, the dominant group, who constitute about 60 percent of the population, are Muslims. In fact, the constitution defines them as Muslims.[26] The political administration is dominated by Muslim Malays, who hold more than 75 percent of the positions in the cabinet ministry. Every student enrolled in all institutions of higher learning, both privately and publicly funded institutions, is required to take courses in Islamic studies and civilizations as core courses. Currently, Malaysia is at the forefront of Islamic banking, Islamic insurance, Islamic health care and the establishment of halal food.

---

[26]Article 160(2) of the Federal Constitution of Malaysia.

Within the legal framework, the sharia court has been established. Although its initial jurisdiction is limited primarily to family law, the influence and the power of the sharia court cannot be undermined, and matters related to Islam cannot be tried and heard in the civil court. The sharia court in Malaysia now has absolute powers in hearing cases related to the Islamic religion. Based on these developments, the former prime minister, Dr. Mahathir Mohamad, declared in September 2001 that Malaysia is an Islamic state.[27]

Furthermore, Malaysia's achievement in Islamization has been held in high regard by other Muslim nations, as reported by Rodney Wilson, who describes Malaysia as "a near ideal Muslim state . . . where the basic Islamic values and tradition are cherished and valued and simultaneously a highly successful modernizing process is going on."[28]

The Christian church in Malaysia faces the extremely challenging task of being a faithful witness as a religious minority in a dominant Islamic context.[29] To cite only two examples of the use of law against Christians, Muslims who convert to Christianity are subject to possible legal punishment[30] and Christian churches are placed under unreasonable zoning restrictions that make building places of worship increasingly difficult.[31]

---

[27]See his *Islam and the Muslim Ummah: Selected Speeches of Dr. Mahathir Mohamad, Prime Minister of Malaysia,* updated ed. (Petaling Jaya: Pelanduk, 2001).

[28]Rodney Wilson, "Islam and Malaysia's Economic Development," *Journal of Islamic Studies* 9 (1998): 259.

[29]For discussion of the challenges and restrictions confronting the church in Malaysia, see Albert Sundararaj Walters, *We Believe in One God? Reflections on the Trinity in the Malaysian Context* (Delhi: ISPCK, 2002), pp. 74-80, 234-84; Göran Wiking, *Breaking the Pot: Contextual Responses to Survival Issues in Malaysian Churches,* Studia Missionalia Svecana 96 (Lund: Swedish Institute of Missionary Research, 2004); and Kairos Research Centre, *Doing the Right Thing: A Practical Guide on Legal Matters for Churches in Malaysia* (Petaling Jaya: Kairos, 2004).

[30]For example, Jamaluddin Othman and Hilmy Nor are Malay Muslims who converted to the Christian faith; Pua Boon Seng is a Christian of Chinese origin. Together with one hundred other political and religious activists, they were detained in 1987 as part of a nationwide operation code-named Operasi Lalang, pursuant to Section 8(1) of the Internal Security Act, 1960, for professing and practicing their religious faith, acts considered threatening to the national security of Malaysia. For further information, see Minister of Home Affairs, Malaysia and Another v. Jamaluddin bin Othman, [1989] 1 *Malayan Law Journal* 418; Hilmy Nor, *Circumcised Heart* (Petaling Jaya: Kairos Research Centre, 1999); and Pua Boon Sing, *Fragments from Kamunting: 325 Days in Police Custody for the Christian Faith* (Serdang: Good News Enterprise, 1990). See also commentary on these cases by Min Choon Lee, *Freedom of Religion in Malaysia* (Kuala Lumpur: Kairos Research Centre, 1999), pp. 85-88. The appeal of Lina Joy, a Malay Muslim converted to Christianity, to remove the word *Islam* from her national identity card was dismissed by the Federal Court, the highest court in Malaysia, in May 2007.

[31]For example, construction of the Church of the Divine Mercy, a Catholic church, was delayed

Paul's declaration that "there is no authority except that which God has established" and that "the authorities that exist have been established by God" in Romans 13:1 clearly puts things in perspective for Christians. It serves as a reminder that the God of whom Paul speaks here is the one who appoints the ruling authorities through political processes (whether they be democratic or otherwise). Yet, this passage reminds Christians that God remains sovereign. Just as Paul addressed the first-century Christians who were a powerless minority under the Roman rule and oppression, this passage also appeals to the Christian minority in Malaysia, and similarly situated Christians, whose ultimate hope is in God alone. Christians are reminded that they are to submit themselves, first of all, to God. Yet at the same time, submission to God does not mean that one will be spared from persecution and suffering as a minority Christian group.[32] Indeed, as Peter urges, if one is going to suffer, it is better "to suffer for doing good than for doing evil" (1 Pet 3:17).

How then would one understand Paul's final exhortation to pay what is due to the empire, be it taxes, revenue, honor or respect? Certainly, Paul would not have been enthusiastic in his support of the Roman Empire. However, he is quick to remind the believers that in regard to what is owed to the empire, such as taxes and revenues, they are to fulfill such obligations as citizens of the empire. In this respect, any civil law that is not against God's commandments is to be observed by the believers. When it comes to giving honor and respect that is due, Paul is less explicit. The question arises in matters where one's loyalty and obligation to God are called into question. In such matters, Paul seems to advocate that honor and respect are not due, or that whatever is due does not include obedience. For example, when confronted with the question of whether minority Christians should evangelize, contrary to the civil law, we have before us the powerful model of the early Christians, who said that "we must obey God rather than human beings" (Acts 5:29) and be prepared to bear whatever consequences may follow. If the ruling authorities have failed to discharge their appointed duties and oppression and injustice are evident, then appropriate actions should also be taken. It is in this regard that Romans 13:1-7 calls the

<hr>

for almost twenty years. See http://www.divinemercyshahalam.com/history.htm.

[32]For further discussion, see Kar Yong Lim, "Is There a Place for Suffering in Mission? Perspectives from Paul's Sufferings in 2 Corinthians," in *The Soul of Mission: Perspectives on Christian Leadership, Spirituality and Mission in East Asia: Essays in Appreciation of Dr David Gunaratman*, ed. Tan Kang San (Petaling Jaya: Pustaka Sufes, 2007), pp. 64-78.

church to speak prophetically to the state. The church is to take a coura-
geous role in denouncing and calling for the elimination of specific abuses
and practices that are contrary to the gospel—whether they are an increase
in corruption and acts of injustice, the erosion of human rights, the sub-
version of for fair and clean elections, or the promotion of the supremacy of
one ethnic group against others, all of which are issues and realities confronting the church in Malaysia. Ultimately, the minority Christians in Malaysia are called to be exemplary witnesses, diligent for the common good
and engaged in good actions (cf. Rom 12:9–13:14). Above all else, the Christians are exhorted to owe no one, including the ruling authorities, anything
except the continuing debt of love (Rom 13:8).

Reading Romans 13:1-7 from within the contemporary West.
Fears of a "post-Christian" state. I (David Smolin) am a citizen of the United
States, a country that historically has been strongly influenced by Christianity, but whose leading cultural and political institutions have in recent
decades been strongly influenced by perspectives that are often at odds
with Christianity. The United States thus bears some similarities to other
parts of the West that are sometimes called post-Christian, although the
levels of Christian religious belief in the United States are much higher than
in most other Western nations. I was born to liberal Jewish parents in New
York City and became a Christian in college. As the grandson of Jewish immigrants who came to the United States just ahead of the Nazi genocide of
the Jewish people, and as an ethnically Jewish Christian steeped in Jewish
Sunday school on the record of Christian historical atrocities against Jews,
I am aware of the dark side of Christendom.

One of the ironies of the perspective of many Christians in the contemporary West is their sense of being under siege and threat in nations that
historically had been parts or extensions of Western Christendom. The fear
of a secular state imposing anti-Christian values is palpable, and even
stronger is a profound sense of loss at not having the anchor of a state and
society supportive of Christian norms. The lack of these governmental and
cultural supports seems to have left many Christians adrift, as if they do not
know how to function without them. Of course some Western Christian
traditions—such as the Anabaptist tradition—have never entrusted themselves to the state or the cultural support of the broader society. However,

even traditions like the Baptist tradition, who theoretically support a strong separation of church and state, seem to find it difficult to identify a clear strategy for dealing with a state and society that are a complex mix of Christian, anti-Christian and non-Christian elements.

Within this setting, it would seem that a properly minimalist reading of Romans 13:1-7 would be of help. The expectations that Romans 13—and indeed, the entire corpus of the New Testament letters—provides for the state are cosmically modest although practically significant. The ruling authorities are neither the founders nor the leaders of the church, and Paul does not charge the state to proclaim the Christian gospel. The state is to punish the evildoer and to protect the good. Seen from within the context of the second table of the law (commandments five through ten of the Decalogue governing relationships between human beings), it would seem to be enough—and indeed a great deal—if the state could, without itself becoming corrupt, effectively check the typical evils of crimes against the human person (murder, assault, sexual assault, etc.) and against property (theft, embezzlement, etc.). There is ample historical precedent for considering matters of the family and marriage to be within the domain of the church rather than the state, providing additional rationale for modest expectations for the kinds of family rules that the state enforces in a diverse society. The church has long understood that there are many evils that in prudence do not come within the jurisdiction of the civil magistrate and many goods that the state is powerless to establish or even further. Freed from the crutches of overreliance on the state, the church within the West may again learn how to walk on its own two feet.

Treatment of minority religions in Western and majority Christian societies. Church and state within Western and majority Christian societies must find an appropriate stance toward other religions, such as Islam, Judaism, Hinduism and Buddhism. Here there are several ironies. For example, within the Malaysian context it is Christians who, despite Muslim opposition, seek to retain the word *Allah* for the name of God, based on the traditional use of that term by Christians and others,[33] while Christians in the West often view *Allah* as a term limited to Islam, a term that names a

---

[33]For a summary of the recent controversy, please refer to the media statement issued by the Christian Federation of Malaysia dated March 30, 2011: http://www.necf.org.my/newsmaster.cf m?&menuid=43&action=view&retrieveid=1284.

God completely different from the Christian God. This common Western Christian stance is based on a linguistic error in its false understanding of the word *Allah* as a term limited to Islam. It also is counterproductive in minimizing the common heritage of Islam and Christianity both worshiping the God of Abraham, the God who is the Creator of the Universe and the Supreme Judge.

It is true, in a sense, that Muslims and Christians and Jews worship the same God, insofar as they all claim to worship the God of Abraham. It is also true, in a sense, that Christians worship a different God from Jews and Muslims, insofar as Christians believe in a triune God of whom Jesus is the incarnate second person. This leads to a rhetorical choice: emphasize the commonality by saying that all worship the same God but understand that God differently, or emphasize the differences by saying that all worship different Gods.

Christians tend to say that they worship the same God that Jews worship because the legitimacy of Christianity is built upon the claim of continuity between the Old and New Testaments, despite the fact that Jews in the Old Testament era generally would not have self-consciously understood themselves to be worshiping a triune God and despite the rejection of the Trinity and Jesus by mainstream Judaism throughout the Christian era. The tendency of some Western Christians to treat Islam differently from Judaism in this regard, and to understand Allah as a completely false and unrelated God, is an easy enough stance to take for Christians in, for example, the United States, but it is not clear that it is helpful to the situation of Christians in majority Islam nations nor overall to Christian-Islamic relations.

The claim that Christianity is a universally valid revelation of God paradoxically requires the utmost care and respect for those of other religions, for in the religious sphere we meet human beings in some kind of spiritual relationship to the divine, even if there are, from a Christian perspective, serious distortions and errors in other religions.

Indeed, Christianity claims that the triune God is the God of all creation. As Paul proclaims, he is not just the God of the Jews, but also of the Gentiles—the nations (Rom 3:29). This global, cross-national, crosscultural Christian claim is constantly met by the belief that Christians are a foreign people preaching a foreign God—as Paul found in Athens (Acts 17:18). This characterization of Christianity as a "foreign" religion that is limited to particular nations, regions, races or peoples, along with the identification of certain nationalities or people as intrinsically of a non-Christian religion (i.e., Hinduism in India, Islam among specific peoples, such as the Malay people in Malaysia), is a serious obstacle to the spread of the gospel. Whenever Christianity or Christ is associated with any kind of racism, with the persecution of or unjust acts taken against non-Christians (Muslims, Jews, Hindus, etc.), or even with ignorant and misleading statements about other religions, it validates this belief that Christianity belongs to "them" and is something that is used against "us." Unfortunately, the centuries of Christendom have produced, not surprisingly, innumerable and notorious acts of persecution and discrimination against specific non-Christian groups. Thus, a Christian state usually is a double-edged sword, for while it has potential for good, it simultaneously creates grave opportunities for evil. Paradoxically, as Christianity assumes political power, the abuses of that power validate the fears of non-Christians and sully the reputation of Christ, creating grave barriers against the further expansion of the gospel. The historical weight of those barriers was recognized by Pope John Paul II when, upon the approach of the third millennium of the church, he called for penitence and the cleansing of the conscience of the church regarding historical sins against, among others, the Jews.

If there is such a thing as a Christian state, or if the state is to act justly as required by Romans 13, then it must exhibit a practice that treats all people as equally made in the image of God. This is why the next topic of "natural law" is so important, for it underscores the universality of the standards to which the state, whether secular, Christian, pagan, Islamic or otherwise, should be held.

ROMANS 2:14-15: NATURAL LAW AND EMPIRE

> Indeed when Gentiles, who do not have the law, do by nature things required by the law, they are a law for themselves, even though they do not have the law. They show that the requirements of the law are written on their hearts, their consciences also bearing witness, and their thoughts sometimes accusing them and at other times even defending them. (Rom 2:14-15)

The foundation for interpreting Romans 2 is the scriptural revelation of God as Creator and Judge, and the scriptural understanding of God's inherent relationship to both his creation and to humankind as made in his image. Natural law[34] is thus not merely a matter of interpreting these few words of Romans or of supplying a proof text, but rather of discerning the worldview of Scripture. Natural law begins in Genesis, not in Romans, and Romans must be read through the lens of Genesis. From this perspective, the plain words of Romans 2:14-15, despite some translation issues, amply support the traditional interpretations of natural law held in common by Augustine, Luther, Calvin and Aquinas.[35]

From this perspective, because human beings are created in the image of God, some true knowledge of the moral law is present in the human heart and conscience, even for those who lack access to written revelation. Moreover, despite Paul's vivid portrayal of the spiritual and moral decline of fallen human beings in Romans 1:18-32, some degree of both knowledge and obedience to the moral law has survived the fall. The image of God has not been totally extinguished in humankind. Even for Calvin, who taught that sin infects every part of the human being, including reason, the fall does not mean that nothing remains of the image of God in humankind. Indeed, this remaining light of the image of God in each human being is a part of what holds us in inherent relationship to God and makes us accountable to God.

This teaching on natural law is foundational for the civil law. It supplies the basis for what Augustine called the possibility of a "common platform" between Christian and pagan regarding "all that concerns our purely human life" and furthers the "earthly peace."[36] Significantly, the Augustinian concept of a common platform is not so rigid as to exclude cultural diversity as embodied by differences in the civil law from nation to nation:

> [The church] takes no issue with that diversity of customs, laws, and tradi-
> tions whereby human peace is sought and maintained. Instead of nullifying
> or tearing down, she preserves and appropriates whatever in the diversities of

---

[34]For additional discussion of natural law in this volume, see "Christian Sources of Insight on Law" in the introduction.

[35]See, e.g., Augustine, *Confessions,* trans. R. Pine-Coffin (New York: Penguin Putnam, 1961), 2.4, p. 47; Thomas Aquinas, *Summa Theologica* 1a2ae, q. 91 a. 1-3; q. 94 a. 4-6; q. 96 a. 4; q. 100 a. 1-5; John Calvin, "Explanation of the Moral Law (The Ten Commandments)," *Institutes of the Christian Religion,* ed. John T. McNeill, vol. 1 (Philadelphia: Westminster, 1960), 2.8.1 and n. 5; John T. McNeill, "Natural Law in the Thought of Luther," *Church History* 10 (1941): 211-27; John T. McNeill, "Natural Law in the Teaching of the Reformers," *Journal of Religion* 26, no. 3 (1946): 168-82; Michael Cromartie, ed., *A Preserving Grace: Protestants, Catholics, and Natural Law* (Grand Rapids: Eerdmans, 1997).

[36]Augustine, *The City of God,* trans. Marcus Dods (New York: Modern Library, 1994), 19.17.

divers races is aimed at one and the same objective of human peace, provided only that they do not stand in the way of the faith.[37]

This concept of an underlying moral unity based on a common human nature, yet expressed in diverse cultural forms and subjected to serious distortion by sin, expresses the complex biblical doctrine of natural law. The concept of natural law stated in Romans 2 creates a necessary context for Romans 13:1-7. Natural law provides a basis for holding governing authorities, including emperors, to account, regardless of the religion of the ruler. Even if emperors are ignorant of the Scriptures, as human beings they have sufficient access to God and the moral law to be held accountable. Thus, the statement in Romans 13 that ruling authorities should punish evildoers but not those who do good works is built upon the supposition in Romans 2:14-15 that Gentile rulers who are ignorant of the Scriptures nonetheless are accountable, as human beings, for knowing the basic moral law. Even pagan emperors are accountable for distinguishing right from wrong and acting accordingly. See also Romans 1:19, 20, 32.

Natural law is thus a central concept for all who seek to hold oppressive rulers to account. It is based on the universality of the Hebrew and Christian God, who is present not only in a specific people, nor only in a specific Scripture, as important as those may be, but whose image is present in every human being. Natural law reminds us of what all people have in common as human beings, despite our very real and important religious differences. For Christian rulers, the moral law is an important reminder that the non-Christians under their authority—the atheist, Muslim, Jew, Hindu, Buddhist and eclectic borrower of this and that—are of the same race and origin as themselves and also bear God's image.

Natural law is an important hedge against simplistic, result-oriented thinking, of the kind that says that the quickest way to advance the kingdom is to do some brutal or immoral act that will accentuate the power or numbers of Christians in this world. The gospel is not a free pass or permission for violating the universal law for kingdom purposes. Indeed, every act committed wrongfully against another individual or group, in the name of God, Christ or the gospel, constitutes a disgrace against the gospel that forms an obstacle to the advancement of God's kingdom.

---

[37]Ibid.

AN ANTI-IMPERIAL READING OF PAULINE ADOPTION TEXTS

In this section, we consider a law-related topic, adoption, that Paul addresses in his letters. This discussion will serve two purposes. First, the subject of adoption raises the question of using the Bible as a basis for advocating specific laws and public policies in contemporary nations. Adoption may seem entirely uncontroversial and unproblematic to many, making it emblematic of the difficulties. Second, the subject of adoption is another example, in an unexpected place, of Paul using Roman emperors, the imperial cult and imperial household as foils against which to demonstrate the superiority of Christ and his kingdom.

The only direct references to adoption in the New Testament occur in five Pauline texts: Romans 8:15, 23; 9:4; Galatians 4:5; and Ephesians 1:5. All five texts concern the relationship of God to his people. The Greek term in the Pauline adoption texts is *huiothesia,* consisting of two parts: *huios* meaning son and *thesia,* from the verb *tithēmi,* which means "to set, put or place." The word literally means to put in the place of a son, and some translate it as "sonship." Regardless of whether "adoption" is always the right translation, Paul is usually understood as using Roman adoption as a metaphor to help Christians understand their relationship to God.[38] Adoption in ancient Rome generally involved an emperor or noble father adopting a young adult son, as a means of obtaining a suitable heir to continue a great Roman family. The persons adopted were generally neither children nor poor nor orphans, and often were related to the adoptive father otherwise through marriage or blood relationship. Adoption thus had nothing to do with providing for parentless minor children. Adoption was particularly prominent in the line of emperors at the time of Paul.[39]

Paul's primary message is that the inheritance the Christian receives from being "adopted" by God would be even greater than the inheritance received by those who were adopted by Roman emperors. Paul is communicating that there is no higher honor than being a Christian, which makes one a coheir with the Lord Jesus Christ, heir of God the Father. The adoption metaphor, like the use of terms such as *lord* (*kyrios*) and *coming* (*parousia*), is once again

---

[38]See David M. Smolin, "Of Orphans and Adoption, Parents and the Poor, Exploitation and Rescue: A Scriptural and Theological Critique of the Evangelical Christian Adoption and Orphan Care Movement," *Regent Journal of International Law* 8, no. 2 (2012): 267, 286-95, http://works.bepress.com/david_smolin/10/.

[39]See ibid., pp. 290-92, nn. 109-16.

a means by which Paul communicates to Gentiles the superiority of the Christian gospel and kingdom to the Roman Empire and imperial cult. For Paul, the adoption metaphor also reinforces the household and family metaphors for the church, under which Christians regard one another as brothers and sisters regardless of diversities in nationality, race and culture—again, an alternative form of unity to that provided by the Roman imperial cult.[40]

The common usage of these Pauline texts to justify modern American and Western forms of adoption of children is problematic.[41] While contemporary Americans think of helpless infants or vulnerable and poor young orphan children when they hear the Pauline adoption texts, such probably never occurred to either Paul or his original readers. To miss the imperial and Roman meanings of adoption is to miss Paul's meaning. To interpret these texts as a call to adopt helpless orphan children is to assert something that was not in the mind or intent of Paul. The application Paul intended and stated was a recognition of the reality of the church as one household and family despite racial, national and cultural differences, not the question of how best to care for orphan children. For churches that claim to care about the word of God, this should matter. It may also make a practical difference, as the biblical methods for assisting orphans, on close examination, may not center on or even involve adoption as practiced in the modern Western world.[42]

These misunderstandings are emblematic of the difficulties that arise when we see a term in the Bible and infuse it with meanings from our own laws and cultures. Adoption has a very particular meaning in the law and culture of the United States, which developed very late in time—between 1850 and 1980—and which is foreign to the law and culture of the Bible, the common law of England and the ancient Roman world. This American form of full, "as if" adoption centers on the legal fiction that the adoptee was born to the adoptive parents and was never born to the original family; this pretense that it is "as if" the adoptee were born to the adoptive parents is protected by a cloak of secrecy preventing the adoptee from ever knowing

---

[40]See ibid., pp. 286-95.
[41]See, e.g., Dan Cruver et al., *Reclaiming Adoption: Missional Living Through the Rediscovery of Abba Father*, ed. Dan Cruver (Adelphi, MD: Cruciform Press, 2011); Russell D. Moore, *Adopted for Life: The Priority of Adoption for Christian Families & Churches* (Wheaton, IL: Crossway, 2009); see Smolin, "Of Orphans and Adoption" (critiquing these works).
[42]See Smolin, "Of Orphans and Adoption," pp. 267-311.

his or her original identity.[43] Claiming biblical support for American law and culture through use of a term that occurs both in the Bible and in our culture, but which had a very different meaning in the Bible, is a pathway for wrongfully using the Bible to justify our own predilections. We cannot properly "hear" the word of God, nor properly apply it to the myriad delicate issues that arise in framing laws, if we infuse our own cultural meanings into biblical terms contrary to their original meanings.

Further, adoption in the contemporary world has very different meanings from culture to culture. For example, Islam generally rejects Western practices of full adoption, preferring something more akin to foster care (*kafalah*); Ethiopian views of adoption and that of many other cultures do not understand adoption to sever permanently the relationship between adoptees and their original families. Presuming that the meaning of the term *adoption* in United States law and culture is the biblical meaning can constitute a kind of cultural hegemony and blindness that can provide a false biblical mandate for overturning the legitimate practices of other cultures, practices that upon examination may prove to be permissible under biblical standards, or even closer to biblical standards than American practices.

Of course the church needs to care for the widow and the orphan, the poor and the vulnerable. However, identification of a biblical term with a distinctly American legal practice confuses efforts to do so rightly, providing us with false biblical justifications for practices that may be helpful, harmful or just one of many ways of accomplishing a proper end.

For purposes of this chapter, the subject of adoption thus demonstrates both the centrality of the anti-imperial theme in Paul and the difficulty of trying to justify or derive specific contemporary laws from the Bible. The same two points are made in the next section, regarding civil litigation between Christians.

CIVIL LITIGATION IN 1 CORINTHIANS 6:1-11

Finally, we consider one of the dilemmas faced by many Christians: can Christians bring one another to court? As we turn our attention to 1 Corin-

---

[43]See Elizabeth J. Samuels, "The Strange History of Adult Adoptee Access to Original Birth Records," *Adoption Quarterly* 5 (2001): 63; Elizabeth J. Samuels, "The Idea of Adoption: An Inquiry into the History of Adult Adoptee Access to Birth Records," *Rutgers Law Review* 53 (2001): 367-437; and E. Wayne Carp, *Family Matters: Secrecy and Disclosure in the History of Adoption* (Cambridge, MA: Harvard University Press, 1998).

thians 6:1-11, we immediately notice that Paul seems to cast litigation in a negative light and church arbitration as a favored position. The problem in the Corinthian church was that some in this Christian community were taking one another to court to be judged by unbelieving judges, and the church did not seem to believe there was anything wrong in doing so. If the early Christians in Corinth did not see such practice to be an issue, why was it that it upset Paul so much, as reflected in 1 Corinthians 6:1-3?

> If any of you has a dispute with another, do you dare to take it before the ungodly for judgment instead of before the Lord's people? Or do you not know that the Lord's people will judge the world? And if you are to judge the world, are you not competent to judge trivial cases? Do you not know that we will judge angels? How much more the things of this life! (1 Cor 6:1-3)

A survey on the function of lawsuits in the Greco-Roman world illuminates the problems addressed within the Corinthian context and helps us understand Paul's meaning.

Why did litigation take place? In an illuminating study, Bruce Winter applies a wealth of information about the operation of the Roman courts to the situation in Corinth.[44] There were many reasons why litigation took place in the Greco-Roman world, including settling scores with political opponents, retaliation for breaches of relationships of trust and obligation, competition for public office, jealousy of a young rising star in civic life, and retaliation against those who interfered with one's political aspirations. All these were considered legitimate reasons for initiating litigation. More often than not, lawsuits were not about seeking justice but were an arena for the battle of personalities and selfish interests where unfair advantage over the opponents was sought. Lawsuits also typically involved assaults of the opponent's character.

Who could be taken to court? In Paul's days, the right to prosecute was not automatically granted to everyone.[45] Generally, lawsuits were conducted between social equals from the elites of the city, or by a plaintiff of superior social status against someone socially inferior. If the defendant was a parent, a patron, a magistrate or a person of high rank, charges could

---

[44]Bruce W. Winter, "Civil Litigation in Secular Corinth and the Church," *New Testament Studies* 37 (1991): 559-72.
[45]For further discussion, see ibid., pp. 561-62.

not be brought against him by those of lower social status, such as children, freedmen, private citizens or men of low rank. Such discriminatory rules protecting members of higher social orders from being taken to law by those of lower social standing were justified by the rationale that those of higher social status should not be publicly shamed. Therefore, a suit against someone of a higher rank would show an unwelcome lack of respect for one's patron or benefactor. As such, law that favored the rich—creditors over debtors, landlords over tenants—seemed to be the norm (see Jas 2:5-7).

What were the purposes of lawsuits? Generally, seeking justice was hardly the reason a case was brought to the civil court. In Paul's day, only people of high social standing were prone to initiate litigation. Social, political and economic elites had the upper hand in the courts because they could capitalize on their influence and wealth. They could also enhance their own reputation by injuring their opponent's character and reputation. They could potentially gain honor by beating a rival down in court. Consequently, the wealthy were able to take unfair advantage of the judicial system by exercising their prestige and influence. If both the plaintiff and defendant were of equal status, law was an arena for the battle of the elites.[46]

This kind of unfair advantage in courts also extended to the choice of a lawyer. A lawyer of humble status might be rejected merely because of the higher status of his opponents. Even the practice of selection of jurors in the Greco-Roman world favored the rich and elites. Jurors were selected from the highest census group of men with wealth as a primary indication, with a minimum wealth indicator of 7500 denarii—twenty-five times the average annual income of an ordinary person.[47] Furthermore, if social standing and status were not enough to weigh the scales of justice, bribery could easily tip the balance.

What others said about the legal system. Evidence indicates that the courts of Paul's days were less than impartial and that substantial corruption existed. For example, Cicero opened his speech to the jury and judges in the prosecution of Verres, a notorious Roman magistrate known for his mismanagement of Sicily, by citing the well-known fact that the courts would never convict any man, however guilty, if he had money.

---

[46]See also Alan C. Mitchell, "Rich and Poor in the Courts of Corinth: Litigiousness and Status in 1 Corinthians 6:1-11," *New Testament Studies* 39 (1993): 562-86.

[47]For further discussion, see Winter, "Civil Litigation," pp. 564-66.

Based on his observation, Cicero also declared that there were three major hindrances in civil litigation, namely, excessive favor, possession of resources and bribery.[48] Seneca related a case of a rich and powerful man daring a poor man to institute proceedings against him. "Why don't you accuse me, why don't you take me to court?" asked the rich man. The poor man responded, "Am I, a poor man, to accuse a rich man?" The rich man exclaimed, "What would I not be ready to do to you if you impeached me, I who saw to the death of a man who merely engaged in litigation with me?"[49]

The case in Corinth. From the survey above, we have seen that unfair advantages in the judiciary system in the Greco-Roman world favored the rich and elites. We have seen how influence, power and wealth could easily bend the rule of law. Therefore, it was not surprising that Paul was exasperated that within the church a Christian brother would take another brother to court. And worse still the case was brought before a nonbelieving judge whose judgment would be biased in favor of the rich and powerful. This background survey suggests that the plaintiff mentioned by Paul in 1 Corinthians 6 likely enjoyed high status and social standing in the Corinthian church. It was most likely that this person had taken one of his peers or a weaker member of the church who was lower in rank and social status to court. Therefore, in this context, the pursuit of litigation had little to do with the pursuit of justice. If the lawsuit was directed against a weaker member of the church, this would likely mean that the defendant would have been victimized by the corrupt court system. As such, Paul's outrage becomes even more understandable. The Christian plaintiff who was of higher social status had become instrumental in inflicting injustice and shame on another fellow believer who did not have equal access to justice.

Paul grieved because believers in the church chose to follow the ways of the world by bringing a trivial matter to court simply to gain some personal benefits and to shame others. Paul was disgusted that someone in the church had the audacity to take a quarrel with a fellow Christian to be adjudicated by unbelievers whose judgment was hardly impartial. Civil litigation between Christian brothers indicated enmity between members and likely caused further discord within the church. And the church failed to intervene. Civil litigation between Christians was another sign that the values of the

---

[48]Cicero, *Pro Caecina* 73.
[49]Seneca the Elder, *Controversiae* 10.1.2, 7.

surrounding culture were still deeply ingrained in many Corinthian Christians. Furthermore, to have members set against each other in court would have seriously undermined the public reputation of the church.

The solution: Paul's use of sibling imagery. Now that we have a glimpse of the problem of the church in Corinth, let us consider how Paul attempted to resolve this issue in 1 Corinthians 6:5-8:

> I say this to shame you. Is it possible that there is nobody among you wise enough to settle a dispute between *brothers*? [In the NIV, the word Greek word for "brothers" is translated as "believers," which loses the force of Paul's family language.] But instead, one *brother* takes another *brother* [Again in the NIV, "brother" is left out in the translation.]—and this in front of unbelievers!
>
> The very fact that you have lawsuits among you means you have been completely defeated already. Why not rather be wronged? Why not rather be cheated? Instead, you yourselves cheat and do wrong, and you do this to your *brothers and sisters*.

In these few verses, the word *brother* appears four times in the Greek text, although this is often made obscure in translations. By using the sibling imagery in addressing the conflicts and disputes in the church, Paul was reminding the Corinthians that relationships between siblings were among the closest, strongest and most intimate of relationships in the ancient world. Siblings were expected to be close, trusting and cooperative, and to stand in solidarity with one another. Siblings were also responsible to advance the family's honor and interest. This meant that a brother was expected not to expose family members to being shamed in front of outsiders.

By addressing the Corinthians as brothers and sisters, Paul was driving home the point that they belonged to one another in this new family or household of God in Christ. As indicated in the prior section, such sibling and familial language for relationships among Christians is a biblical application of the Pauline language of being adopted by God. In this new family, all social and economic boundaries that divided the community were being overcome. All the ethnic boundaries that prevented its growth were being broken down. As brothers and sisters, they were to treat one another with respect and honor. They were to protect one another and build up one another. They were to help the weaker and poorer brothers. As such, the family image is a very powerful metaphor evoking not only the bonds of affection

Paul had for the Corinthians but also the ties that bind the members of the Christian community together. As a family, the Corinthians should uphold the values of togetherness, goodwill, protection, provision, honor, respect and love. As such, each member of this family must do all he or she could to live up to this expectation and to guard this relationship jealously.

That's why in an environment where lawsuits, divisions, disputes over food, abuse of the Lord's Supper and spiritual gifts were threatening this familial bond, Paul used a language of kinship and endearment to encourage and rebuke the Corinthians (see 1 Cor 1:10; 8:13; 11:33-34; 12:1). Paul recognized that the most serious threat came from within the community, and not without. Thus, Paul admonished the church for failing to exercise arbitration among members of the Christian community and prohibited disputes from being brought to the civil courts.

MOVING TO OUR PRESENT DAY

Based on this background, one can see that the application of Paul's words on civil litigation could vary greatly depending on the circumstances. Thus, where Christians are a vulnerable minority and the courts are often corrupt, the circumstances would parallel those that Paul addressed, and his admonitions against Christians going to court against one another would appear directly applicable. It can be dangerous and counterproductive in such circumstances for Christians to take their disputes with one another outside of the church into the courts of an often-hostile nation or society. Under such circumstances, it becomes important to develop dispute-resolution capacities within the churches.

On the other hand, trying to apply Paul's words where Christians have composed the majority for hundreds of years is more difficult. In such circumstances, the legal system presumably would have been deeply influenced by Christianity. Civil political and legal institutions may properly be viewed as performing the function of dispute resolution for a Christian society. While the church itself would remain a separate institution from the civil legal system, Christians could view the civil legal system, within its own proper jurisdiction and function, as Christian. In addition, since the vast majority of persons in the society would be Christian, the judges would most often be Christians and the laws most often made by Christians. The entire concept of Christians bringing their disputes before nonbelievers assumed by Paul would be inapplicable.

Often in societies with a long historical Christian heritage, the courts and legal system are considered secular. Such a conception of secularity, however, can embody the institutional separation of church and state, the conception of civil law as having functions distinct and separate from that of the institutional church, and the concept of all persons as being equal before the law, all of which are defensible in Christian terms. These kinds of distinctions do not mirror the situation in Paul's day, nor do they parallel Paul's categories. Thus, it would be wrong to infer from Paul's words a premise that the state has no proper role in dispute resolution in a majority Christian society. Further, it would seem odd to infer from Paul's words a requirement that church courts would be the only legitimate forums to settle disputes in majority Christian societies. Paul simply was not addressing the question of where institutionally to place the dispute-resolution function in societies in which most of the people belong to the church.

To the contrary, Paul's admonitions in 1 Corinthians 6 assume the anti-imperial perspective discussed throughout this chapter. To seek justice or dispute resolution from the civil magistrate or courts in Paul's day was to entrust oneself to this "evil empire," and to sue a Christian brother in such courts was to expose such a brother to the power of corrupted judges and juries. Indeed, the extreme distrust of Paul for the legal systems of the Greco-Roman world reinforces the interpretation of Romans 13 presented above, for if Paul really believed that the law courts would punish the evil and reward the good, he surely would not warn to the same degree against Christians using those courts. Instead, Paul presumes, as does James (Jas 2:5-7), that the law courts found in the empire are corrupt and consistently fail to fulfill the dictates of Romans 13.

The question of whether Paul's words have a renewed meaning in purportedly post-Christian societies is significant. In these instances, the legal systems and laws have been influenced by Christianity through a long historical process, and certain ideals of justice may in significant part survive a loss of faith. One cannot simply apply Paul's words literally to such a situation; on the other hand, one cannot deny the possibility that Paul's words need to be given greater application in some such contexts. In addition, as disputes over issues related to marriage and the family accelerate, there may be occasion for renewed attention to traditions of investing religious courts with jurisdiction over some such matters. Situating dispute resolution of certain kinds within church courts may be a part of weaning the church in the West from its overreliance on the state, and situating certain kinds of disputes within religious courts may be a way of maintaining civil peace in societies with significant religious diversity.

Conclusion

The New Testament letters were written to churches constituting a tiny, multicultural religious minority within the larger Roman Empire. Under these circumstances, the letters do not provide direct guidance on the question of how Christians in power might rule or legislate. The most direct political concerns of the letters address survival as minorities within an empire that at best was indifferent and at worst genocidal toward them. In this way, the setting of the letters and their immediate, practical concerns align much more closely with Christians who constitute vulnerable minorities in their societies.

Despite this setting, there is, underlying the letters, a cosmic and global vision that would create a comic contrast with the modest reach and situation of the churches of that day, if we did not know the incredible story of the subsequent growth of the church. This cosmic and global vision certainly implicates the political and the legal. However, untangling the various strands and meanings of this vision so that it can be applied in particular times and situations is more than an act of interpretation; it requires acts of lived faith, wisdom, courage and discernment, under the empowerment of the Holy Spirit.

We end with a note from 1 John:

> Do not love the world or anything in the world. If anyone loves the world, love for the Father is not in them. For everything in the world—the lust of the flesh, the lust of the eyes, and the pride of life—comes not from the Father but from the world. The world and its desires pass away, but whoever does the will of God lives forever. (1 Jn 2:15-17)

John's use of "the world" and "love" of "the world" echoes Paul's use of the Roman Empire as a foil, and John's negative description of the world is a good description of the ethos of the Roman emperors, military, nobility and leadership. John may have had in mind the way that Satan tempted Jesus by offering him all the kingdoms of this world. The temptations of political power would not be an issue for Christians for hundreds of years, and yet John's words resonate through the centuries. Of course hidden within this passage is the classic dialectic of the church being "against the world for the world,"[50] for the Gospel of John declares that God "so loved the world" that he sent Jesus to save it (Jn 3:15-17).

Ultimately, then, getting politics and law right is a spiritual struggle, for it situates Christians squarely between the proper love of others, which they are commanded to practice, and the temptations of power, pride, greed and lust endemic to political power, which Christians are commanded to renounce. This spiritual struggle will last until Jesus returns to institute the true reign of God, which ultimately is the only fully biblical and fully satisfying political solution. For whether Christians rule or are ruled by others, the results (as history shows and the Bible indicates) are mixed at best and too frequently disastrous. For if there is anything the Bible teaches clearly enough about politics and law, it is that political rule by the people of God is not the same thing as being ruled by God himself.

---

[50]Cf. Peter L. Berger and Richard John Neuhaus, eds., *Against the World for the World: The Hartford Appeal and the Future of American Religion* (New York: Seabury, 1976).

9

EXPECTATION AND CONSUMMATION

LAW IN ESCHATOLOGICAL PERSPECTIVE

John Copeland Nagle and Keith A. Mathison

T HE BIBLE CONCLUDES with the book of Revelation, whose fantastic imagery has long been a source of confusion and excitement. Its contemporary application is famously contested. As one commentator asks, "What do multiheaded beasts and warriors in blood-drenched robes have to do with the modern condition of the church or of the world?"[1] A similar question may be asked of the Old Testament book of Daniel, which contains its own apocalyptic images and whose influence can be seen in John's account in Revelation.

The goal of this chapter is to determine what the books of Daniel and Revelation can teach us about civil law. On the surface, this appears to be a daunting task since these two books, unlike Exodus or Deuteronomy, for example, do not contain extensive lists of God's laws for Israel or explicit applications of those laws. But when we look at Daniel and Revelation in the context of what the entire Bible teaches on the subject of law, we can discern some important implications about how the law sometimes responds to unfounded eschatological arguments that insist that a particular

---

[1]Ben Witherington III, *Revelation* (New York: Cambridge University Press, 2003), p. xi.

activity will result in "the end of the world." Daniel and Revelation also show us how abusive leaders manipulate the law to their own ends, and how faithful communities are nonetheless able to persevere.

THE BIBLICAL CONTEXT

In order to understand what Daniel and Revelation might contribute to our understanding of civil law, it is helpful to have a basic grasp of the relationship between the law and the prophets. God revealed the law to Israel through Moses in the context of establishing a covenant with his people. The Mosaic covenant provided a law for a people that God had already redeemed on the basis of his earlier covenant with Abraham (Ex 20:2). The Mosaic law included promises of blessings for obedience and warnings of judgment for disobedience (e.g., Lev 26; Deut 28). Israel, as a nation, would be corporately blessed if it adhered to the law of God, but if the nation rejected God's law, it would be punished. If it remained recalcitrant, the ultimate punishment would be exile from the land (e.g., Deut 28:64).

The history of Israel, recorded in the books of Joshua through Kings and more fully described in chapter two of this book, presents a nation in almost continual rebellion against God. After the death of Solomon, the nation divided into a northern kingdom (Israel) and a southern kingdom (Judah). The northern kingdom rejected God's law from the beginning. God then began to send prophets who acted as covenant prosecutors, calling Israel to repent, return to God and obey the law.[2] They warned that a failure to do so would result in judgment and exile. The prophets Amos, Hosea and Micah came to the northern kingdom of Israel with these warnings. They went unheeded, and the curses of the covenant were poured out on the nation. Israel was soon overrun by the Assyrians and destroyed in 722 B.C.[3]

The southern kingdom of Judah was not as consistently wicked as Israel and had periods of revival under godly kings such as Josiah. Over time, however, the people of Judah also followed in the footsteps of Israel and violated God's law. The prophets Isaiah, Zephaniah, Jeremiah and Ezekiel (and probably Joel) were all sent by God to Judah to warn the nation that it

---

[2]Willem A. VanGemeren, *Interpreting the Prophetic Word* (Grand Rapids: Zondervan, 1996), p. 37.

[3]Iain Provan, V. Philips Long and Tremper Longman III, *A Biblical History of Israel* (Louisville, KY: Westminster John Knox, 2003), pp. 259-71.

would suffer the same fate as the northern kingdom if repentance were not forthcoming. Judah, too, failed to repent and fell to Babylon in 587/586 B.C.[4] The prophet Daniel was among those deported to Babylon during these turbulent times. In his case, we witness a prophet of God outside the Promised Land, living under a godless tyrant. The apostle John, one of the twelve disciples of Jesus and author of the only New Testament book described as a prophecy, found himself in a situation similar to that of Daniel, living under the tyranny of a pagan empire (Rome) and forced into exile (on the island of Patmos).

A Brief Introduction to Daniel and Revelation

Before we proceed to look at Daniel and Revelation more closely, it must be noted that commentators have applied a large number of interpretive approaches to these two books. As a result of their inherently difficult literary form, a variety of end-time views have arisen over the course of church history, and these views affect how one might relate the content of Daniel and Revelation to contemporary history and contemporary issues. It may be of some benefit to describe briefly each of the main eschatological views and how those views might affect the way their adherents approach structural problems in society.

Eschatological views are often described in terms of the millennium—the thousand-year reign of Christ described in Revelation 20. Many Christians hold a position known as premillennialism.[5] According to the premillennial view, Jesus Christ will return at some point in the future and will establish his kingdom on earth. This kingdom will last for a thousand years. This view is described as premillennialism because Christ returns *before* (pre-) the millennium. Generally speaking, premillennialists (especially dispensational premillennialists) believe that things in the present age are going to go from bad to worse and that efforts to improve conditions on earth before Christ's return amount to little more than "polishing

---

[4]Ibid., pp. 271-85.

[5]A classic defense of premillennialism is John F. Walvoord, *The Millennial Kingdom* (Findlay, OH: Dunham, 1959). More recent defenses of the premillennialist view may be found in Donald K. Campbell and Jeffrey L. Townsend, eds., *The Coming Millennial Kingdom: A Case for Premillennial Interpretation* (Grand Rapids: Kregel, 1997); and Craig L. Blomberg and Sung Wook Chung, eds., *A Case for Historic Premillennialism: An Alternative to "Left Behind" Eschatology* (Grand Rapids: Baker Academic, 2009).

brass on a sinking ship."[6] For some premillennialists, attempts to create a more just society in the current age are a waste of time—true justice will come only in Christ's reign. This tendency is exacerbated for those premillennialists (present, it seems, in almost every age) who believe that Christ's return is imminent. Other premillennialists, however, recognize that it is not for Christ's followers to know the time of his return (Acts 1:7). His return may be far in the future, and love of neighbor requires that Christ's followers concern themselves with injustice.

Other Christians believe that the millennium described in Revelation 20 is a symbolic description of either the entire period of time between Christ's first and second advent or (less often) the last thousand years before Christ's second advent. Strictly speaking, all those who believe this view could be termed *postmillennialists* in one sense because they believe that Christ returns *after* (post-) the millennium. However, in the twentieth century, those who believe that Christ returns after the millennium began to distinguish between postmillennialism and amillennialism.[7]

Generally speaking, postmillennialists and amillennialists agree on the *timing* of the millennium (both agree that Christ returns after the millennium). They disagree, however, about the *nature* of the millennium. Amillennialists tend to view the millennium as more of a heavenly reality and do not see it having a great influence on common earthly affairs until

---

[6]According to dispensational premillennialism, the present church age will end with the rapture of the church, which, along with the appearance of the antichrist, will indicate the beginning of the seven-year Great Tribulation on earth. The tribulation will end with the battle of Armageddon, in the midst of which Christ will return to destroy his enemies. The nations will then be gathered for judgment. Those who supported Israel will enter into Christ's millennial kingdom, and the rest will be cast into Hades to await the last judgment. Christ will sit on the throne of David and rule the world from Jerusalem. Israel will be given the place of honor among the nations again. At the end of the millennium, Satan will be released and will lead nonbelievers in rebellion against Christ and the new Jerusalem. The rebellion will be crushed by fire from heaven, and Satan will be cast into the lake of fire. The wicked will be brought before the Great White Throne, judged and cast into the lake of fire. At this point the eternal state will commence.

[7]Amillennialism sees Revelation 20 as a description of the spiritual reign of Christ with the saints throughout the entire present age, which is characterized by the parallel growth of good and evil. The present millennial age will be followed by the second coming of Christ, the general resurrection, the last judgment and the new heavens and earth. Like amillennialism, postmillennialism teaches that the "thousand years" of Revelation 20 occurs prior to the second coming. Some agree with amillennialists and see it as concurrent with the entire present age, while others say that it is the last thousand years of the present age. According to postmillennialists, the Holy Spirit will draw unprecedented numbers to Christ through the preaching of the gospel before the second coming.

Christ returns to consummate the kingdom.[8] Postmillennialists tend to be much more optimistic about the potential earthly effects of Christ's present heavenly reign.[9]

Daniel. It is important to understand the mixed genre of the book of Daniel. The book is set within the context of the sixth-century exile.[10] The first six chapters narrate events dating from 605 (the year of Daniel's deportation) to 536 B.C. These chapters may be described as court narratives, detailing the interaction between Daniel and a foreign court.[11] The prophecies in the last six chapters look to events beyond the time of the exile. The genre of these chapters is usually characterized as apocalyptic.[12] The Greek word translated "apocalyptic" means "revelation" or "unveiling," and apocalyptic literature usually involves revelations concerning the last days given to the prophet through a heavenly messenger in a dream or vision. The visions found in apocalyptic literature are usually couched in vivid and highly symbolic language, making them difficult to interpret. The Society of Biblical Literature has proposed the following helpful definition of *apocalyptic:* It is "a genre of revelatory literature with a narrative framework, in which a revelation is mediated by an otherworldly being to a human recipient, disclosing a transcendent reality which is both temporal, insofar as it envisages eschatological salvation, and spatial insofar as it involves another, supernatural world."[13]

Daniel 3 tells of the refusal of Daniel and his friends to obey the king's order to commit idolatry (a clear act of civil disobedience). Daniel 4 and 5 both describe acts of divine judgment against arrogant human kings. The visions in the final six chapters are among the most difficult to understand

---

[8]A good defense of amillennialism may be found in Kim Riddlebarger, *A Case for Amillennialism: Understanding the End Times* (Grand Rapids: Baker, 2003).

[9]A good defense of postmillennialism may be found in John Jefferson Davis, *The Victory of Christ's Kingdom: An Introduction to Postmillennialism* (Moscow, ID: Canon, 1996). For a helpful overview of the various millennial views, see Cornelis P. Venema, *The Promise of the Future* (Carlisle, PA: Banner of Truth, 2000), pp. 189-243.

[10]The dating of the book of Daniel is a hugely complicated and controversial question and beyond the scope of this chapter. One's conclusion regarding the date of Daniel does not seriously affect the substance of the argument in this chapter. For an overview of the question of Daniel's date of composition, see the standard commentaries, such as Joyce G. Baldwin, *Daniel,* Tyndale Old Testament Commentaries 21 (Downers Grove, IL: InterVarsity Press, 1978), pp. 35-46.

[11]Ernest Lucas, *Daniel,* Apollos Old Testament Commentary 20 (Downers Grove, IL: InterVarsity Press, 2002), p. 25.

[12]Baldwin, *Daniel,* p. 46.

[13]Cited in John J. Collins, *The Apocalyptic Imagination: An Introduction to Jewish Apocalyptic Literature,* 2nd ed. (Grand Rapids: Eerdmans, 1998), p. 5.

in all of Scripture. Daniel 7 echoes Daniel 2 in describing a series of four human kingdoms followed by the establishment of the kingdom of God. Daniel 8 is a vision concerning the Medo-Persian and Greek Empires. It concludes with a vision about Antiochus Epiphanes, the Greek ruler who severely persecuted the Jews in the second century B.C.[14] Daniel 11 also describes the wickedness of Antiochus Epiphanes as well as another king who acts in the same evil manner.

Revelation. John describes the book of Revelation as a prophecy (Rev 1:3; 19:10; 22:7, 10, 18, 19). It is, then, the only New Testament prophetic book, and it is, like Daniel, an apocalyptic prophecy. Apocalyptic prophecies differ somewhat from the other prophetic books. Most of the Old Testament prophets acted as covenant prosecutors, calling God's people to repent, act justly and turn back to the law of Moses. Apocalyptic prophecies tend to focus more on future events. This difference is not absolute, however, because a focus on future events is also found in the nonapocalyptic prophets.[15] The difference is one of degree. In addition, while God tends to speak directly to the other prophets, he sends angels with messages to Daniel and John.

The date of the book of Revelation is debated. Most contemporary scholars argue that the book was composed around A.D. 95–96, during the latter part of the reign of Domitian. A strong argument can also be made, however, for dating the book sometime between A.D. 64 and 70, during or just after the reign of Nero.[16] The authors of this chapter take the position that the book of Revelation was written during or just after the reign of Nero. This is an admittedly minority view that affects the way we read Revelation, but it is not possible to avoid taking a side on this question. Whichever position one takes regarding the date of the book of Revelation will heavily influence the interpretation of the book and thus its application.[17]

If Revelation is dated during or soon after the reign of Nero (and we emphasize the *if*), then it shares something in common with many of the

---

[14]John H. Hayes and Sara R. Mandell, *The Jewish People in Classical Antiquity: From Alexander to Bar Kochba* (Louisville, KY: Westminster John Knox, 1998), pp. 49-59.

[15]On the nature of prophecy, see VanGemeren, *Interpreting the Prophetic Word*, pp. 18-99; O. Palmer Robertson, *The Christ of the Prophets* (Phillipsburg, NJ: P & R, 2004), pp. 9-90.

[16]For example, see Stephen S. Smalley, *Thunder and Love: John's Revelation and John's Community* (Milton Keynes: Nelson Word, 1994), pp. 40-50.

[17]For a summary of the case for an early date, see Keith A. Mathison, *From Age to Age: The Unfolding of Biblical Eschatology* (Phillipsburg, NJ: P & R, 2009), pp. 644-47.

Old Testament Prophets. Like them, it was written in the years immediately preceding an invasion of the land and the destruction of Jerusalem. Like them, it contains oracles concerning this imminent historical judgment, and like them, it also contains oracles concerning a future restoration beyond the period of judgment.

The first major section of Revelation contains a vision of Christ and messages to the seven churches of Asia (Rev 1:9–3:22). This is followed by John's initial vision of heaven (Rev 4:1–5:14), which introduces a series of three sevenfold judgments. The judgments associated with seven seals are first (Rev 6:1–8:5). The judgments associated with the seven trumpets follow (Rev 8:6–11:19). Before describing the third series, John reveals the conflict of God's people with the dragon and the beast (Rev 12:1–15:4). The dragon symbolizes Satan, while the beast is arguably symbolic of the Roman Empire. The judgments associated with the seven bowls conclude this section (Rev 15:5–16:21). The judgment of the great harlot Babylon is described next (Rev 17:1–19:10), followed by the transition from Babylon to the new Jerusalem (19:11–21:8). In the last major section of the book, the new Jerusalem is described (21:9–22:9).

The final chapters of Revelation bring the entire story of Scripture full circle. Whereas Genesis 1–2 opens the Bible with the story of the original creation, Revelation 21–22 closes the Bible with the promise of a new creation. The original creation was to be God's kingdom. Adam was to have dominion over creation as God's vice-regent (Gen 1). All of his worldly, cultural labors were to be carried out under the sovereign rule of God, but Adam rebelled. Satan usurped God's rule, and death fell upon all humankind (Gen 3). Throughout Scripture, God works toward redemption, showing that his original intention for creation will not be thwarted. The second Adam, Jesus the Messiah, is obedient, and through his suffering, death, resurrection and ascension, the kingdom of God and a new creation are inaugurated.[18]

There is an "already" and a "not yet" aspect to both the kingdom of God and the new creation. Both were inaugurated with the death, resurrection and ascension of Jesus Christ. He has already been given all authority in

---

[18]See G. K. Beale, *A New Testament Biblical Theology: The Unfolding of the Old Testament in the New* (Grand Rapids: Baker Academic, 2011). Beale does a masterful job demonstrating how all the Old Testament promises concerning the kingdom, the new creation, the outpouring of the Spirit and more are inaugurated in the first advent of Christ and consummated at his second advent.

heaven and on earth (Mt 28:18), and we reign with him, but the last enemy has not yet been destroyed, and during this entire present age, he is putting all his enemies under his feet (1 Cor 15:25-26). Already we are a new creation in Christ (2 Cor 5:17), but creation still groans and has not yet experienced full deliverance from the bondage of the curse (Rom 8:18-23).

There is, therefore, both continuity and discontinuity between the present creation and the new creation, just as there is both continuity and discontinuity between our present bodies and our resurrection bodies (1 Cor 15:35-49).[19] While the degree of continuity between this creation and the new creation is disputed, the existence of continuity provides incentive for our work in this world. If we believe that the present creation, like our present body, is to be transformed rather than destroyed, we have one more incentive to press on without giving up in despair.[20]

WHAT DO DANIEL AND REVELATION HAVE IN COMMON?

Before we can look at what Daniel and Revelation contribute to discussions of civil law, we must look at what these books have in common. First, and most obviously, both books contain extensive symbolic descriptions of evil, beast-like human kingdoms.

Daniel received the vision described in Daniel 7 in the first year of Belshazzar (Dan 7:1). In the vision, Daniel sees the winds of heaven stirring up the sea (Dan 7:2), and then he sees four great beasts arise from the sea itself.

> And four great beasts came up out of the sea, different from one another. The first was like a lion and had eagles' wings. Then as I looked its wings were plucked off, and it was lifted up from the ground and made to stand on two feet like a man, and the mind of a man was given to it. And behold, another beast, a second one, like a bear. It was raised up on one side. It had three ribs in its mouth between its teeth; and it was told, "Arise, devour much flesh." After this I looked, and behold, another, like a leopard, with four wings of a

---

[19]Traditionally, Lutherans (among others) have argued for almost complete discontinuity, while most (not all) in the Reformed tradition have argued for a continuity comparable to that which will exist between the present body and the resurrected body. Just as the body is transformed while retaining a continuity of identity, so too will the creation be transformed. See Herman Bavinck, *Reformed Dogmatics*, ed. John Bolt, trans. John Vriend (Grand Rapids: Baker Academic, 2008), 4:716, and Louis Berkhof, *Systematic Theology* (Grand Rapids: Eerdmans, 1991), p. 737.

[20]This is not to say that Lutherans and others who argue for little or no continuity between the present creation and the new creation have no incentive for their work in this world. It is merely a different incentive.

> bird on its back. And the beast had four heads, and dominion was given to it. After this I saw in the night visions, and behold, a fourth beast, terrifying and dreadful and exceedingly strong. It had great iron teeth; it devoured and broke in pieces and stamped what was left with its feet. It was different from all the beasts that were before it, and it had ten horns. (Dan 7:3-7)[21]

Here, according to many commentators, Daniel describes the Babylonian, Medo-Persian, Greek and Roman Empires as beast-like creatures rising from the sea.[22] Compare this dramatic vision to John's vision in Revelation 13:1-4.

> And I saw a beast rising out of the sea, with ten horns and seven heads, with ten diadems on its horns and blasphemous names on its heads. And the beast that I saw was like a leopard; its feet were like a bear's, and its mouth was like a lion's mouth. And to it the dragon gave his power and his throne and great authority. One of its heads seemed to have a mortal wound, but its mortal wound was healed, and the whole earth marveled as they followed the beast. And they worshiped the dragon, for he had given his authority to the beast, and they worshiped the beast, saying, "Who is like the beast, and who can fight against it?"

In this passage, John describes what many believe to be the Roman Empire as a beast with ten horns and seven heads rising from the sea (Rev 13:1-2).[23]

Both books also describe tyrants who demand idolatry. In Daniel 3, we read of Nebuchadnezzar's command to worship a giant image of gold.

> King Nebuchadnezzar made an image of gold, whose height was sixty cubits and its breadth six cubits. He set it up on the plain of Dura, in the province of Babylon. Then King Nebuchadnezzar sent to gather the satraps, the prefects, and the governors, the counselors, the treasurers, the justices, the magistrates, and all the officials of the provinces to come to the dedication of the

---

[21]Unless otherwise indicated, all Scripture quotations in this chapter are from the ESV.

[22]See, for example, Baldwin, *Daniel,* pp. 161-62, and Edward J. Young, *The Prophecy of Daniel, a Commentary* (Grand Rapids: Eerdmans, 1949), pp. 150, 163.

[23]See, for example, R. H. Charles, *A Critical and Exegetical Commentary on the Revelation of St. John,* International Critical Commentary (Edinburgh: T & T Clark, 1920), 1:345; Henry Barclay Swete, *Commentary on Revelation: The Greek Text,* 3rd ed. (1911; reprint, Grand Rapids: Kregel, 1977), p. 161; George R. Beasley-Murray, *The Book of Revelation,* rev. ed., New Century Bible (Grand Rapids: Eerdmans, 1978), p. 209; David S. Clark, *The Message from Patmos* (reprint, Grand Rapids: Baker, 1989), p. 86; David E. Aune, *Revelation 6–16,* Word Biblical Commentary 52B (Dallas: Word Books, 1998), p. 735; and Robert H. Mounce, *The Book of Revelation,* rev. ed., New International Commentary on the New Testament (Grand Rapids: Eerdmans, 1998).

image that King Nebuchadnezzar had set up. Then the satraps, the prefects, and the governors, the counselors, the treasurers, the justices, the magistrates, and all the officials of the provinces gathered for the dedication of the image that King Nebuchadnezzar had set up. And they stood before the image that Nebuchadnezzar had set up. And the herald proclaimed aloud, "You are commanded, O peoples, nations, and languages, that when you hear the sound of the horn, pipe, lyre, trigon, harp, bagpipe, and every kind of music, you are to fall down and worship the golden image that King Nebuchadnezzar has set up. And whoever does not fall down and worship shall immediately be cast into a burning fiery furnace." (Dan 3:1-6)

Revelation 13 describes a second beast who makes the earth and its inhabitants worship the first beast.

Then I saw another beast rising out of the earth. It had two horns like a lamb and it spoke like a dragon. It exercises all the authority of the first beast in its presence, and makes the earth and its inhabitants worship the first beast, whose mortal wound was healed. It performs great signs, even making fire come down from heaven to earth in front of people, and by the signs that it is allowed to work in the presence of the beast it deceives those who dwell on earth, telling them to make an image for the beast that was wounded by the sword and yet lived. And it was allowed to give breath to the image of the beast, so that the image of the beast might even speak and might cause those who would not worship the image of the beast to be slain. (Rev 13:11-15)

The reference here to the worship of the beast is arguably a reference to the Roman imperial cult.[24]

In both books, the refusal of the faithful to participate in idolatry results in vicious persecution. When they refuse to commit sin and they disobey Nebuchadnezzar, Daniel and his friends are cast into a fiery furnace (Dan 3:19-23). In Revelation, the beast makes war on the saints (Rev 13:7). Revelation is filled with references to persecution and martyrdom. The letter to Smyrna encourages believers to be faithful unto death (Rev 2:10). In the chapter describing the judgment of the fifth seal, John sees "the souls of those who had been slain for the word of God and for the witness they had

[24]For the Roman imperial cult, see S. R. F. Price, *Rituals and Power: The Roman Imperial Cult in Asia Minor* (New York: Cambridge University Press, 1984); Stephen J. Friesen, *Imperial Cults and the Apocalypse of John: Reading Revelation in the Ruins* (New York: Oxford University Press, 2001); and Ittai Gradel, *Emperor Worship and Roman Religion* (New York: Clarendon Press, 2002).

borne" (Rev 6:9). Babylon the great is described as being "drunk with the blood of the saints, the blood of the martyrs of Jesus" (Rev 17:6). Daniel and Revelation, then, have in common their emphasis on the persecution of believers, and they have in common the call to remain faithful to the end.

IMPLICATIONS FOR CONTEMPORARY CIVIL LAW

The application of the books of Daniel and Revelation to the civil law is difficult for the same reasons that understanding the theological messages of these books can be challenging. Civil courts are most likely to cite Daniel and Revelation when they quote people who suffer from delusions and other mental illnesses.[25] But the misuse of these prophetic books should not deter us from seeking to identify their proper uses. In this section, we discuss two themes from Daniel and Revelation that are especially relevant to the civil law in the twenty-first century: (1) how the law should respond to apocalyptic claims asserting that human actions could destroy the world, and (2) how to respond to an unjust state that demands its subjects' complete allegiance, and even worship.

God is in control of the end of the world. There are many ways to read the prophecies and apocalyptic visions in Daniel and Revelation. The lesson that is common to all of them is that God is sovereign over the world as it exists today and over what will happen to it in the future. This provides a sense of comfort for those who believe in God and are faithful to his purposes. That sense of providential control is absent from most discussions of civil law today. What the law once characterized as "acts of God" are now viewed sometimes as events with a human cause and, thus, a human agent

---

[25]See, e.g., Hayden v. Henderson County Jail, 2007 U.S. Dist. LEXIS 64329, 21 (E.D. Tex. 2007), describing a prisoner's "rambling and incoherent dissertation on topics" including "the Four Horsemen of the Apocalypse in the biblical Book of Revelation"; In re Lawley, 179 P.3d 891, 895 (Cal. 2008), quoting a murder defendant's assertion that "unidentified persons had framed him for the murder because he had angered them with his efforts to go down in history as 'the Beast in Revelations'"; T.A.L. v. P.L.H., 2010 Mo. App. LEXIS 1277, 3 (Mo. Ct. App. 2010), reviewing the termination of parental rights of a mother who had "'made odd statements to Jefferson City police officers about the book of [R]evelation . . . in the Bible'"; and State for the Best Interest & Prot. of W.Y., 2003 Tex. App. LEXIS 7653, 10 (Tex. Ct. App. 2003), upholding the civil commitment of an individual who, during the commitment proceeding, "borrow[ed] the trial judge's Bible and then read a long passage from Revelation, chapter twelve. He explained that the passage is about his life and the woman in the passage was with him in his cell while he was locked up."

who may be held responsible for them.[26] Daniel and Revelation thus join an ongoing debate about the meaning and purpose of human history, taking the side of those who believe that all of history involves the unfolding of God's divine purposes.

The apocalyptic character of much of Daniel and Revelation is designed to reveal the workings of God: past, present and future. As one biblical scholar observed, "The essence of apocalyptic is direct access to the heavenly world and its divine truths."[27] But that does not mean that reading these two books will immediately result in a clear human understanding of precise future events and exactly when they will occur. The historical experience in trying to understand the details of the prophecies contained in Daniel and Revelation demonstrates the folly of trying to predict the future. For example, when writing after World War I about Revelation 13, an otherwise valuable commentary asserted that a federation of nations would arise "out of the old Roman empire. It will be Satanic in origin and character, and will in fact be the devil's last card, if I may borrow such an expression, before he is obliged to admit complete defeat."[28] Similarly, the reported court decisions include repeated assertions by parties that a social security number is the mark of the beast described in Revelation, as well as what turn out to be inaccurate claims that Revelation teaches that the world will end on a specific date.[29] One writer concluded that there is "a near 100 percent failure rate when matching up images and events in Revelation with particular historical figures."[30]

Students of the biblical apocalyptic literature are not the only ones to advance contested claims about the end times. There are many secular counterparts who insist upon their own apocalyptic visions. Here we see the importance of apocalyptic thinking for the civil law. Consider three claims about the future that have shaped the law since the beginning of the twentieth century. The devastation of two world wars and the ensuing de-

---

[26]See generally Kenneth T. Kristl, "Diminishing the Divine: Climate Change and the Act of God Defense," *Widener Law Review* 15 (2010): 325.

[27]Smalley, *Thunder and Love*, p. 25.

[28]H. A. Ironside, *Revelation*, rev. ed. (Neptune, NJ: Loizeaux, 1996), p. 147.

[29]See, e.g., Seaworth v. Pearson, 203 F.3d 1056, 1057 (8th Cir. 2000), social security number as mark of the beast; and Risenhoover v. England, 936 F. Supp. 392, 396 (W.D. Tex. 1996), noting that the Branch Davidians "prophesied that the end of the world, as foretold in the Bible's Book of Revelations, would commence on April 22, 1959."

[30]Witherington, *Revelation*, p. xi.

velopment of nuclear weapons resulted in widespread concern about the apparently imminent end of the world. Nuclear weapons and other weapons of mass destruction presented the first threat of devastation on a truly global scale. Numerous international legal treaties and domestic laws sought to avoid that result, including the treaties establishing the League of Nations after World War I and the United Nations after World War II, and the arms control and nuclear nonproliferation treaties negotiated during and after the Cold War. The threat such legal instruments sought to avoid was the end of the world caused by human warfare using such terrible, unprecedented weapons.

By the 1970s, environmental threats began to replace a nuclear holocaust as the most likely cause of planetary destruction. Numerous secular environmental prophets warned that humans could not survive if we exhausted the earth's natural resources. In 1972, the Club of Rome reported on *The Limits of Growth,* concluding that "if the present growth trends . . . continue unchanged, the limits to growth will be reached sometime within the next one hundred years. The most probable result will be a rather sudden and uncontrollable decline in both population and industrial capacity."[31] Barry Commoner's *The Closing Circle* prophesied that present trends would "destroy the capability of the environment to support a reasonably civilized human society," leaving only "a kind of neobarbarism with a highly uncertain future."[32] Such a fate could be avoided, these writers insisted, only by enacting stringent laws limiting the growth of human population, regulating the exploitation of natural resources and prohibiting the spread of pollution.

Climate change has displaced more general warnings of the environmental consequences of economic growth as the source of an imminent environmental apocalypse. Prominent environmental law scholars have observed that "climate change comes draped in claims of apocalypse"[33] and that "the worst-case scenarios projected by the scientific community are biblical in proportion."[34] Al Gore's movie *An Inconvenient Truth* (2006)

---

[31]Donella H. Meadows et al., *The Limits to Growth: A Report for the Club of Rome's Project on the Predicament of Mankind* (New York: Universe Books, 1972), p. 29.
[32]Barry Commoner, *The Closing Circle: Nature, Man, and Technology* (New York: Knopf, 1971), pp. 217-18.
[33]Jedediah Purdy, "The Politics of Nature: Climate Change, Environmental Law, and Democracy," *Yale Law Journal* 119 (2010): 1122.
[34]Jeffrey J. Rachlinski, "The Psychology of Global Climate Change," *University of Illinois Law Review* 2000 (2000): 299.

warns that rising sea levels and changing temperatures could result in the deaths of millions of people and "send our planet into a tailspin of epic destruction." Another activist group sees "a high probability that . . . the human species may not survive into the foreseeable future" unless we change our ways.[35] Scientists and environmentalists fear that the continued emission of greenhouse gases will so fundamentally alter the earth's climate that it could become uninhabitable. Mike Hulme describes such claims as "catastrophic climate change" (as distinguished from ordinary climate change), and he explains how "presaging apocalypse" is one of the "ideas of climate change" (as distinguished from an objective truth about climate change) that shapes perceptions.[36] Again, law is posited as playing a crucial role in the world avoiding this fate. The international debate over a new climate-change treaty yielded countless assertions that the fate of the world was in the hands of the world leaders who met at Copenhagen in 2009. Failure to reach an agreement was inconceivable to those who shared that understanding, but failure occurred. The years following Copenhagen produced more modest ambitions for law's response to climate change, and soul-searching among those who watched in disbelief as their apocalyptic claims were ignored.

Daniel and Revelation have much to teach today's secular prophets of the end of the world. As one biblical scholar put it, "Theology is more important than chronology."[37] The long history of failed attempts to use Revelation to predict the end of the world serves as a cautionary tale for efforts to use the law to respond to the latest vision of the world's purportedly imminent demise. We cannot know when the events described in Daniel will (or did) occur, but we can be sure that God is working out his purposes in the world today and that he will continue to do so until the end of the age.

That knowledge should not encourage a passive acquiescence in the face of injustice, nor should it deter us from faithful obedience to God's commands. The ongoing discussions among Christian communities about how to respond to climate change and other environmental harms still feature

---

[35]See Sarah S. Amsler, "Bringing Hope 'To Crisis': Crisis Thinking, Ethical Action and Social Change," in *Future Ethics: Climate Change and Apocalyptic Imagination*, ed. Stefan Skrimshire (New York: Continuum, 2010), p. 13.

[36]Mike Hulme, *Why We Disagree About Climate Change*, Cambridge: Cambridge University Press, 2009), p. 345.

[37]Smalley, *Thunder and Love*, p. 151.

numerous disagreements about the role of science and environmental law, but none of them embrace the caricature of Christians not caring about this creation because Revelation teaches that a new one will follow. This caricature is most frequently seen in the repeated misquotation of a statement attributed to former Secretary of the Interior James Watt that "after the last tree is felled, Christ will come back."[38] In fact, Watt said, "I do not know how many future generations we can count on before the Lord returns; whatever it is we have to manage with a skill to leave the resources needed for future generations."[39]

Even as we are cautious about the chronology, we should remember the theology contained in Daniel and Revelation. Both books illustrate God's profound concern about the future of humanity and the rest of his creation. Thus it is right, in the words of current legal thinking, to emphasize the impact of our laws and other actions on future generations. Yet we cannot know exactly how our actions will affect those who are as yet unborn, just as we cannot know the timing or even the full meaning of the events described in Daniel and Revelation. Both books, in sum, encourage us to use the civil law with care and humility about the future that is in God's loving hands.

A cautionary note on the abuse of the law. The Bible concludes, and thus this book concludes, with a cautionary note. The civil law is not a force for good in Daniel or in Revelation. Instead, in both books the state employs law for its own ends with little regard for biblical principles of justice. The state assumes complete power, and wields it with abandon. Any book, such as this one, that seeks to recover the Bible's insights into the positive development of the civil law must recognize the abusive power of the law as well.

Consider the story told in Daniel 3. The king calls all the leaders—including the judges and magistrates—to fall down and worship the golden image that the king set up, on pain of being thrown into the furnace. The king is filled with rage when Shadrach, Meshach and Abednego disobey his command. The king's "primary concern is with their public conduct, rather than their private beliefs. . . . Religion is acceptable as long as it is a matter of private belief and does not lead people to challenge the assumptions and values of their society

---

[38]Glenn Scherer, "The Godly Must Be Crazy: Christian-Right Views Are Swaying Politicians and Threatening the Environment," *Grist Magazine,* October 27, 2004, http://www.resilience.org/stories/2004-10-26/godly-must-be-crazy (purporting to quote Watt, emphasis omitted).

[39]Briefing by the Secretary of the Interior: Oversight Hearing Before the House Commission on Interior and Insular Affairs, 97th Cong. 37 (1981) (statement of James G. Watt, Secretary of the Interior).

by what they say or do."[40] But once they survive the furnace, the king issues another decree to destroy anyone who insults their God.

The persecution of the faithful by secular authorities is a persistent theme in Revelation as well. The seven churches that receive the letters contained in Revelation 2 and 3 all endure persecution by the Roman government. The imagery of the beast that appears in Revelation 13 offers another account of the destructive power of the state. Like the king in Daniel, "the beast is a symbol of the perpetual deification of secular authority."[41] The historical period described in Revelation was one of emperor worship and a state willing to punish those who defied its commands.

Daniel and Revelation are thus instructive because they give us insight into what it is like to live under the laws of wicked tyrants, and they provide encouragement to persevere. Whereas the laws of the Pentateuch describe Israel's life under the rule of God, Daniel and Revelation give us a glimpse of life under the rule of the beast. Daniel and Revelation describe civil law gone awry under godless despots and tyrants. They describe human kingdoms governed by the antilaw of the anti-Christ. This antilaw exalts those who do evil while persecuting those who do good.

Christians are strangers and exiles, and sometimes find themselves living under tyrannical regimes that persecute believers. In the twentieth century, Nazi Germany and the Soviet Union are just the most obvious examples of states that sought to impose their will on all who were subject to their authority. Other states have already taken their place in the twenty-first century. But as Richard Bauckham cautions,

> it is a serious mistake to suppose that Revelation opposes the Roman Empire solely because of its persecution of Christians. Rather Revelation advances a thorough-going prophetic critique of the system of Roman power. It is a critique which makes Revelation the most powerful piece of political resistance literature from the period of the early Empire. It is not simply because Rome persecutes Christians that Christians must oppose Rome. Rather it is because Christians must dissociate themselves from the evil of the Roman system that they are likely to suffer persecution.[42]

---

[40]Lucas, *Daniel*, p. 95.
[41]Stephen S. Smalley, *The Revelation to John: A Commentary on the Greek Text of the Apocalypse* (Downers Grove, IL: InterVarsity Press, 2005), p. 337.
[42]Richard Bauckham, *The Theology of the Book of Revelation*, New Testament Theology (New York: Cambridge University Press, 1993), p. 38.

Or, as Stephen Smalley explains, "The key political issue in Revelation is power; and there is a sense in which the book is chiefly concerned with this question." Moreover, "the vision of the Apocalypse challenges the church, as well as society, to use its power with *justice.*"[43]

The demands of such a state present a dilemma for those who deny its ultimate authority. On the one hand, H. A. Ironside wrote that the removal of Christians from government "would be like the breaking of a dike, permitting the rushing waters of anarchy to sweep over every land. Think how evil will then be intensified. . . . With the preservative power of righteousness gone, the masses of men will be given up to corruption and violence."[44] And we must recall that Daniel and his friends served under the king of Babylon.

But there are dangers in participating in an unjust state as well. Ben Witherington notes that "one of the major functions that Revelation can serve for the Christian community today is a warning against too much assimilation into the dominant non-Christian culture." He adds that "apocalyptic literature is, by its very nature, resistance literature."[45] The famous story in Daniel about the king consigning Shadrach, Meshach and Abednego to the furnace for disobeying his laws is matched by innumerable stories since then of people who were executed for their opposition to an unjust law. Even government workers like Daniel and his friends disobeyed the state when commanded to sin against God, and they were willing to face the consequences for that disobedience. But even if the state threatens less dire consequences, individuals must struggle to know when to engage in civil disobedience to the state's laws. In making that decision, we do well to remember Revelation's admonition that "for the cowardly, the faithless," and those who choose the side of sin instead of the side of righteousness, "their portion will be in the lake that burns with fire and sulfur, which is the second death" (Rev 21:8).

Resistance to the state sits uneasily with a role in shaping the state's laws. That does not present a problem for those who live in states that do not involve their people in making their laws. It is more complicated for those who live in states that rely on public participation to make and implement

[43]Smalley, *Thunder and Love,* pp. 178-79.
[44]Ironside, *Revelation,* p. 148.
[45]Witherington, *Revelation,* pp. 110, 160.

the law. There is at least one more response (even a *requirement*) in addition to participation and resistance. We should pray for the peace of Babylon (Jer 29; cf. 1 Tim 2:1-2).

CONCLUSION

Daniel and Revelation will continue to be sources of mystery and speculation for the rest of human history. The books have prompted endless efforts to know a future that only God knows. We can do our best to craft laws to prepare for that future, but we should recognize the limits of our prophetic abilities. And we must heed the warnings in both books that the state does not always employ law for beneficial means. There is a wealth of insight throughout the Bible to aid us in shaping civil law even for those who live in a society that is radically different from the one that was familiar to the biblical writers. But the warnings of Daniel and Revelation, whatever their precise meaning, caution us against relying too much on law and the power of the state. As we await the new Jerusalem described in Revelation 21 and the return of Jesus promised in Revelation 22, we are charged with both encouraging and resisting the state as it exercises power, at times in the just and at times the unjust application of civil law. May God guide us as we discern how to respond in the world in which we live.

ACKNOWLEDGMENTS

We WOULD LIKE TO THANK Pepperdine's Herbert and Elinor Nootbaar Institute on Law, Religion, and Ethics and Provost Darryl Tippens for funding this project. Thanks as well to Deans Ken Starr, Tom Bost, Deanell Tacha and J. V. Fesko for their support. We are also indebted to Don Buffaloe for his assistance in tracking down numerous volumes and journals from a variety of disciplines. Finally, a special thanks to Brannon Ellis and his colleagues at InterVarsity Press for their thoughtful editorial assistance.

LIST OF CONTRIBUTORS

Leslie M. Alford, PhD, is a scholar in Christian spirituality, pastoral care and counseling and has taught at Pepperdine University in the School of Law and Seaver College.

Roger P. Alford, JD, is professor of law at the University of Notre Dame School of Law.

Barbara E. Armacost, JD, is professor of law at the University of Virginia School of Law.

Randy Beck, JD, is the Thomas O. Marshall Professor of Constitutional Law at the University of Georgia School of Law.

William S. Brewbaker III, JD, is the William Alfred Rose Professor of Law at the University of Alabama School of Law.

Robert F. Cochran Jr., JD, is the Louis D. Brandeis Professor of Law and the director of the Herbert and Elinor Nootbaar Institute on Law, Religion, and Ethics at Pepperdine University School of Law.

Peter Enns, PhD, is affiliate professor of biblical studies at Eastern University.

Kar Yong Lim, PhD, is lecturer in New Testament Studies and director of postgraduate studies at the Seminari Theoloji Malaysia (Malaysia Theological Seminary).

V. Philips Long, PhD, is professor of Old Testament at Regent College (Vancouver, British Columbia).

Tremper Longman III, PhD, is the Robert H. Gundry Professor of Biblical Studies at Westmont College.

Keith A. Mathison, PhD, is director of curriculum development for Ligonier Ministries and an associate editor of *Tabletalk* magazine.

James W. McCarty III is a PhD candidate at Emory University.

John Copeland Nagle, JD, is the John N. Matthews Professor of Law at the University of Notre Dame School of Law.

Joel A. Nichols, JD, is associate dean for academic affairs and professor of law at the University of St. Thomas (Minneapolis, Minnesota).

David Skeel, JD, is the S. Samuel Arsht Professor of Corporate Law at the University of Pennsylvania School of Law.

David M. Smolin, JD, is the Harwell G. Davis Professor of Constitutional Law and director of the Center for Children, Law and Ethics at the Cumberland School of Law, Samford University.

David VanDrunen, JD, PhD, is the Robert B. Strimple Professor of Systematic Theology and Christian Ethics at Westminster Seminary California.

Dallas Willard (1935–2013), PhD, was professor of philosophy at the University of Southern California for forty-eight years.

John Witte Jr., JD, is Jonas Robitscher Professor of Law, Alonzo L. McDonald Distinguished Service Professor, and director of the Center for the Study of Law and Religion at Emory University.

GENERAL INDEX

SCRIPTURE INDEX